EVANGELICAL PROTESTANT GIFTS TO RELIGIOUS EDUCATION

Dedicated to Peggy
Other than Jesus, she is God's greatest gift of grace.

EVANGELICAL PROTESTANT GIFTS TO RELIGIOUS EDUCATION

RONNIE PREVOST

Smyth & Helwys Publishing, Inc.
6316 Peake Road
Macon, Georgia 31210-3960
1-800-747-3016
© 2000 by Smyth & Helwys Publishing
All rights reserved.
Printed in the United States of America.

The paper used in this publication meets the minimum
requirements of American National Standard for Information
Sciences—Permanence of Paper for Printed Library Materials.
(pbk. : alk. paper)

Library of Congress Cataloging-in-Publication Data

Prevost, Ronnie, 1949–
  Evangelical Protestant gifts to religious education / Ronnie Prevost.
  p. cm.
  1. Christian education—Philosophy.
  2. Evangelicalism.
  I. Title.
  BV1464 .P74 2001
  268'.804—dc21   2001018386
                                                                          CIP

ISBN 1-57312-345-5

CONTENTS

Preface vii

Acknowledgments ix

Chapter 1
    Dimensions of Evangelical Protestantism 1

Gifts of Commonality

Chapter 2
    A Common Core 31

Chapter 3
    A Common Purpose 39

Chapter 4
    Drinking from Their Own Wells 47

Gifts of Diversity

Chapter 5
    Drinking from Others' Wells 57

Chapter 6
    Ecumenicity for Learning 65

Chapter 7
    Variety of Resources for the Church 73

Chapter 8
    Variety of Resources for Theological Higher Education 81

Chapter 9
    Choice in Expression of Spirituality 89

Chapter 10
    Demanding Developmental Sensitivity 99

Chapter 11
    Personalized Approach to Response and Expression 107

Gifts of Function

Chapter 12
    Purposeful Bible Study 117

Chapter 13
    Focus on Relationships 125

Chapter 14
    A Balance of Inward and Outward Nature of Spirituality 135

Chapter 15
    Purposeful Study of Moral and Ethical Issues 145

Chapter 16
    Vision for Growing the Kingdom of God .153

Gifts of Opportunity

Chapter 17
    Opportunity for Response 163

Chapter 18
    Opportunity for Service 171

Chapter 19
    Opportunity for Leadership 179

Chapter 20
    Opportunity for Cultural Sensitivity 187

Chapter 21
    Separation of Church and State 195

PREFACE

Almost three years ago James Michael Lee came to me with the idea for this book. I was interested that he broached the subject with me because it indicated, of course, how he categorized me as a scholar, religious educator, and Christian. The issue is one of personal identity, and a few words of reflection on this may help the reader better understand my perspectives shared herein.

The matter of personal identity has been a longtime struggle for me. Part of the reason, according to developmental psychologists, would relate to both my being the middle of three sons (no sisters) and my having had to deal (during early adolescence) with serious health issues. Reared in a devout Christian home, I was converted at the age of seven and first felt God's call to ministry at nine. These latter two factors did, in some sense, seal my identity. Being always the curious one, however, I always wanted to know more about what it meant to be a Christian, a Baptist, and a minister. My identity was to be honest and genuine. That was and is my intent.

Moving out of middle age and toward senior adulthood, I would describe myself as basically a simple person and prefer to describe myself in simple terms. Further, I find myself increasingly inclined to eschew labels and focus on issues. This has posed serious problems for me over the last twenty years. During that time the larger faith family in which I grew up has been embroiled in controversy over labels as well as matters of theological and ecclesiological substance. While serving on the faculty of The Southern Baptist Theological Seminary, I received an anonymous theological "survey" that ended with the question, "Are you liberal, moderate, or conservative?" My response (given somewhat tongue in cheek) was: "I am biblically conservative, which drives me to be theologically moderate and socially liberal."

My point is that, by many definitions, I am an Evangelical Protestant. However, there are those Evangelical Protestants who may disagree with me on certain issues and, so, would not include me as one of theirs. Nevertheless, being included in Evangelical Protestantism bestows me with familiarity and personal interest. Likewise, being excluded accords a certain objectivity. I beg all of the above.

Lastly, readers may detect a certain passion in what I have written. My passion derives from that of which I am convinced and that to which I am committed: the Lordship of Jesus and the authority of the Bible under that Lordship. These key issues compel me to take most seriously the principle of the priesthood of all believers on which my dedication to Christian education is founded.

I do not claim nor intend that what follows is the only appropriate view of any of the matters I describe. As with any book, other writers will have varying perspectives. These are mine.

ACKNOWLEDGMENTS

There are many who—past and present and either knowingly or unknowingly—have made this book possible and are deserving of thanks. First, a tremendous debt of gratitude is owed those forebears in the faith whose lives and writings bear testimony of what it means to be a real Baptist. They are my heroes and have inspired a lifelong quest to be worthy of the gifts of legacy and example they have given me. Many of these are known by name: John Smyth, Thomas Helwys, Henry Dunster, Elizabeth Backus, John Leland, Edgar Young Mullins, George Truett, Will Campbell, and others. Of course, there is a great company of those whose names today are known but to God. Thanks to them for their sacrifices.

Second, there remain those many contemporaries who have been my peers in the struggle to maintain our rich heritage as Baptists—especially as it relates to genuine authority of Scripture. Among these are my colleagues at The Southern Baptist Theological Seminary (1984–1990) and Midwestern Baptist Theological Seminary (1994–1995). Thanks to all of you for your courage, faithfulness, support, and companionship. Battles may have been lost, but in the Bible God assures us that ultimate victory over evil is ours.

There are many educators and religious educators—past and present—to whom I am indebted for their examples and influence. Among these are John Amos Comenius, Paolo Friere, Findley B. Edge, Sara Little, Thomas Groome, James Michael Lee, and Maria Harris.

Thanks also to my beloved and treasured colleagues at Hardin-Simmons University and its Logsdon School of Theology. This is indeed a wonderful place to call home.

To my secretary, graduate assistant, student, and friend, Spencer Wagley—thank you for all your hard work in support of my writing this book and in the preparation of this manuscript. I flatter myself by pointing to you as part of my own legacy and gift to religious education.

To Peggy Prevost, my wife and the one to whom this book is dedicated—thank you for everything. I love you.

Last, but foremost—thanks and glory be to my Lord, Redeemer, and Friend, Jesus. Thank you for your many gifts of grace.

[CHAPTER 1]

DIMENSIONS OF EVANGELICAL PROTESTANTISM

The task of defining Evangelical Protestantism may be described as either quite simple or as incredibly difficult. It may be so easy as to say that it is self-defining in that a faith group—or, an individual—is Evangelical Protestant if it (or the person) wishes to say so. However, there is no ruling authority nor are there absolute guidelines by which "all may know" conclusively whether this group or that is "certifiably Evangelical Protestant"—at least not with which all concerned would agree. The term could describe the various Reformed churches, Mennonites, Baptists, charismatic Roman Catholics, Pentecostals, Wesleyans, and many other assorted individual faith communities. Also included, by some definition, would be some denominations and churches such as the Worldwide Church of God (a member group of the National Association of Evangelicals), formerly considered "cults" even by some of their fellow Evangelical Protestants.

There are levels of disagreement and tension within some faith groups over whether or not they are, indeed, Evangelical Protestant.[1] Some would claim it as a badge of honor and distinctiveness. Others see it as an admission of being schismatic and would prefer to be known as "mainline." In reality, the term Evangelical Protestant originates and stands outside the parameters of the church and/or denominations proper and might even be said to transcend the issue of denomination. Herein lies the problem.

When most people find themselves at a loss to describe a physical object, they can at least do so in (perhaps approximate) terms of dimensions that help one understand the size, appearance, or position of the object. So, to make our task less daunting, we prefer to write not in terms of definition, but of dimensions. In this chapter we will examine the historical dimensions of Evangelical Protestantism for an understanding of common and diverse historical moments and movements that have given rise to that multifarious body. Next, we will study theological dimensions, again to see and understand commonly held doctrinal tenets and those on which there is particular disagreement among and within Evangelical Protestant faith groups. By looking at the ecclesiological dimensions we seek to discern what Evangelical Protestants perceive as a true church, the appropriate role of a church, the role of the individual believer in the life of the church, and how varying forms of congregational and denominational polity and governance have arisen among Evangelical Protestants despite the theological commonalities. The section on sociopolitical dimensions refers to how Evangelical Protestants address the moral issues affecting society as a unit and why those particular issues are addressed as opposed to others. By examining the personal-ethical dimensions, on the other hand, we will explore those personal moral issues on which Evangelical Protestants tend to speak publicly.

By many definitions, these same dimensions are similar to the concerns and the curricula of the religious education that arises in most faith communities. Examining these dimensions and their interplay can help one develop a greater understanding of from where Evangelical Protestants came, what they believe, how they operate, what concerns them about people and society, and what they see as their mission in the world. That is, the juxtaposition of these on the life of the denomination or church will determine how, why, what, and whom they will teach—and who will do the teaching (as well as how all of that will be determined). Thus, such can also provide a solid foundation and perspective from which to consider Evangelical Protestant gifts to religious education.

HISTORICAL DIMENSIONS

[PRE-REFORMATION]

Well before the onset of the Reformation there were many who struggled with the hierarchical structure of the Roman Catholic Church of the time. Some opposed the Church's power to impose liturgical forms, others the Church's control of dogma, still others more specifically what they saw as corruption in church offices (especially those of the papacy and the priesthood) and abuse of certain powers such as indulgences and inquisition. Some of these identifiable pre-Reformation "Protestants" were the Waldensians, Lollards, and Hussites.

Waldenses. Also known as Waldensians and the "Poor of Lyon," the followers of Peter Waldo or Valdez date to the late twelfth century near Lyon, France. In terms of doctrine they were relatively orthodox; they eschewed personal wealth and called on the Church to do the same. This doctrine was based on their understanding of scriptural demands, for they held that the Bible was to be the exclusive source of doctrinal and ethical teaching for the individual and the Church. They functioned as itinerant Bible teachers, encouraging families to worship together and read, study, and memorize Scripture. Though forbidden in their work by the Third Lateran Council and Pope Alexander III, the Waldenses continued their work outside the institutional church and, so, were excommunicated by Pope Lucius III in 1184 and subsequently forced into the Alps to escape persecution. Descendants of the original Waldenses continued to suffer even into the sixteenth century as the Reformation began in full force.

Lollards. The Lollards were adherents of the teachings of the fourteenth-century English Oxfordian scholar and teacher John Wycliffe. Wycliffe's teachings reflected those of the Waldenses, especially that of authority of Scripture over any human authority, and compelled him to translate the Bible into his native English and to send out his disciples as wandering preachers. The Lollards used their nomadic lifestyles to disseminate evangelistic tracts.

Hussites. John Huss (or Jan Hus) was a Bohemian priest/scholar of the late-fourteenth and early-fifteenth centuries. Studying at the University of Prague under one of Wycliffe's former students, he came to appreciate Wycliffe's teachings. Huss (who later would be excommunicated and executed) and his followers believed that Jesus Christ was the head of the church rather than the pope and that, under the Lordship of Christ, the "law" for the church was the Bible and, in particular, the New Testament. This Hussite perspective was of particular significance against the backdrop of the papal struggle within the Church at the time: the Great Schism. This was a period of thirty years during which French and Italian factions battled over papal candidates. Rival popes declared each other anti-popes. Church unity was virtually nonexistent, and Church leadership was in disarray and was increasingly secular.

Mysticism, Humanism, and Other Forces. With the Church so weakened, the vacuum of power began to be filled—over the ensuing centuries—by a rising nationalism and the expansion of power among the various princes of Europe. Also, there had been developing for some time mystical theology that focused on the nature of the divine/human relationship. Though some mystics (Bonaventura, Thomas a Kempis, etc.) were strict in affirming this relationship through more formal church structures, Meister Eckhart and others were open to the possibility of aspects of the relationship being transacted outside the sacraments and directly between the two parties. The late fourteenth century saw the onset of the Renaissance and its emphasis on human values, concerns, and worth and on looking to classical writings in their original languages. This movement was the impetus for Christian humanist writers such as Erasmus. The confluence of these forces with the growing discontent represented by the Waldenses, Lollards, Hussites, and others resulted in a Church and Europe ripe for reform.

[REFORMATION]

Imbued by the Renaissance interest in the classics, all the leading reformers affirmed the Bible as their authority. Their view of the Bible as uniquely authoritative formed the bases of their disputes with the Church at many points of faith and practice. However, the early reformers, such as Martin Luther and Ulrich Zwingli, and others, such as John Calvin and Menno Simons, can each be seen as characterizing and as having significant influence on their particular followers (and those of others) in specific areas of theology.

Martin Luther. Luther's conflict with the Church was especially rooted in his understanding of biblical teachings related to soteriology. Even before Luther, Hildegard (1098–1179), a German Benedictine abbess and mystic, called for the authority of Scripture to be recognized as superseding that of priests, especially regarding salvation. Luther himself had developed misgivings about those aspects of church doctrine influenced by Aristotle and Scholasticism, preferring the mysticism of Augustine. His study of Paul's letter to the Romans particularly moved him to oppose what he saw as the church's "works righteousness." Luther's *Ninety-Five Theses*, posted on the castle church door at Wittenburg in 1517, called into question the system of indulgences and proposed that "the whole life of the faithful be an act of repentance."[2] There developed at the core of Luther's theology and concern the doctrine of justification by faith in Jesus Christ. Rather than finding salvation in obedience to church-decreed ritual, Luther held to a salvation of grace and personal experience and responsibility to God. On this foundation each believer would be at liberty to function as an individual priest, that is, serving God and others unimpeded by externally imposed barriers and restrictions.

Luther would prove to be concerned with influencing culture to preserve reform. His prolific writing on education rose from his awareness of the importance of education in reforming the church, changing society, and serving as a stage from which his theological reforms would be launched.

Ulrich Zwingli. The Swiss theologian and reformer, Ulrich Zwingli, is the antecedent of the "Reformed" Protestant tradition as Luther is of the "Lutheran" tradition. Zwingli was a contemporary of Luther (the two were born just a few weeks apart) and, like Luther, had been educated in the humanist scholarly tradition (though more Thomist than Luther). He agreed with Luther in believing—based on his understanding of the Bible— in justification by faith. However, Zwingli offered a distinct ethical-social alternative since he differed from Luther in his concern with the reform of society as an end in itself and not just as a means to extend and preserve individual personal reform. That is, for Zwingli, the spiritual accord found in the faith community (the church) should find both a parallel and expression in the social concerns of the civic community. One expression of this was Zwingli's militant patriotism that would find him twice serving as a military chaplain: first, with Italian troops and at the appointment of the Pope; and later, after his break with the church of Rome, with a Protestant army in the battle of Kappel (1531) in which he would be killed.

The canton of Zurich would prove to be somewhat a laboratory for Zwingli's social reforms, especially as a result of the findings of the Zurich town council subsequent to the First Zurich Disputation (1523). The council had called for the debate, but—consistent with an earlier ordinance of the city that obligated all preaching to be consistent with Scripture—required that all arguments be based solely on the Bible. A representative of the local bishop challenged the council's right to adjudicate a theological matter, but Zwingli concurred with the form and purpose of the council. Further, Zwingli would be chosen to serve on the board of the Zurich schools. It was through this office that Zwingli exerted his influence in reforming the entire educational system of Zurich. He gave special attention to the development of a theological institute that would produce ministers who reflected his Reformed perspective.

Zurich would eventually be isolated from the other Swiss cantons which would remain Catholic. However, Zurich sought to exert its influence on its neighbors through economic sanctions that would become additional catalysts for the military struggle in which Zwingli would die.

John Calvin. John Calvin was born in France and would be a child of eight when the Reformation began. He would also be trained and educated in the classical tradition and would embrace Reformation doctrine in 1533. From that time he preached, wrote, and taught in support of Reformation theology and, in 1536 (the year he finished writing his seminal work, *Institutes of the Christian Religion*) arrived in Geneva. He quickly became involved in the developing theocracy of Geneva, but would be exiled from the city for a brief time over issues of liturgy and discipline. Calvin's return to Geneva was made possible by a shift in civic and ecclesiastical power, which he used as the opportunity to establish the Geneva Academy, a comprehensive and clergy-controlled system that included primary through university education.

Calvin shared with the earlier reformers a high regard for Scripture as foundational for all faith and practice. His view of human nature—total depravity—did not require abandonment of the classics, though they were limited by their human nature and origins. For Calvin, however, it was the divinely inspired Scriptures that would reveal truly and consistently accurate knowledge. The reliability of Scripture not only arose from its divine origin, but also was beyond human reason. Belief in the veracity derived from the presence of the Holy Spirit rather than reason, because, "the testimony of the Spirit is more excellent than all reason...[and] the Word will not find acceptance in men's [sic] hearts before it is sealed by the inward testimony of the Spirit."[3]

Calvin also concurred with other Reformers in that grace and faith were at the center of his soteriology and, through his perspectives on providence and the sovereignty of God, his voice characterizes the reformed doctrine of predestination and election. He held that the proper role of government was as a natural extension of God's reign and with the expressed purpose of maintaining order and establishing "right" religion. It was by this means that, for Calvin, the "elect" would work to bring about God's kingdom. Calvin's legacy to Evangelical Protestantism was conveyed through subsequent reformers and Protestants throughout Europe and, among present Evangelical Protestants, is viewed as either the *sine qua non*, a distortion of Scripture, or—at least—a matter of heated debate.

Anabaptists. Early in the Reformation there developed within the Protestant ranks a singular schism beyond the particular disagreements that existed among the followers of Luther, Zwingli, and Calvin. In Zurich, led by Conrad Grebel, Felix Manz, and Balthsar Hubmaier, dissent arose regarding scriptural teaching on baptism. While Zwingli held to infant baptism, these dissenters countered that there was no scriptural basis for the practice, refused to exercise it—hence the name by which they and their followers would be known: Anabaptists—and spoke out instead for baptism of believers only. The split became formal in 1525, when, after a public debate on the matter between Zwingli and this faction, the Zurich government required all children to be baptized and banished some Anabaptist leaders while issuing gag orders to others.

Viewed with disdain and often persecuted by both Catholic and fellow Protestants alike, the Anabaptists were at the heart of the movement known as the Radical Reformation. Among the most effective theologians and leaders among the early Anabaptists were Hubmaier and Jacob Hutter. However, both were executed without having written prolifically: Hubmaier burned at the stake at the age of 48 (his wife was drowned three days later), and Hutter tortured and then burned to death at the age of 36.

Mennonites. Menno Simons, however, was an Anabaptist leader and theologian who lived to old age and, so, was a more copious writer and more influential on the theological legacy of the Radical Reformation. Trained as a Roman Catholic priest, he served as such until his study of the Bible caused him to question various liturgical and sacramental matters. The death of his brother among the other militant Anabaptists at Munster precipitated a spiritual crisis in Simons' life that within a few months resulted in his leaving the Catholic church.

Simons was the progenitor of the Anabaptists known as Mennonites. His influence is to be seen not only in them but also in many other Evangelical Protestants (e.g., Baptists) of today. Simons differed significantly (as noted) on baptism from the other Reformers, but little on issues of authority of Scripture and soteriology, except in terms of stress and terminology. According to historian Timothy George, "Although Luther described himself as 'born again,' and both Zwingli and Calvin commented on Jesus words to Nicodemus, Menno placed the greatest emphasis on the necessity for the new birth."[4] Also, he was concerned that the believer's outward life would give evidence of the inward, personal experience with God.

Simons' particular broader influence, and that of the other early Anabaptists, deals with ecclesiology. Widely accepted in the days of the Reformation was the notion that had existed from the time of Constantine that a nation could be "Christian." This idea continued to find expression among Luther, Zwingli, Calvin, and their followers as well as the Roman Catholics with whom they had split. Simons and the Anabaptists, however, contended that the true "church" was to be found only within the fellowship of believers consciously and personally committed to the Lordship of Jesus Christ. The implications of this belief carried beyond the simple issue of expression and recognition of the church in the local sense. It required a church and individual Christians to be free to believe and to practice that faith according to the dictates of the conscience as informed by Scripture. Although to them the state was ordained by God, its role was not to be one of duress or intimidation.

[POST-REFORMATION]

Subsequent to the Reformation there continued to arise movements and individuals that would influence those groups that could be identified as Evangelical Protestants today and provide bases for both further commonality and further difference of belief among those so classified. Among these movements was the Pietism that rose in the seventeenth century and Pentecostalism that developed in the nineteenth century.

Pietism. Much of the impetus for Pietism was a response to a perceived overemphasis on theological intellectualizing within Protestantism. Early Pietist leaders, theologians, and writers such as Jacob Spener, August

Hermann Francke, and Nicholas von Zinzendorf underscored and sought a renewed emphasis on the authority of Scripture, salvation as a rebirth, corporate and individual inward devotional life, and outward acts of spiritual and social ministry that demonstrated (and/or were the fruit of) the inner experience and growth. Both early and contemporary Wesleyanism trace their roots to Pietism through John Wesley, who was directly influenced by Zinzendorf. Important to note at this point is the Arminian perspective injected into the Evangelical Protestant tradition by the Wesleyan movement. Other, perhaps more direct, historical media through which the various forms and currents of the Protestant Reformation—especially that of the Calvinist bent—have affected various Evangelical Protestant groups today would be the Puritans and others of like mind.

Pentecostalism. The rise of Pentecostalism has either directly or indirectly affected some current Evangelical Protestant faith groups. Pentecostalism as a movement among contemporary Christians has its foundations primarily in Wesleyan groups (and revivals in Kansas and North Carolina) in the mid-to late-nineteenth century, but exploded on the broader American scene in southern California with the Azusa Street Revival of 1906. The Pentecostal emphasis on the work of the Holy Spirit in and through salvation, sanctification, and liturgy also has provided fodder for both agreement and disagreement among Evangelical Protestants as a group and as a distinguishing mark for some particular Evangelical Protestant individuals, denominations, and churches.

The thought of various persons from these historical streams coalesced into the contemporary movement known as Evangelical Protestantism. The precipitant was a reaction to the so-called "liberalism" of German theology and higher biblical criticism and culturally-perceived modernity.

THEOLOGICAL DIMENSIONS

Since there is no controlling authority among Evangelical Protestants, both those within and those outside Evangelical Protestantism perceive and describe its theological dimensions in a variety of ways. Alister McGrath, drawing on other Evangelicals such as Carl F. H. Henry and J. I. Packer, outlines six "fundamental' convictions":

- The supreme authority of Scripture as a source of knowledge of God and a guide to Christian living
- The majesty of Jesus Christ, both as incarnate God and Lord and as Savior of sinful humanity

- The Lordship of the Holy Spirit
- The need for personal salvation
- The priority of evangelism for both individual Christians and the church as a whole
- The importance of Christian community for spiritual nourishment, fellowship, and growth[6]

Donald G. Bloesch takes a different approach. Characterizing Evangelicalism and Catholicism as "two themes in the Christian symphony," he describes the theological orientation of Evangelical Protestants in opposition to that of Catholicism. For Bloesch, the primary concerns of Protestant Evangelicalism are as follows:

- to be rooted in "the primitive message of the New Testament"
- to assert "the particularity of the historical revelation as attested in Scripture"
- to live out a "concern…with outreach and mission"
- to emphasize in theology and piety the vicarious atonement of Christ[7]

Similarly, Bloesch goes on to contrast Protestant Evangelicalism with "Liberalism" by outlining the doctrinal tenets of the former this way:

> Among these [tenets] are the absolute sovereignty and transcendence of God; the divine authority and inspiration of Scripture; the radical sinfulness of man [sic]; the deity of Jesus Christ; His vicarious, substitutionary atonement; the eschatological and superhistorical character of the kingdom of God; a final judgment at the end of history; the realities of heaven and hell; and evangelization as the primary dimension of the Christian.[8]

Though certainly not speaking for those Evangelical Protestants not a part of its fellowship, the National Association of Evangelicals adopted a "Statement of Faith" that reads:

- We believe the Bible to be the inspired, the only infallible, authoritative Word of God.
- We believe that there is one God, eternally existent in three persons: Father, Son, and Holy Spirit.
- We believe in the deity of our Lord Jesus Christ, in His virgin birth, in His sinless life, in His miracles, in His vicarious and atoning death through His shed blood, in His bodily resurrection, in His ascension to the right hand of the Father, and in His personal return in power and glory.

- We believe that for the salvation of lost and sinful people, regeneration by the Holy Spirit is absolutely essential.
- We believe in the present ministry of the Holy Spirit by whose indwelling the Christian is enabled to live a Godly life.
- We believe in the resurrection of both the saved and the lost; they that are saved unto the resurrection of life and they that are lost unto the resurrection of damnation.
- We believe in the spiritual unity of believers in our Lord Jesus Christ.[9]

Kenneth O. Gangel and Christy Sullivan are helpful in delineating the theological foundations of Evangelical Protestantism in terms of these questions and answers:

- *Whom do we worship?* (A God who is revealed through nature, but also through special revelation—particularly through the Bible—and through historical statements of the Christian faith.)
- *What is the state of humanity before God?* (Persons created by God in His image, but who have by nature and by volition disfigured the divine image and separated themselves from a holy God through sin.)
- *What is the relationship between God and humanity?* (In mercy and grace God has taken the initiative to restore the relationship between Himself and sinful humanity, and this restoration is made possible only through a spiritual re-birth at which point a person is adopted as a child of God.)
- *What is the goal of our instruction and means of growth?* (Spiritual formation—also known as sanctification—which is a process of individual and corporate maturity in which one increases in God-likeness.)
- *What is the source of our knowledge?* (The Bible, inspired by God and authoritative "when properly understood [the reader/interpreter being assisted by "proper interpretative tools" including textual and higher biblical criticism], not only in matters of faith and practice, but also in matters relating to history and science.")[10]

Al Mohler affirms the " 'three marks' of evangelical identity" adopted by a conference called by Evangelical Protestant leaders Carl F. H. Henry and Kenneth Kantzer:

- belief in the gospel as set forth in Scripture (salvation by grace through grace by faith)
- commitment to the basic doctrines of the Bible as found in the Apostle's creed and other historic confessions (the "material or content principle")

- an acknowledgment of the Bible as the authoritative and final source of all doctrines (the "formative or forming principle")[11]

Pollster and researcher George Barna described the definition for "evangelical" used by Barna Research Group (whose clients have included such diverse clients as the Billy Graham Evangelistic Association, Focus on the Family, CBN, and the Disney Channel and whose surveys have been used extensively by Evangelical Protestant churches and denominations of various stripes) as a parameter for its research not in terms of a relationship to denominational identity or church membership or attendance. For Barna, evangelicals "say their faith is very important to their life…believe they have a responsibility to share their faith in Christ with non-Christians…believe in the existence of Satan…believe that eternal salvation is gained through God's grace alone, not through human efforts…believe the Bible is accurate in all it teaches…choose an orthodox definition of God."[12]

These lists and perspectives evidence the theological dimensions of Evangelical Protestantism as continuing to center on issues of Scripture, soteriology, and personal faith. Each of these dimensions has particular significance and implications for current Evangelical Protestants and, sometimes, serves as grist for the mill of controversy even within the Evangelical Protestant community.

For many Evangelical Protestants, the authority of Scripture is rooted in its reliability and trustworthiness. The Scriptural foundation of this doctrine is found in 2 Tim 3:16 in which Paul writes to his protégé, Timothy, that Scripture is "inspired" or "God-breathed." The nature of biblical inspiration would be described by most Evangelical Protestants in terms of some form of verbal, plenary inspiration. Simply stated, this means:

> All that is found within the canon is Scripture, the product of the oversight of the Holy Spirit…[and] Rather than asserting that God dictated every word…the [Holy] Spirit superintended the process of word selection and word order to the extent that they are capable of communicating the intended meaning of the text.[13]

Two other descriptors of the Bible (but not found in it) are often used by Evangelical Protestants: infallible and inerrant. Historically, the issues of infallibility may be seen as a continuing expression of the Reformation refutation of the infallibility of either popes or councils. To Grenz, "the declaration, 'the Bible is infallible,' means that these writings are 'not liable to deceive.' Because the Spirit moved in the lives of the authors, the product can be trusted. The writers do not intend to lead their readers astray."[14] This seems to be the perspective of James P. Boyce, nineteenth-century Baptist theologian to whom many current Southern Baptists point as an example of what they see as "traditional" Baptist theologians and as a theological link to Evangelical Protestants, in his "A Brief Catechism of Bible Doctrine": "*How much does it [the Bible] teach us?* It teaches us all that is necessary about God, our duty to Him, our condition as sinners, and the way of salvation."[15]

Many current Evangelical Protestants, however, see the term as synonymous with inerrancy.[16] It is this particular expression that, though simply stated means "free from error," leads to much further debate even among Evangelical Protestants. That the concept of inerrancy finds its roots in the Enlightenment rationalism of John Locke is ironic since many Evangelical Protestants point to the Enlightenment itself as the foundation for the "secular humanism" so despised by many Evangelical Protestants and so demeaned in the rhetoric of their leaders and polemicists.

In 1978 the International Conference on Biblical Inerrancy (ICBI) met in Chicago and included persons from a broad spectrum of denominational and theological perspectives, but all concerned with the defense biblical inerrancy. Their concern was "to define, defend, and apply the doctrine of biblical inerrancy as an essential element of the authority of Scripture and a necessary ingredient for the health of the church of Christ in an attempt to win the church back to this historic position."[17]

Many who choose to use the word "inerrant" to describe the Bible go on to use conditional statements to describe either implicitly or explicitly what inerrancy is not. For instance, Gangel and Sullivan (referring to Paul D. Feinburg) refer to eight of these limitations.[18] Grenz describes a four-point continuum of inerrantist perspectives.[19] Robert Preus has offered not only six corollaries to biblical inerrancy, but also twelve "adjuncts" to the doctrine, which (at the very least) hermeneutically conditionalize the term.[20] The 1978 (ICBI) conference (mentioned above) produced "The Chicago Statement on Biblical Inerrancy," which uses the terms "inerrant," "infallible," and "authoritative" in a variety of ways—in relation to one another. This statement is comprised of nineteen separate articles, each of which states what is claimed and what is denied by inerrancy. Even this document allows for considerable disparity among its claimants and can be construed at various points as being at odds with itself.[21]

Whatever the Evangelical Protestant view of the particular areas of the doctrine, the authority of Scripture is not widely held in isolation from an appreciation for and acknowledgment of the value of historical theology and scholarship for hermeneutical assistance. Nevertheless, the Bible is still the touchstone. Therefore, it is this holding to both the authority of Scripture and the efficacy of traditionally understood theology that impels Evangelical Protestants toward orthodox doctrines of God, Jesus, virgin birth, humanity, sin, atonement, and so on. The very root of the meaning of authority as applied to Scripture can be illustrated by how Evangelical Protestants perceive its use as a moral primer. That is, since it is inspired (i.e., "breathed by God")—as both document and as a moral authority—it has as its own source the God who best understands how the universe is made and how it functions. Since it was given by the Creator as a blueprint for how the created is to live and relate to the rest of creation, it applies to every portion of a person's life as both individual and as a part of formal and informal social and faith groupings. Therefore, the understanding of Evangelical Protestants is that the authority of Scripture has implications of cosmic proportions, but at the immediate and personal level.

However, there are many issues of "Bible doctrine" on which Evangelical Protestants can and do have differing hermeneutical perspectives and seriously disagree. Interestingly, some of the more biblically "conservative" (or more accurately called "literalist") Evangelical Protestants claim the Bible is quite clear in its meaning, thereby aligning themselves historically more with an aspect of Roman Catholicism rejected by the Reformers.[22]

Not surprisingly, then, Evangelical Protestant views of soteriology grow out of the traditional interpretations of the Bible and reflect traditionally understood Reformation orthodoxy, although common among Evangelical Protestant theologians is the varying selection of and hermeneutical "spin" given to particular biblical passages that they reference in building their theologies. They tend to be consistent on the effect of total depravity (at least some form of it), sin, separation from God and the need for regeneration, and the initiative of God in effecting that regeneration through vicarious or substitutionary atonement.

Total depravity can speak to either "the corruption at the very center of man's [sic] being," or "the infection in every part of man's being," or "the total inability of sinful man to please God or come to him unless moved by grace," or "the idea of the universal corruption of the human race," but does not necessarily mean "that there is no natural goodness or freedom remaining in man."[23]

Sin itself is understood in reference to total depravity not only as particular overt acts on the part of a person, but also—and seminally—as the inward attitude of unbelief and of rebellion against God's order, will, and commands. The result of this sin in the life of the individual is often understood among Evangelical Protestants in terms of a separation from God that can be characterized in such metaphors as alienation (from God and from others), condemnation (punishment), enslavement (to forces of evil), and depravity (incapacity for solving this human dilemma apart from the power of God).[24] These and other biblical metaphors describing the effect of sin and helpless humanity betray the individual's need for salvation (i.e., regeneration, being "converted," "saved," or "born-again").

Evangelical Protestantism holds that, by some definition, regeneration comes as the result of the confluence of personal awareness of sin, repentance, and (in faith) accepting the truth and the historical claims of the gospel and its claims upon the life of the individual. How and to what degree God took the initiative in regeneration depends on the specific Evangelical Protestant orientation to Calvinist or Arminian theology.

Further, for Evangelical Protestants the salvific core of the gospel is to be found in the substitutionary or vicarious atonement. By this they simply mean that in his suffering and death on the cross, Jesus Christ, took on himself the punishment due sinful humanity. By this act, God has made available the means by which the individual's separation from God can be overcome. This, too, is expressed among and by Evangelical Protestants variously as justification, salvation, and so on, often depending on the particular biblical image or metaphor for sin or its effect that has been used.

The generally accepted Evangelical Protestant concept of personal faith naturally grows out of that basic understanding of the individually rooted, subjective, inner experience. This does not mean that it is comprehended as being without some form of outward expression. Rather, it is variously construed among Evangelical Protestants to be experienced and expressed (individually and corporately) in and through sanctification (variously understood forms and process of spiritual growth, cleansing, and renewal) and in action (such as diverse acts of evangelism, service, and missions). Nor does this mean that Evangelical Protestants are denying at this point the Reformation heritage of justification by faith alone. Borrowing from John Gerstner and reflecting on and responding to issues surfaced by the dialogue among the biblical epistles of Romans and James (and various scholarly perspectives regarding their respective dates and interpretations), Luther, and Calvin, R. C. Sproul explains the matter in terms of the relationship and interplay that exist among the concepts of justification, faith, and works. For Gerstner and Sproul, the existing Roman Catholic doctrine held that faith and works produced justification. In contrast, the Reformation view was that both justification and works were products of faith.[25] Even Luther's disdain for the epistle of James ("a right strawy epistle" according to him) should not be construed as his repudiation of good works on the part of the Christian, but of "works- righteousness."[26]

The key point of commonality here is that of personal experience. Despite the many areas and degrees of doctrinal differences among Evangelical Protestants, they all affirm either directly or by clear implication that one's faith experience is deeply personal and, at the most basic level, absolutely individual. However Christian faith may be expressed and nurtured in the corporate context, that faith must first be arrived at individually.

Sanctification, too, is comprehended in many different ways among Evangelical Protestants, though always as an act of God through the Holy Spirit. The more Arminian would hold that sanctification is somewhat of a higher stage or step than justification in the salvation process. Those of a more Calvinist or Reformed background would hold that sanctification is "the concrete enactment of justification in our lives" and that it "signifies the personal or interior appropriation of the fruits of justification."[27] Evangelical Protestants agree that—however they are otherwise understood—salvation, regeneration, justification, and sanctification are all inwardly and individually experienced but outwardly expressed both individually and corporately (i.e., in fellowship, relationship, and concert with others of the church).

ECCLESIOLOGICAL DIMENSIONS

Another cluster of doctrinal issues about which Evangelical Protestants are concerned and that demonstrate both unity and disagreement among them relates to ecclesiology—the study of the church. Historically, however, among Evangelical Protestants little attention has been given to developing a thorough ecclesiology. Some even point to this shortcoming as one reason for the current decline in concern for denominational identity and involvement among many professing Christians.[28]

One obvious consistency among Evangelical Protestants is that their doctrinal stances regarding the church hold in balance two basic elements: (1) biblical authority (for understanding biblical images of the church and biblical teachings on both the nature and the mission of the church) and (2) respect for a personal faith that transcends and can set one apart from traditionally understood doctrinal parameters of the institutional faith community with which the individual identifies. For example, there exist two documents both of which have their respective geneses among Evangelical Protestants and have as their signatories leading Evangelical Protestants of differing backgrounds and one Evangelical Protestant leader, J. I. Packer, signed both. Significantly, they differ on the basic issue of whether or not the Roman Catholic church can be construed as a "true" church in other than the purely institutional sense. One document, *Evangelicals and Catholics*

Together: The Christian Mission in the Third Millennium, was developed over a two-year period beginning in 1992, each of those participating doing so as individuals and not as representatives of their distinct denominations. This statement accepts as true church any who accept in faith Jesus as Lord and Savior and on this basis explicitly includes Evangelical Protestants, Roman Catholics, Eastern Orthodox, and non-Evangelical Protestants.[29] At about the same time, on the other hand, Evangelical Protestants Michael Horton and J. I. Packer (who signed the previously mentioned statement) produced a differing document, *Resolutions for Roman Catholic and Evangelical Dialogue*. This latter paper declares that the doctrine of justification by faith alone is foundational to being a true church and, so, "disqualifies [the Roman Catholic Church] as an acceptable Christian communion," though it allows that among the individual communicants within the Roman Catholic church, "there are many Christians."[30]

The word "church" and cognates such as *cirche* (Middle English) and *cirice* (Old English) are derived from the Greek term *kuriakos* and (ultimately *kurios* or "master" or "lord") refer to the more institutionalized concept of church as an organization, building, or denomination[31] in the sense that it is something that "belongs to the Lord."[32] Evangelical Protestant ecclesiology, however, rises from a rejection of what is seen as misguided ideas or images of "church" (as simply a social club or a corporation). Though there are certainly other images for the church derived from the Old and New Testaments, the one most central to Evangelical Protestant notions of the church is based on an understanding of the Greek word, *ekklesia*. Usually translated "church" in the New Testament (hence the term "ecclesiology," which refers to the doctrine of the church), the word literally means "called out," and the connotation is that of "a public assemblage summoned by a herald." So, in the Evangelical Protestant view, "*ekklesia* in the New Testament means that congregation which the living God assembles around His Messiah Jesus."[33] Evangelical Protestants recognize the Old Testament roots of *ekklesia* in the concept of the people of God and continue to understand the word in various understandings of the church as both realized and eschatological expressions and manifestations of the Kingdom of God.

The ecclesiological focus among Evangelical Protestants is almost always on the local church. Nevertheless, the common practice is for local Evangelical Protestant churches and individuals to be touched and to seek either a formal or informal association with a wider like-minded body. This, too, they see as a biblical model in that the book of Acts and a number of Pauline passages recall occasions when local bodies of believers joined others in some form of fellowship and/or physical, moral, or spiritual support and accountability. Some Evangelical Protestants refer to their broadly based fellowships by the term "convention," "association," or "conference" and choose to reserve the term "church" for use in the local context only. Others use "church" in reference to both the local and general body.

According to Stanley Grenz, the appropriate role of a church is first to glorify God:

> The ultimate motivation for all church planning, goals, and actions must center solely on our desire to bring glory to God. We must direct all that we say and do as the eschatological covenant community toward this ultimate purpose, namely, that God be glorified through us. Because this is our ultimate goal, we must carefully monitor the various dimensions of church life, seeking to bring everything under this one priority.[34]

This purpose of glorifying God is accomplished by the church not only through worship, but also through such means as mutual betterment among members of the church by acts of service, encouragement, observance of biblically mandated rituals, moral and doctrinal accountability, and so on. It is also achieved through the church—corporately and as individuals—by proclaiming to the world the many facets of gospel as experienced through personal salvation, by being a prophetic voice, and by acts of ministry to the ends of meeting the world's needs.

Most Evangelical Protestants acknowledge that unity among believers is an ideal, not only as a biblical mandate, but also as a more efficient and effective means by which to live before and minister to the world. However, there is wide disagreement on viable and appropriate bases, levels, areas, and means of expressing this unity through ecumenicity. Also, since the inward and the personal are such vital parts of the Evangelical Protestant experience, there seems to exist deep within the hearts of Evangelical Protestants the fear that unity may require an unacceptable conformity.

A consistent Evangelical Protestant strategy to accomplish what unity is possible, then, is to base that unity on clearly understood and stated areas of agreement on biblical doctrine. Those Evangelical Protestants concerned with declining interest in denominational identity still call for Scripture to be the basis of all statements of common faith.[35]

While it may be safely assumed that most, if not all, Evangelical Protestants would agree that the church—though of divine origin—manifests diverse qualities of a human institution (i.e., structure, organization as a response to human need for such), they would insist that both the local and universal expressions of "church" be biblically-modeled. So, there are among Evangelical Protestants types of ecumenical statements, organizations, para-church groups, trans- and inter-denominational alliances and efforts. One example is the National Association of Evangelicals, which is comprised of nearly fifty member denominations of varying traditions, but which are in close agreement on basic doctrines shared even by those Evangelical Protestants who are not members of the NAE.

Evangelical Protestants' orientation toward scriptural authority and personal experience incline them toward the free church tradition, although within some churches and denominations identified corporately as Evangelical Protestant there may exist some form or level of hierarchy within the larger faith community or within the context of the local church itself. Similarly, though many of these also claim the Bible as exclusive authority, they still insist on adherence to creeds and/or confessions of faith as means to maintain identity and order and discipline within the body. Often the problem for denomination and local church alike is in finding a balance between the two highly-valued concepts.

Because of the broad emphasis among Evangelical Protestants on the biblical (and Reformation) principle of priesthood of all believers, leadership among most of them is seen as something to be shared (at least to some degree) by clergy and laity. At this point of doctrine, as at many others, there remains among Evangelical Protestants great variety of interpretation. Some, for instance, interpret the Bible (especially the New Testament) as calling for diversity of gifts, function, and roles among believers, but not a hierarchy of clergy and laity. These particularly, though not necessarily denying an appropriate role and function for the professional minister, call for all church members to function as ministers and, so, for shared leadership in all areas of church life. Others, though not disallowing priesthood (and equality) of all believers, interpret the Bible as setting up certain members of the church in particular roles of authority with definite supervisory responsibility over the others. Most of these, though, will still involve the laity in some roles of significant leadership in the church. Remember at this point that what has been noted are varieties of structured or institutional responses to questions of leadership in the church. There also exists among individual church leaders (professional as well as lay) along the already-described spectrum yet another continuum of personal preferences and styles of leadership from the authoritarian to the inclusive. However, at this point most of these would admit to at least some degree of influence on the part of "secular" management theories, etc.

One example of a biblical conundrum, the answer for which can differ widely from one Evangelical Protestant to another (and has served to divide churches and denominations within Evangelical Protestantism), is an additional leadership-related issue. There is a wide variance among Evangelical Protestants regarding feminism and the Bible teaching on appropriate leadership roles for women in the church. There is a distinct tension between Paul's constraints on women in passages such as 1 Tim 2:12 and 1 Cor 14:34 and Paul's liberation of women (and others) in passages such as Gal 3:28 and Rom 12:6-8. Three stances on the issue can be said to characterize the contrasting Evangelical Protestant views on women in the church. There are those that, referring to passages such as 1 Tim 3:1-13 and 1 Cor 14:34, would deny any place for women as either ministers (especially as pastor or senior minister or any position of authority over men—some even take it so far as to prohibit women from having a voice or vote in church business meetings and conferences) or as lay leaders such as deacons. There are others, some of whom would be labeled "feminist," who encourage women to function in any role of ministry (as either clergy and laity) for which they are equipped and to which they are led. These rely particularly on biblical passages that clearly identify women among the leaders of God's people in both the Old and New Testaments. They also refer to passages such as Joel 2:28 (which is quoted in Acts 2:17), and Galatians 3:28. There are also those Evangelical Protestants who hold both views in tension, accepting that there is legitimate biblical evidence on both sides and, so, consider it a matter for decision by individual persons and churches. Yet others, who might themselves be personally convinced regarding one of the antithetical interpretations, regard the matter as "marginalia" and call for fellow Evangelical Protestants to avoid focusing on issues that are not central to faith.[36]

Within the contexts of some denominations and churches identified as Evangelical Protestant this issue among others has become somewhat polemical and schismatic and often a test of faith and fellowship. Some have noted the irony that, despite the anti-feminist stance of many staunch Evangelical Protestants, the roots of feminism can be traced to the egalitarian nature of American Evangelical revivals over the past two centuries such as those manifested in revivals led by Evangelical Protestant icon Charles G. Finney.[37]

SOCIOPOLITICAL DIMENSIONS

The struggle for Evangelical Protestants is in the confluence of their understanding of biblical standards for morality with an increasingly heterogeneous world. Like their Reformation forebears, Evangelical Protestants envision themselves as not only harbingers, but also catalysts and change agents in bringing about or calling the world to God's kingdom on earth. Most Evangelical Protestants would agree with what Donald G. Bloesch wrote more than ten years ago: "What is missing in so much current spirituality is the ethical or prophetic note."[38] A similar tone was heard from what James Davison Hunter describes as the "three waves of evangelical political activism":

- the 1920s in which the uniting concerns were Darwinism, Prohibition, and Roman Catholicism
- the 1950s in which the concern was socialism/communism
- the 1980s in which the concern was what was perceived as a general decline in cultural morality[39]

Certainly the antecedents of today's Evangelical Protestants demonstrated concern with the political, legal, social, and moral issues of their day. Historically, Evangelical Protestants were to be found on both sides of issues such as slavery (and the subsequent civil rights struggle), public education, religious liberty/separation of church and state, humane treatment of animals, enforced observance of the Sabbath, feminism, and war and peace. (They tended to be more of one voice on prohibition, though there were some who stood out in dissent.) Significantly, however, they tended to speak out on these issues—at least officially—as individual denominations, churches, or persons.

Aware of the increased complexity of the contemporary sociopolitical scene, today's Evangelical Protestants are more apt to be of the Christ-against-culture mentality. There is great variety among theologians to whom Evangelical Protestants are beholden for their sociopolitical views. Some hearken to Walter Rauschenbusch, Jurgen Moltmann, and Langdon Gilkey; others to John R. W. Stott, Jacques Ellul, and (even) Hans Küng.[40]

Most Evangelical Protestants speak "prophetically" on and to sociopolitical issues not only individually, but also more often deliberately in concert with other faith groups—both fellow Evangelical Protestants as well as others with whom they would disagree doctrinally. An example of the latter situation is that in which Richard Mouw called for dialogue and common ministry between Evangelical Protestants and Roman Catholics on addressing the issue of poverty. His call rose from a concern that Evangelical Protestants base their attitudes and actions regarding the poor on a more biblically-derived theology. For Mouw, it is by this means that Evangelical Protestants will be more consistent with their theological roots, discover areas of theological/ethical common ground on the issue with Roman Catholics, and develop stronger responses and alternatives to theological approaches to poverty (e.g., liberation theology) at which Evangelical Protestants are at variance.[41]

Evangelical Protestant statements of sociopolitical cooperation with groups not so aligned are usually accompanied with a further declaration outline and description of doctrinal differences. For example, in 1995, Dallas Theological Seminary, a bastion of Evangelical Protestantism, issued a statement in response to the earlier-mentioned 1994 document on Evangelical/Roman Catholic cooperation, *Evangelicals and Catholics Together: The Christian Mission in the Third Millennium*, a document in which the seminary was not involved nor did it contribute. This response was generated by "a growing concern" among seminary alumni and supporters. In its statement the Dallas Theological seminary recognized that "Evangelicals and Roman Catholics share much in common on moral and social issues and can often cooperate in these areas" and went on to indicate as areas of common concern and agreement secularism, humanism, "false religions," abortion on demand, and pornography and to "remind Evangelicals that Roman Catholics are our allies in the fight to reclaim the basic moral and spiritual values under assault in our society." The seminary, however, pointing particularly to doctrines of justification, baptism, authority of Scripture, and priesthood of all believers, also asserted that "theological differences between Evangelicals and Roman Catholics remain significant and must not be minimized," but allowed "that a number of Roman Catholics are trusting in Jesus alone for their salvation and are truly 'born again.'"[42]

The National Association of Evangelicals (NAE) states its social concerns this way: "We stand committed to biblically defined family values, the sanctity of human life, and human rights."[43] In "An Evangelical Manifesto" the NAE also affirmed specifically "the pursuit of biblical justice (i.e., ministry to the poor)."[44] Other Evangelical Protestants would agree with both of these statements, but would state the issues differently. Roberta Hestenes, president of Eastern College, contributing to the Evangelical Protestant periodical, *Christianity Today*, wrote:

> Evangelical Christians have serious and important contributions to make on the major issues of human dignity and purpose, environmental stewardship, the roles of men and women, the strengthening of families, and the building of Christian community and service centered on the values of the kingdom of God.[45]

Martin Marty notes that the vague nature of Evangelical Protestantism predisposes the movement to diverse hermeneutical perspectives, especially about sociopolitical issues. He observed that the Evangelical Protestant community includes "varied attitudes toward feminist and liberationist hermeneutics [and]...various justifications for diverse social programs, from *Sojourners, The Other Side*, Jacques Ellul, John Howard Yoder, and Mark Hatfield to the Quite Far Right."[46] The spectrum Marty cites includes periodicals and individuals identified as "far left" and as "far right" on sociopolitical issues such as hunger, homelessness, distribution of wealth, abortion, and war and peace. For example, the organization that publishes the magazine *Sojourners*, often labeled as "liberal" because of its political stands against the arms race and the interventionism of U.S. foreign policy (especially in the Western Hemisphere), and bases its corporate political perspective on their understanding of Scripture, had its origins at Evangelical Protestant Trinity Evangelical Divinity School.[47] Other persons could also be given as similar embodiments of the sociopolitical diversity among Evangelical Protestants: Tony Campolo, Ron Sider, James Dobson, Pat Robertson, Jerry Falwell, *Focus on the Family*, World Vision, and others. Other sociopolitical issues with which today's Evangelical Protestants are increasingly concerned would be euthanasia, pornography, and environmentalism among others. Here, too, Evangelical Protestants prefer to ally themselves on these issues with other Evangelical Protestants. For example, environmentalism, characterized by some as a "liberal" issue, is the obvious concern of the Christian Environmental Studies Center, sponsored by various Evangelical Protestant colleges and allied with the Evangelical Environmental Network.[48] Faithful to their Evangelical Protestant regard for authority of Scripture, common questions among these refer to human responsibility in stewardship of God's creation as taught through the Bible. Again, there are also alliances on this and other sociopolitical issues with non-Evangelical Protestants, but where this occurs caveats are almost inevitable.

Further, many Evangelical Protestants can be found among the leaders and supporters of groups as diverse as the Christian Coalition on the one hand and the Baptist Joint Committee on Public Affairs and Americans United for Separation of Church and State on the other. These distinctive and divergent groups differ significantly on matters of public policy regarding religious liberty and separation of church and state. They differ most in terms of interpretation of the establishment and free exercise clauses of the First Amendment of the U.S. Constitution. Their respective stances on the general issues and on particular U.S. Supreme Court cases are rooted in their understanding of the original intent of the framers of the Constitution, but is significantly flavored by the sociopolitical traditions of their respective faith groups (and, in some cases, sub-groups within the contexts their denominational bodies). Those of the Christian Coalition tend to envision the United States as more "accommodationist." That is, their focus on the free exercise clause and their desire to be instruments of creating within the context of the nation an expression of the Kingdom of God compels them to be more accepting of governmental accommodating religion (especially that of the Christian persuasion—and, more specifically that of the Evangelical Protestant bent). As "separationists," those who support the Baptist Joint Committee on Public Affairs and Americans United for Separation of Church and State hold that freedom (expressly religious freedom) is always endangered when government and religion delve into and try to control either indirectly or directly the affairs of the other. This leads them to understand the First Amendment as calling for separation of church and state. Though these respective stances lead to significantly differing approaches to questions regarding prayer and Bible reading in public schools, state-funded support of parochial schools, and so on. Evangelical Protestants within each group will almost invariably support their immediate and traditional views not only with legal citations, but also with biblical texts that provide the doctrinal bases for the traditional perspectives of their faith perspective.

A further understanding of the sociopolitical diversity and the degree of individual political activism that exists among Evangelical Protestants can be had by reminding oneself that concurrently sitting in our nation's capital were President Bill Clinton, Vice-President Al Gore, Speaker of the House Newt Gingrich, and Senate President Pro Tem Strom Thurmond—all Southern Baptists and, as such, labeled by many as Evangelical Protestants. This same contrast can be drawn between former President Jimmy Carter (who addressed the issue of being "born-again" in his first campaign) and presidential aspirant Pat Robertson who supported Ronald Reagan's successful run for the presidency against the incumbent Carter.

One writer has observed that a significant difference in the way Evangelical Protestants have chosen to operate on the sociopolitical arena is through direct and indirect lobbying efforts. "While there was only one Evangelical lobbying effort in existence at mid-century, by 1982 there were twenty-seven and most of those had emerged since 1971."[49] Another means by which many politically right-wing Evangelical Protestants have advanced their sociopolitical agenda is through primary and secondary education. Many have established their own systems of parochial schools either as part of the ministry of an individual church or as the joint effort of like-minded persons in a community. Though in some areas many of these were founded in the 1960s and 1970s to avoid racial integration and/or to sidestep busing for that purpose, the purpose of these schools is today more uniformly to offer an alternative to what they perceive as a pervasive "secular humanism" in the public schools and to transmit their view of "traditional values." Another widespread effort among right-wing Evangelical Protestants (both those who sponsor their own schools and those who do not) to convey their values is to influence public school boards by bloc voting for board members and by regularly petitioning and (sometimes vociferously) influencing school boards in meetings. There is also among Evangelical Protestants particularly a distinct trend toward home-schooling their children. Despite these conspicuous approaches to education taken especially by right-wing Evangelical Protestants, there remain many of that particular branch as well as the more moderate and relatively "left-wing" Evangelical Protestants who support public schooling through a more traditional approach. Despite these differing strategies, all would find a justification for their respective alternatives in a theological base derived from an understanding of various biblical texts.

PERSONAL-ETHICAL DIMENSIONS

Evangelical Protestants tend to decry what they see as a decline in personal morality just as they do in corporate society and to attribute that decay to what they call "moral relativism." They justify their own moral judgments on what they consider the moral absolutes as they find them in Scripture.

Those personal moral issues on which Evangelical Protestants tend to speak publicly and the means by which they do so are also influenced, as they see it, by an understanding of Scripture. For Evangelical Protestants, their emphasis on "holy living" is based on the inward faith experience. This personal relationship with God juxtaposed with a scripturally-based understanding of God's character as morally perfect requires that "God's disposition toward creation [become] the standard by which we will be judged and we judge all human conduct."[50] The process by which this works in the life of the believer and by which the lifestyle is transformed is a part of the aforementioned sanctification.[51] Such is expressed among them in varying ways somewhat dependent on their particular views of sanctification as noted earlier in this chapter.

Evangelical Protestants voices are to be heard particularly on such traditional moral issues as sexuality (especially homosexuality, premarital abstinence, and fidelity within the context of marriage), pornography, drinking, and gambling. They speak out on these issues, too, in a variety of ways both individually and corporately: through one-issue-oriented organizations of which they are a part and/or support, through denominational emphases and conferences, through thematic and Bible study curricula, through the broadcast media they support, and (especially within the contexts of the local church and at denominational meetings) through preaching.

Each of these means of addressing issues is seen by Evangelical Protestants as an opportunity for personal response in the form of joining one's voice and "standing up and being counted" in defense of biblically-based morality. However, each also affords occasions for conviction (i.e., consideration of personal guilt and the resulting awareness and concern for personal repentance), confession, expression of repentance, and rededication of oneself to a life more reflective (or expressive) of their personal relationship with Jesus.

The "True Love Waits" movement among the youth of differing denominations and churches (Evangelical Protestant and beyond) is an example of an Evangelical Protestant approach to sexuality—specifically in terms of sex education and premarital sexual abstinence. Originating with a Southern Baptist, the program leaves the specific design of the program up to the local church but seeks to emphasize biblical teaching on sexuality and to offer youth the opportunity to explore the application of those teachings in their own lives. One singular characteristic of many "True Love Waits" programs and emphases is the occasion for participants to respond by inviting them to sign a card indicating (before their peers, church, and parents) their commitment to premarital sexual abstinence. Some offer other means of response in addition or as an alternative to that of the commitment card. Some even include the youth wearing a ring similar to a wedding band as an indication and a reminder of their commitment.

Though they often eschew the liturgical calendar in planning their curricula, common among Evangelical Protestants is the inclusion in their dated Sunday School/Bible study curricula regularly (i.e., at particular times of the year) occurring lessons on specific personal moral issues. Sometimes curricula will provide for "special lessons" on personal moral issues that can be used in diverse settings and over varying lengths of time. Again, though dealing with many differing personal moral concerns, such lessons will almost invariably involve first a study of Scripture passages that (by some interpretation at least) speak to the issue at hand. Almost as certain will be a concluding call for both inward and outward response on the parts of individual participants.

For some Evangelical Protestants, it was the "retreat into liturgy" among Roman Catholics and mainline Protestants that has detracted from the proclamation of moral teaching within those bodies. In response, their call (as Evangelical Protestants) is for "biblical preaching [that consists of] the diligent and faithful exposition of the biblical text, taking into consideration its literary and historical background as well as assessing its theological significance for the present age."[52] It is in this framework that many Evangelical Protestants would see themselves as claiming (or reclaiming) the liturgical/homiletical expression of their historical and theological heritage.

Within the context of preaching and liturgy whether in the local church or at a large meeting, Evangelical Protestants are especially characterized by regular times of commitment, usually in the form of the "invitation" time at the end of a sermon. Some even describe this as the most important moment in a worship service. Though such would be described as hyperbole by most Evangelical Protestants, they would agree on the importance of personal response to the biblical message whatever the means by which that message has been received. This somewhat theologically based argument is augmented by the practical in that, even though it can be simply an avenue of catharsis, it can also open doors for counseling and other types of ministry, therapy, and learning.

NOTES

[1] Some excellent examples of the diversity of faith perspectives and expressions found within the Evangelical Protestant fellowship are described in *The Variety of American Evangelicalism*, edited by Donald W. Dayton and Robert K. Johnson (Knoxville TN: University of Tennessee Press, 1991).

[2] Martin Luther, "The Ninety-Five Theses, 1517," *Documents of the Christian Church*, 2nd ed., selected and edited by Henry Bettenson (London: Oxford University Press, 1967) 186.

[3] John Calvin, *Institutes of the Christian Religion*, 1.7.4. The translation is that of Ford Lewis Battles in The Library of Christian Classics (Philadelphia: Westminster Press, 1960) 1:79.

[4] Timothy George, *Theology of the Reformers* (Nashville: Broadman Press, 1988) 266.

[5] Unfortunately, the term "Fundamentalism," especially as applied within the context of Christian Protestantism, is often seen as being synonymous with Evangelical Protestantism. Several points are worth noting. First, Christian Fundamentalism exists in many forms. Second, there are those within the Evangelical Protestant family who would accept both terms for themselves. Third, others reject the label but accept Fundamentalists as legitimately part of the Evangelical Protestant community. Finally, a few others (including this writer) reject many Fundamentalists as true Evangelical Protestants because their foundational authority rests not in Scripture, but in their interpretation of Scripture.

[6] Alister McGrath, *Evangelicalism & the Future of Christianity* (Downers Grove IL: InterVarsity Press, 1995) 55-56.

[7] Donald G. Bloesch, *Essentials of Evangelical Theology* (San Francisco: Harper & Row, 1978) 1:9.

[8] Ibid., 14.

[9] National Association of Evangelicals, *"NAE Statement of Faith," An Evangelical Manifesto* (Wheaton IL: National Association of Evangelicals, 1996, accessed online 11 May 1998) <http://nae.goshen.net/naemanifesto.html>.

[10] Kenneth O. Gangel and Christy Sullivan, "Evangelical Theology and Religious Education," *Theologies of Religious Education*, ed. Randolph Crump Miller (Birmingham AL: Religious Education Press, 1995) 59-68.

[11] R. Albert Mohler, "A Call for Baptist Evangelicals and Evangelical Baptists: Communities of Faith and a Common Quest for Identity," *Southern Baptists & American Evangelicals: The Conversation Continues*, David S. Dockery, ed. (Nashville: Broadman Press, 1993) 238.

[12] Associated Baptist Press, "Researcher Defines 'Born-Again' Terminology," 12 March 1998.

[13] Stanley J. Grenz, *Theology for the Community of God* (Nashville: Broadman & Holman, 1994) 518-19.

[14] Ibid., 519.

[15] James P. Boyce, "A Brief Catechism of Bible Doctrine," appendix to *Abstract of Systematic Theology* (1987) (reprint, Escondido CA: den Kulk Christian Foundation) ii.

[16] Richard Land, "Response to 'A Brief History of Inerrancy, Mostly in North America,'" *The Proceedings of the Conference on Biblical Inerrancy, 1987* (Nashville: Broadman Press, 1987) 43n.

[17] Norman L. Geisler, ed. *Inerrancy* (Grand Rapids: Zondervan, 1979) ix.

[18] Gangel and Sullivan, 69-70.

[19] Grenz, 519-22.

[20] Robert Preus, "The Inerrancy of Scripture," Proceedings, 47- 55.

[21] For example, while Article XII holds that inerrancy extends to the field of science, Article XIII denies that the Bible is to be held to "standards of truth that are alien to its usage or purpose" and that "inerrancy is negated by Biblical phenomena such as...observational descriptions of nature." This is at best unclear and at worst contradictory. Cf. "The Chicago Statement on Biblical Inerrancy," Geisler, 496.

[22] Bernard Ramm, *The Evangelical Heritage* (Waco TX: Word Books, 1973) 31-32.

[23] Bloesch, 1:90-91.

[24] Grenz, 268-75.

[25] R. C. Sproul, *Faith Alone: The Evangelical Doctrine of Justification* (Grand Rapids: Baker Books, 1995) 155-56.

[26] Bloesch, 1:35.

[27] Ibid., 2:45.

[28] Stanley J. Grenz, *Revisioning Evangelical Theology: A Fresh Agenda for the 21st Century* (Downers Grove IL: InterVarsity Press, 1993) 164.

[29] Sproul, 26-29.
[30] Ibid., 44-47.
[31] *Merriam-Webster's Collegiate Dictionary*, 10th ed. (1995), s.v. "church."
[32] William F. Arndt and F. Wilbur Gingrich, *A Greek-English Lexicon of the New Testament: and Other Early Christian Literature*, 4th ed. (Chicago: University of Chicago Press, 1957) 459.
[33] William C. Robinson, "The Nature of the Church," *Christian Faith and Modern Theology*, ed. Carl F. H. Henry (Grand Rapids: Baker Book House, 1964) 389.
[34] Grenz, *Theology*, 635.
[35] Grenz, *Revisioning*, 164-65.
[36] McGrath, 147.
[37] Donald W. Dayton, *Discovering an Evangelical Heritage* (New York: Harper & Row, 1976) 85-91.
[38] Donald G. Bloesch, *The Future of Evangelical Christianity: A Call for Unity and Diversity* (Colorado Springs CO: Helmers & Howard, 1988) 134.
[39] James Davison Hunter, *Evangelicalism: The Coming Generation* (Chicago: University of Chicago Press, 1987) 117-25.
[40] Bloesch, *Essentials*, 2:164-67.
[41] Richard J. Mouw, "Toward an Evangelical Theology of Poverty," *Christian Faith and Practice in the Modern World*, Mark A. Noll and David F. Wells, eds. (Grand Rapids: Eerdmans, 1988) 218-38.
[42] Dallas Theological Seminary, "Response to the Discussion of Evangelical/Roman Catholic Cooperation" (Dallas: Dallas Theological Seminary, 1995, accessed on-line 11 May 1998) <http://www.bible.org/cam/romcath/romanca3.html>.
[43] National Association of Evangelicals, "Attending to Human Concerns" (Wheaton IL: National Association of Evangelicals, 1996, accessed on-line 23 October 1998) <http://nae.goshen.net/values/values6.html>.
[44] National Association of Evangelicals, An Evangelical Manifesto (Wheaton IL: National Association of Evangelicals, 1996, accessed on-line 11 May 1998) <http://nae.goshen.net/naemanifesto.html>.
[45] Roberta Hestenes, "Important Contributions," Christianity Today 36 (5 October 1992): 24.
[46] Martin E. Marty, "The Years of the Evangelicals," The Christian Century 06 (15 February 1989):172.
[47] Randall Balmer, *Mine Eyes Have Seen the Glory: A Journey into the Evangelical Subculture in America* (New York: Oxford University Press, 1989) 213.
[48] Cf. Christian Environmental Studies Center, Montreat College; http://cesc.montreat.edu.
[49] Hunter, 127.
[50] Grenz, *Theology*, 124.
[51] Ibid., 578.
[52] Bloesch, *Future*, 146.

GIFTS OF COMMONALITY

[CHAPTER 2]

A COMMON CORE

One obvious way to discuss Evangelical Protestants gifts to religious education is to begin with what stands as the axis around which Evangelical Protestant doctrine and practice revolve. The Evangelical Protestant perspective on authority of Scripture provides a common core and, as an example, is a significant gift to all of religious education, regardless of faith orientation. That is, as a gift to religious education, it reminds any faith community of the need for a core language, a core curriculum, a core authority, and a core experience to educate more effectively in the faith.

A CORE LANGUAGE

Imagine the difficulty of teaching any subject without a common language. Language can be simply understood as the medium through which ideas are communicated in symbols (words, characters, etc.), idioms, grammar, and syntax. Any one of these elements alone significantly impacts how the ideas being communicated are understood by both the sender and the receiver.

For example, in most U.S. schools when one speaks of teaching grammar the reference is to the teaching of *English* grammar (and *American English* at that). Anyone who has studied English grammar and, subsequently, other language such as the Romance languages of Spanish, Italian, and French will attest to the tremendous differences that can and do exist among the grammars of these various languages despite their own shared roots in Latin. Even more significant are the differences among the grammars, characters, and idioms of the biblical languages of Greek and Hebrew and other languages such as Mandarin or Cantonese Chinese and Japanese. What teacher would try to teach specifics of grammar without regard to which language was at issue?

Language is a powerful communicator of ideas, but the gap that occurs among participants when there is no common language negates that power. For Evangelical Protestants, their belief in the authority of Scripture provides a type of common language. That is, both in a given generation and across generations (regardless of time) Evangelical Protestants can more readily find themselves in dialogue with others regarding matters of doctrine and practice (i.e., ideas) because the Bible provides them with a common language.

To discuss these issues is to discuss the Bible. Despite the significant hermeneutical differences that can and do exist among Evangelical Protestants and even within their respective fellowships and within and across generations, their exchange of ideas will ultimately rest on understandings of scriptural teachings. This is related to the concept of a common authority that will be discussed subsequently, but may be seen at an arguably more superficial, utilitarian level.

Part of the purpose of every religion is the transmission of ideas. Sometimes the ideas are shared so as to explain the religion to those outside its community. They are also dispersed with an eye toward converting others to the faith. And, especially within the aegis of religious education, the concepts of the religion in question are passed on to subsequent generations. Whether as an apologetic, missionizing, or didactic tool, any religious education requires a common language in some form. Just as a teacher cannot teach grammar without reference to which language is at issue, so there can be no effective religious education without reference to that which most unites and is most universally held by the faith community.

For most, it will be whatever canon they claim and share. They will find this common language at the core of who they are and whatever they will accomplish as a teaching community. Evangelical Protestants evince an understanding of this with their use of the Bible. Their gift, then, is a reminder that the effective and efficient communication of ideas and concepts required by religious education must rise out of a common language, whatever that language may be and whatever form it may take.

A CORE CURRICULUM

Most schools have what they call their "core" courses or curriculum. Typically and by some definition, these courses reflect those areas of skill, knowledge, or understanding the school desires to have been attained by *all* its students. These cores can be said to reflect the respective schools' understandings of its mission and purpose and to serve as a unifying influence among faculty and students alike. They are important expressions of the commonality that makes each respective academic community exactly that: a group with a common base of perspective that is shared and, so, is unified. Also, as with a common language, a school's core curriculum provides the basis for further dialogue among differing majors and disciplines, particularly in a liberal arts environment. The value is that among students of diverse vocational interests and goals, there remains some common perspective that enables them to appreciate and communicate with each other as they compare, contrast, and otherwise discuss areas, problems, and issues of mutual concern. This enables more creative and synergistic approaches to problem-solving.

Evangelical Protestants have found, in their common language as described above and in elements of their other points of commonality as described below, a type of core curriculum that offers them at least some similarity of perspective despite the quality and quantity of their otherwise differing practices and thought. Though their divergences of interpretation, application, and denomination can (and do!) divide them deeply, this "core curriculum," as in a school, provides a means by which Evangelical Protestants can communicate and deliberate together regarding matters of education, fellowship, and mutual concern.

As a larger religious community, Evangelical Protestants do not stand alone in their many types or degrees of diversity. This seems to be universal among religions having many adherents. Therefore, these religions, too, are in need of rediscovering their particular "core curriculum" to facilitate the dialogue necessary for quality education and creative responses as their religion confronts, responds to, and interacts with the world. This gift of Evangelical Protestants to religious education, then, is their testimony to the importance of rediscovering (perhaps recovering) the core curriculum of any religious community to its educational enterprise.

A CORE AUTHORITY

The word "authority" has myriad connotations. It can conjure up military images of a type of line of command, refer to citations in research or legal works, or even allude to certain freedoms, powers, or rights granted an entity. All these, of course, reflect the etymology of the word found in the root "author," which bespeaks origins and source.

Authority is a pedagogical issue at many points. First, akin to the core curriculum described above, there must be a source—a point of origin, if you will—for curricular decisions. The parameters and course of the curriculum must be decided. Without some means by which to define and delimit the curriculum, the whole educational enterprise becomes much too nebulous for its goals and objectives to be identified. So, there must be some authority somewhere to serve this purpose of defining the curriculum.

An authority can also serve to determine to some degree what pedagogical form or forms will be used. As an obvious example, the authority (author, source, origin) of the pedagogical form called the "Montessori method" was/is Maria Montessori. Above and beyond the issue of curriculum, this method or form is characterized by Montessori's specific approach to realist education that would, for her and her disciples, enable a child to discover her/his world by clearing that which would impede the child from that discovery. It may be argued that differing circumstances may call for differing pedagogical forms or methods. However, there still must be a source by which even that determination will be made.

Further, an authority also must decide what content is to be taught even within the context of a given curriculum. For instance, in a "typical" classroom, the teacher—as the authority—must decide what part of the curriculum is to be taught on a particular day and time. This is usually expressed in the lesson plan and is one of those areas where a teacher must be especially mindful not only of the curriculum, but also of the readiness and the needs of the students, for here these two factors are brought to confluence.

An authority serves as the source of a call to action and a certain degree of freedom within the scope of pedagogy. Learning is most purposeful when, within the context of the lesson, there is some measure of a charge for the student to do something with what has been learned. When followed, this call to action both provides for reinforcement of what has been learned and frees the student for further learning through his/her application of the learned principles in life situations not covered or spoken to in a formal lesson.

Authority also speaks to the matter of discipline. Though the nature of the relationship of discipline to pedagogy is debatable, it is clear that any educational setting will have basic parameters that govern interpersonal and group relationships, be the understanding of those parameters formal or informal, stated or understood. The authority is that which dictates those principles and standards for behavior.

Finally, an authority is also that to which one refers in substantiation of a stand one takes academically. Whether in the development of a paper or a discussion, those who make a statement that either may be out of the ordinary or seek to establish a matter of fact are normally expected to cite their authority. Some of the type questions that are being asked are: "Who says that this is so?" "Who are they that they have knowledge of this?" "What gives that source the right to make that claim?"

All these facets of authority are vested by Evangelical Protestants in Scripture—specifically for them understood to be the Christian Bible—and lie at the core of what they mean by authority of Scripture. The Bible is, for Evangelical Protestants, the authority from which their curricula rise and, in fact, ultimately serves as the core curriculum for virtually all of what they do educationally. In many differing ways and to various degrees, the Bible also serves as an authority for pedagogical methods and forms. For instance, the norm for most books on "Christian education" is to include chapters or sections on teaching methods found in the Old Testament as well as in the life of Jesus and those of the Apostles. Further, the Bible serves most educational efforts of Evangelical Protestants as the primary content. That is, even those lessons and other curricula that may be thematic will still focus, by some measure, on biblical hermeneutics and teaching. Though this certainly can be described as an "authoritative call to action," despite the narrowly-understood hermeneutical perspective of some Evangelical Protestants, it also offers the individual tremendous freedom within biblically-understood and -prescribed parameters. This would be especially so among those Evangelical Protestant fellowships that emphasize soul-competency and/or priesthood of all believers. This freedom notwithstanding, there Biblical authority provides Evangelical Protestants with a basis for both individual and corporate discipline. Ideally applied, the Bible defines areas of responsibility and accountability for God-to-individual, person-to-person, and group-individual relationships. As a matter of discipline, it further provides the structure and basis for a type of transgenerational relationship among the family of faith (even across centuries and millennia). By this, it enables a generation to be faithful to its heritage while speaking to its contemporary culture and generation. Finally, for Evangelical Protestants, Scripture is a core authority in that matters of doctrine, conscience, experience, and conduct, both personally and corporately, are ideally to be substantiated by legitimate use and understanding of biblical passages.

These Evangelical Protestant applications of biblical authority are accompanied by obvious dangers of abuse of Scripture or using Scripture to abuse people. However, it is this threat that bespeaks the immediacy and the comprehensive nature of biblical authority and, so, compels the study and teaching of the biblical witness. That is, for Evangelical Protestants, since the Bible is such an authority, in some manner and to some degree it speaks to every area of life rendering its study and application imperative.

Pedagogically, the gift of Evangelical Protestants to the education of other religious communities at this juncture is that of a testimony to immediacy, interest, and investment. A truism is that any student of any subject will study and learn more effectively when the subject is a matter of immediate interest, application, and investment. This could be said also regarding the vitality of a religion or faith alone. With no compelling reason for application to one's life, a religion or faith will become a sterile philosophy. This gift, then, also takes the form of a challenge to the educators of whatever faith to seek the core authority of their religious community and heritage and let that shape and inform their pedagogy. By doing so, religious education can more effectively render its faith relevant to any given generation and society.

A CORE EXPERIENCE

A common, core experience results from and in pedagogical encounters of varying sorts. First, in an educational event or activity the student, hopefully and potentially, will engage the material/content, any other students, and the teacher. The students as a group will also engage the material/content and the teacher. Additionally, the student(s) and the teacher are involved with the content/material as yet another body or entity. This emphasis on the role of education in facilitating and otherwise directing and administrating personal and social dimensions of various experiences is at the heart of pragmatism's basic pedagogical approach. For the pragmatist, this enables and empowers the student to discover solutions to problems they face whether those solutions are innovative and creative or rooted in tradition.

One pedagogical concept or approach that illustrates in microcosm (i.e., the classroom) the educational value of a common experience is that of the "Advance Organizer." Developed by educational theorist David Ausubel, the purpose of the advance organizer approach is to enable learners to add to and organize their knowledge so that more information is stored and that this information can be processed by the learner as future situations require. It can be a wonderful means by which a content area with many ancillary principles and applications is taught.

Advance organizers are used in many forms and in many instances. Here's an example of how an advance organizer could be employed: A teacher involved in outdoor education has three basic teaching goals for her class. One is that her students grasp and can describe the complexity of the relationships that exist among the *flora* and *fauna* of the environment. The other is that her learners can describe how human incursions can negatively and positively impact the environment.

In anticipation of a field trip—an extended hike on a wilderness trail— she describes and explains the concepts in her goals and tells them that these are principles they will see being played out around them on their hike. As the hike progresses, she points out examples of those principles and describes the processes involved in each specific situation.

Anthropologically, any religion can be described as a set of common experiences and values that, by some definition, speak to issues of the transcendent. Religion has always served as that part of a culture that—along with other cultural characteristics such as values and rituals—sets patterns for human behavior and enables people to deal with living in the world that surrounds them. From this perspective, the issue for religion is to help people deal with the supernatural world or the transcendent, both of which are aspects of the world people consistently find to be beyond their control. Therefore, all religions and all religious education are based somewhat on what comprises a core experience or set of experiences. The same is true among Evangelical Protestants.

For Evangelical Protestants, it is their common (and, to some degree, commonly understood) experience that provides a core to their pedagogy. This experience is what they refer to as salvation and/or, as noted in the opening chapter, being "born again." They may differ (sometimes fractiously) along multiple lines about some facets of salvation (e.g., the meaning and/or role of providence and "election" in the salvific or redemptive process, preferred models of the atonement, etc.). However, Evangelical Protestants almost universally would agree that the common, core experience of salvation is, at least in theory, a basic, unifying influence. This core experience of salvation, in which a person consciously and voluntarily enters into a personal relationship with God is, for Evangelical Protestants, basic to all other human needs and issues. It is through this experience that persons engage not only God and Scripture, but also other Christians and the world and non-Christians in ways different than before. They will find more motivation to learn and to join, especially with others of more similar faith, in religious education for the purpose of engaging personal and social problems with people of similar experience and perspective.

This perspective of core experience can and (unfortunately) sometimes does result among some Evangelical Protestants in an exclusivity and arrogance that many others find both anathema and repugnant. However, its value as an implicitly motivating factor should not be lost. Rather, as a gift it is a reminder to all of religious education of the importance in any faith group of connecting their pedagogy to basic core experiences, giving their students reasons to learn as they engage their faith and bring it to bear on their circumstances and their world.

[CHAPTER 3]

A COMMON PURPOSE

Another gift Evangelical Protestants offer to the religious education of any faith group is found in the role their sense of common purpose serves in all they do, especially in the way they view and what they do in their own efforts of religious education. It exemplifies how a common purpose shared within and among individuals and congregations can serve as a catalyst for clarifying identity, the impetus for growth, and the motivation for cooperation.

PURPOSE AND ORGANIZATIONAL BEHAVIOR

Purpose, by expressing an organization's basic commitments and values, is a potent cohesive force. It provides the framework by which those involved are able to develop a shared vision, understanding, and ownership of group relationships, strategies, and goals. Such investment is the catalyst for the coalescing of the objective, affective, and active energies within and among the group and furnishes the means by which even particular, individual performance is directly and clearly related to that of the organization. Also, clarifying, stating and committing to common purpose enable more sufficient internal and external audits and evaluations at both the corporate and individual levels.

This understanding of a synergistic approach driven by common purpose has, over the past twenty years, grown in popularity in the business world—especially in the manufacturing sector. Sometimes expressed as TQM (Total Quality Management) or CQI (Continuous Quality Improvement), the point of the paradigm is to identify and "totally" and "continuously" commit and work toward a common purpose as expressed in terms of a target group (i.e., customers), outcomes, or processes.[1] Corporations that have styled and managed themselves this way have found the method to enable them to be more flexible and responsive and to access and utilize the abilities of their workers more effectively.

One good example of how this works is found in the football program at the small university at which I teach. Each spring the team participates in a conditioning program designed to increase the players' strength, quickness, and endurance. Each player sets personal performance goals in the various areas and exercises on which they work. Toward the end of this program the team divides into units: offensive line, defensive line, defensive backfield, etc. Separately the units discuss their purpose as part of the team and develop specific unit performance goals for each game in the fall. They discuss together how these unit goals play a part in the goal of the team as a whole—winning a national championship. As individuals, as units, and as a team, this system that emphasizes common purpose with specific, demanding goals is much more effective than the generalized "work hard" or "do your best" in motivating the student-athletes (all our athletics programs are NCAA Division III—nonscholarship) and in producing a higher level of output (ours has been one of the strongest NCAA Division III football programs in the nation).

Rather than imposing uniformity across the spectra of organizational concerns, purpose actually warrants and empowers creativity in particular circumstances and situations faced by specific units within the group. Focusing on common purpose is a holistic approach to "keeping the main thing the main thing," fosters among individuals and smaller units a sense of investment, and enables the organization to evolve and to be more dynamic.

PURPOSE AND EDUCATIONAL OBJECTIVES

Common purpose is also a powerful tool for education. In the form of a common vision it both motivates and unifies. Expressed as an educational objective, common purpose directs vitality, emphases, and priorities. Educational contexts can express or utilize purpose in various ways.

In the mid 1950s and early 1960s Benjamin S. Bloom, David R. Krathwohl, and others developed taxonomies of educational objectives within three domains of learning: cognitive, affective, and psychomotor. Bloom's book, published in 1956, dealt with the objective domain. Krathwohl's, published in 1964, was concerned with the affective domain. Their aim was to help educators clarify objectives so that they may be placed appropriately within the larger context of the educational process and that they might be measured properly. They also intended to remind educators that the entire educational process should, in some sense, be centered around purpose. For instance, a curriculum or a classroom might modify and employ any one of Bloom's educational objectives within the objective domain as an explicitly stated purpose either within a class session or over the course of a term (or series of terms). The usefulness in clarifying students' understandings of the instructor's expectations are obvious, especially in specifying observable behavior. Krathwohl's descriptions of objectives in the affective domain are useful in relating to common purpose, but in ways differing from that of the objective. The affective domain can be seen as facilitating movement from one becoming aware of a common purpose to, ultimately, that common purpose being characterized by and in that person's life.

RELIGIOUS EDUCATION AS AN OPEN SYSTEM

Relating more specifically to religious education, Timothy Arthur Lines described an open system as a "more promising" model. He noted that the dynamic relationship existent among structure, function, and purpose (and those, corporately, with the environment) defined such a system and observed that such allowed for more interaction with the surroundings. He also allowed that a totally open system is a "theoretical construct" and that a system totally open would lose its identity as differentiated from that of its milieu.[2] The dynamism is lost due to a lack of limitations.

One image that illustrates this principle is that of burning gasoline in an internal combustion engine. A gallon of gasoline poured out on the ground or in a large barrel would burn if a lighted match were thrown on it. However, the unconstrained energy released from the gasoline would be dissipated, and little work would be realized. On the other hand, that same amount of gasoline, injected in measured amounts and burned within the confines of the cylinders of an engine, harnesses and channels that energy and can power an automobile for miles.

The loss of identity (and constraint) in a totally open system would both rise from and lead to loss of purpose. This can be seen to be at the root of and as the unifying factor among the "Flaws in Church Education" identified by Charles R. Foster: loss of corporate memory, irrelevance of teaching from the Bible, subversion of Christian educational goals, cultural captivity of church education, and collapse of the church's educational strategy.[3] Further, much of what Foster (in a chapter titled "A Guide to Revisioning Local Church Education") suggests by which future Christian education can deal with and/or eliminate those flaws, is a process toward discovering/rediscovering common purpose.[4]

Recapturing a sense of purpose (in the form of shared vision) is, by many definitions, also that for which Thomas Groome calls in his "shared praxis" approach to religious education. As with Foster's "revisioning," Groome's five movements of shared praxis outline a method by which persons are called to discover, engage, and respond to common purpose (in Groome's words, "shared vision").[5]

THE COMMON PURPOSE OF EVANGELICAL PROTESTANTS

The one vision or purpose most shared and held in common among Evangelical Protestants can be found in the term used to differentiate them from other Protestant Christians. At this point one must understand that in accepting or using the term "evangelical," Evangelical Protestants are not necessarily claiming an exclusivity among Christians (though, unfortunately, either overtly or by implication, some do). Rather, the matter is seen as one of both understanding and emphasis.

The term "evangelical" derives from the New Testament Greek word *euangelion* ("gospel" or, literally, "good news"). The term "gospel" has various meanings among Evangelical Protestants yet, by some definition, always in connection with an understanding of the Kingdom of God. While some may interpret the Kingdom of God only in the eschatological sense (very few would see it as present solely in the ministry of the historical Jesus), most Evangelical Protestants would take the approach of "realized eschatology," seeing it as the manifestation of God's influence on contemporary human pursuits and God's rule in human hearts and actions.

At this point Evangelical Protestants can and often do differ as to weight or priority given one approach to or element of the gospel (sometimes to the exclusion of the other). As noted in chapter 1, some Evangelical Protestants will accentuate the salvific aspect of the gospel, emphasizing (to the point of exclusivity with some, almost so with others) the spiritual reconciliation between God and persons made possible by the redemptive act of Jesus in his crucifixion. Others stress the social aspects of the gospel, founding this on Jesus' own observation that he had come to proclaim jubilee. Among Evangelical Protestants, however, this would rarely be done to the point of singularity.[6]

Most Evangelical Protestants make a concerted effort to bring about a type of balance between these two general approaches, though probably most would give at least a degree of primacy to the salvific. Some would see social action as the means by which to gain opportunity to spread the salvific message. Others see the salvific aspect of the gospel as that which transforms the person and motivates him/her toward fulfilling the part of the gospel that speaks to social action. Yet others see the two in a more holistic way and would hold that they are inextricably intertwined. In terms of their common core, these differences find their implicit or explicit foundations in divergent hermeneutical approaches to the Bible.

COMMON PURPOSE AND RELIGIOUS EDUCATION

Whatever their dissimilarities at the points above, Evangelical Protestants, by definition, see their common purpose as that of proclaiming—by word or action—the gospel. It is this common purpose, however it may be understood, that drives all they do, especially in areas of religious education.

In the congregational setting it is both the means and the goal toward which education works and will usually, in some form or fashion, be understood to permeate all of congregational life. Although she is a Roman Catholic and not an Evangelical Protestant, Maria Harris's holistic model for religious education found in her 1989 book, *Fashion Me a People: Curriculum in the Church*, is useful as a framework for grasping how this works in Evangelical Protestant churches. In *Fashion Me a People*, Harris suggests five interrelated and intertwined curricular forms that shape the intentional and the unintentional educational ministry of a church: *koinonia*, *leiturgia*, *didache*, *kerygma*, and *diakonia*.

In their various respective expressions each one of these—in Evangelical Protestant churches—finds at its very heart the common purpose of gospel proclamation. *Koinonia*, inclusive of worship, is that which leads the church toward the realization of fellowship, commonality, or community in the truest sense and in its many implications. *Leiturgia* also involves worship, but more centrally, and is that in which the congregation focuses on the development of the spirituality in its various personal, corporate, inward, and outward dimensions. *Didache* speaks to that which is explicitly taught, whatever the context: schooling, preaching, or formal educational curriculum. Further, its more immediate concern relates to issues of the doctrinal and moral teachings of the faith community. *Kerygma* is the curricular form that is the most prophetic in that the main issue is that of the congregation sharing, within and outside of its immediate fellowship, a "word from God." The challenges of *kerygma* would include those of authentic theological reflection and the summons to public action. *Diakonia* calls the congregation to embody the servant model in which it seeks to meet, individually and corporately, the many and differing needs of the community, society, and world, in which it resides.

Whatever the religious educational context within a "typical" Evangelical Protestant church, teaching regarding fellowship or community (i.e., that which is the basis for their unity) *is* the gospel in terms of both shared experience and shared task. This is the main thrust in worship, prayer, and Bible study. It is why most Evangelical Protestant churches will devote significant time and energy in training congregants in conversion-oriented evangelism. Once converts are made, Evangelical Protestant churches usually provide some form of catechetical instruction for the purpose of consolidating gains, confirming the convert's experience, and equipping and motivating the convert for personal evangelistic efforts. This is especially true among those Evangelical Protestant fellowships that give particular emphasis to the doctrine of the priesthood of all believers. At this juncture it is important for one to recognize that, though the vast majority of Evangelical Protestant churches are, to varying degrees, formally or informally involved in meeting differing needs in their respective communities (and around the world), Evangelical Protestants see conversion-oriented evangelism as service in that it meets what they see as the deepest and most significant and eternal of human needs (i.e., that of a redemptive relationship with God). In like manner, in teaching and training its members to be a prophetic voice, for Evangelical Protestant churches this "word from God" will emanate from their respective aforementioned emphases and understandings of the gospel.

Since there are, within the larger body of Evangelical Protestantism, ample multifarious forms, hermeneutical and theological approaches to facilitate differing means of interchange with its surroundings, it can be seen as an open system (whether or not those involved see it as such). This allows for the rich diversity that characterizes Evangelical Protestantism. Though some within their family are nonplused and frustrated by the complexities that also result from that multiformity, it establishes conditions that have tremendous potential in nurturing vitality and growth within individuals and at many levels of corporate life. Yet, what keeps Evangelical Protestantism from moving toward a totally open system (and, perhaps in the eyes of many, it does not keep them far enough from it) is the vision of and commitment to the common purpose found within its framework. Similar to the image of engine cylinders harnessing the power of gasoline, the common purpose of Evangelical Protestants found in proclamation of the gospel allows the individual and corporate fires to burn while providing a level of control to render useful the energy generated by those fires.

A religion can, through processes such as institutionalization, find itself becoming a closed system. In doing so, it is in danger of refusing any dialogue with its environment and thus loses its relevance and vitality. In this context the religion's educational efforts degenerate into indoctrination with a restrictiveness that strangles and with little, if any, awareness of or sensitivity to what is happening in the lives of its adherents. A star that may have once burned brightly, that religious education inevitably collapses into a black hole into which all that comes near are absorbed and from which radiates only enough energy to indicate that it (perhaps) exists.

On the other hand, a religion that seeks to be totally open with no sense of purpose will inevitably lose its identity and deteriorate into an ill-defined shadow. The goals, strategies, etc. of its religious education are doomed to become an amorphous quagmire of fuzziness and imprecision. Since it stands for nothing, this type of religious education will be unable to utilize and channel the corporate and individual gifts and energies of its adherents as teacher or students. The result is that it will lack any significant relevance and force, much less realize even a modicum of synergy. What light it might shed is so dim as to be lost in that of its surroundings.

The sense of common purpose among Evangelical Protestants is a significant gift to religious education with many implications that give rise to or influence other gifts it offers. Its immediate importance is that it calls any faith community be more dynamic as an effective open system. Concurrently (and importantly), it is also an example of how through its religious education that faith can both move beyond narrowly-understood minutiae—either within or beyond a specific faith community—while (as with common authority) maintaining its identity and keeping in touch with its roots. In leading and helping its faith community discover, claim, and focus on common purpose as the means by which to find that balance and to avoid falling into triviality whatever the expression or cause, religious education will be an agent of the relevance, dynamism, and synergy.

NOTES

[1] Dan Ciampa, *Total Quality: A User's Guide for Implementation* (Reading MA: Addison-Wesley Publishing Co., 1991) 6-7.

[2] Timothy Arthur Lines, *Systemic Religious Education* (Birmingham AL: Religious Education Press, 1987) 45-48.

[3] Charles R. Foster, *Educating Congregations: The Future of Christian Education* (Nashville: Abingdon Press, 1994) 22-35.

[4] Ibid., 136-55.

[5] Thomas Groome, *Christian Religious Education: Sharing Our Story and Vision* (San Francisco: Harper & Row, 1980) 207-223.

[6] To use the term "never" rather than "rarely" is tempting and probably would be safe given our understanding of the self-defining parameters that characterize Evangelical Protestants. As noted in chapter 1, anyone may claim for themselves the appellation "Evangelical Protestant" with impunity. Nevertheless, given the generally understood connotations of the various terms, it would seem aberrant if not paradoxical that one who emphasizes the social aspect of the gospel to the exclusion of the salvific would wish to be known as Evangelical Protestants.

[CHAPTER 4]

DRINKING FROM THEIR OWN WELLS

The latter half of Genesis 26 contains a very telling story about the patriarch Isaac that serves as a framework for understanding yet another Evangelical Protestant gift to religious education. The account deals with conflict over the wells dug by Isaac's father, Abraham. Water was a valuable commodity to the herdsman of the area. The Philistines and others who were envious of the water resources that had been left to Isaac filled in many of the wells. According to verses 19-33, Isaac's response was to redig and rename the wells left to him by his father. He also dug and named new wells, some of which were sources of further contention with the surrounding people. It was out of his redigging his father's wells and digging some of his own that Isaac found the nurture he and his herds needed. Further, it is significant that immediately subsequent to this story (and, it may be claimed, as its climax), in vv. 23-25, one reads of Isaac's encounter with a theophany at Beersheba. In this event God confirmed Isaac as Abraham's successor. There Isaac settled, signified by his building an altar, pitching his tent, and digging a well. The connotation for Isaac was that, by these actions, he was claiming God as his own and confirming his own part in covenant with God.

In summary, he was truly finding a "place to call home" not only physically, but also spiritually. The well would provide the water from which he and his herds would drink for physical sustenance. The spiritual wells from which he would drink could be found in four related and overlapping but somewhat distinct sources: the altar as a token reminding Isaac of his covenant with God, the covenant itself as an expression of the relationship God desired with Isaac, the personal nature of the covenant and that relationship, and the person and character of God.

THE ROLE IN SPIRITUAL FORMATION

Susanne Johnson draws on this rich image in book *Christian Spiritual Formation in the Church and Classroom.* Johnson's purpose for the book was to explore the dimensions of spiritual formation as the crux or nexus of Christian education. Shying away from popular or trendy concepts of spirituality, but still seeking to address the issue, Johnson defines the term as "our self-transcendent capacity as human beings to recognize and to participate in

God's creative and redemptive activity in all of creation."[1] As Paul Tillich, H. Richard Niebuhr, and others have described faith (though not salvific faith) as a universal, so Johnson does spirituality. In further similarity with Tillich's and Niebuhr's respective views of faith, Johnson also writes that, by its definition, personal spirituality is not all-encompassing. Rather, for each individual it is more a peculiar and continuing journey of spiritual renewal.

Also important to note is that Johnson's particular interest is not simply spirituality or spiritual formation in general. Her prevailing interest is in the distinct nature of Christian spiritual formation and how it might be addressed by Christian religious education. Nevertheless, as we will see, her imagery (and that of the Isaac story from which hers is drawn) is fruitful both toward understanding how Evangelical Protestants work at this point and, in turn, how this is helpful to (more specifically) Jewish and Christian religious education, though also to religious education in general.

The opening chapter of *Christian Spiritual Formation* is titled "Drinking from Our Own Wells." In the chapter Johnson used the metaphor to describe the intensely personal nature of religion and religious expression in terms of a human pilgrimage toward authentic spiritual self-transcendence. However, she does not deny, but affirms, the role and the importance of the community as both as a contributor to and the context within which the individual spiritual formation occurs. Admittedly, a certain tension between the personal and the corporate dimensions of spirituality is inevitable. However, a balance can be found in which personal spiritual formation is nurtured and realized through individual appropriation befitting of Scripture as well as the tradition and culture that have borne the individual. Disparaging any of those determinants is neither necessary nor desirable. Instead, the faith community—realized in terms of either the heritage one receives or the present congregation of which one is a part—can and should be the setting (a "safe place") for discussing and exploring questions that both lead to and rise from spiritual formation, i.e., those of doctrinal, political (in the sense of social action), and liturgical importance.

EVANGELICAL PROTESTANT THEOLOGY AND CHRISTIAN SPIRITUAL FORMATION

Three particular theological concepts—*imago dei*, sanctification, and priesthood of all believers—must be addressed to comprehend and clarify how "drinking from one's own wells" can be a helpful paradigm if religious education on any level is to influence spiritual formation positively. The first has to do with what is meant by people being created "in the image of God." Rooted in Gen 1:26-27, this biblical teaching, sometimes known as *imagio dei* has had various interpretations over the centuries among Jews and Christians. Those diverse hermeneutical approaches have included elements related to issues of the capacity of human beings for dominion, rationality (i.e., that relating to intelligence, or affection, or morality—or all of these), and creativity. For the most part, the multifarious doctrines that have developed regarding *imagio dei* have been mixtures of those elements, but have almost always shared the basic understanding that it has something to do with humans (though some would deny women's participation in being created in God's image, holding it more exclusively for men) as distinct and set apart from the rest of creation and as spiritual personalities with at least some degree or expression of the power of will. Important to religious education is how one Christian saint, Augustine of Hippo, viewed *imagio dei*. Augustine saw the potential of this rational nature to be used as an agent of commonality by which people could relate to God, thus evoking the tension between faith and reason. It should also be noted that there is a wide spectrum of beliefs about the effect of "the Fall" (i.e., the coming of sin into the world) on the image of God in humans. Some believe that sin obliterated the image, while others hold that it was—to varying degrees of understanding—damaged, but not irreparably.

The second theological concept deals with salvation or redemption not just as conversion, but as formation or growth. The term most often used in Christian circles at this point is "sanctification." *Sanctus*, the Latin root of the term, is usually translated "holy" and has the immediate connotation of someone or something being set apart. As a Christian doctrine, sanctification is generally understood to have to do with an individual being made into a better, more moral person in the broadest sense of the term. The theological process would be that of, beyond the initial point of conversion, the image of God being restored or rediscovered within the individual so that the person is more like God and, so, more set apart (i.e., more "holy"). Though most Evangelical Protestants and other Christians would agree that the work of sanctification resides mostly within and comes from God, they would also generally concur that there are important roles to be played by both the individual and the congregation through different forms of nurture, discipline, and education. There are disagreements among Christians in general and Evangelical Protestants in particular regarding various dimensions of sanctification such as the proportional efforts of and roles played by God and people in the process of sanctification and whether or not the process can be completed within the span of an earthly life.

One educational principle quite related to that of sanctification is characterization. The ultimate step or highest level in David R. Krathwohl's (1964) taxonomy of educational objectives in the affective domain, characterization involves the individual's consistency in behavior that manifests evidence of the beliefs, convictions, and values that have been received and otherwise internalized. The point is not necessarily that these behaviors are universally consistent with the stated beliefs, but that they are consistently lived out to the degree that they are seen as peculiar traits of the individual.

The third theological concept is the priesthood of all believers. The term has roots in both the Old and New Testaments. For example, in Exod 19:6, in establishing covenant with Israel, God declares to the people through Moses, "You will be for me a priestly kingdom and a holy nation," and in the New Testament, specifically 1 Pet 2:9, the church (i.e., the church universal or all of Christians) is described as "a chosen race, a royal priesthood." This doctrine is of special importance to most Protestants, whether Evangelical or mainline. Although the doctrine of the priesthood of all believers has critical corporate implications, its two primary dimensions relate to personal freedom and personal responsibility. The former basically means that each believer has the freedom and capacity for direct access to God with no human intervener. The latter asserts that, in terms of one's religious or spiritual life and growth, every believer (and, by implication, each person—even those outside the family of this faith) is responsible and accountable to God. The priesthood of all believers can be most obviously expressed in the contexts of a "free church" or one whose governance is congregationally-oriented. This would be the case with most Evangelical Protestants. However, it can be expressed in many ways—particularly in the sense of its most private and personal aspects—in a congregation or faith community that works within a hierarchical and/or sacramental paradigm.

For Evangelical Protestants, these three doctrines characterize and engage the "wells" from which one can "drink" to nurture one's own spiritual formation and growth. Though the relationship is also much more complex than what follows, one way to explain or illustrate how an Evangelical Protestant might view the interconnectedness among these sources is to look at them in reverse order. It is the priesthood of all believers that calls the individual to fulfill his or her personal responsibility to work toward spiritual formation and, importantly, underscores the God-given capacity for accomplishing what part of that task is dependent on one's individual efforts. Further, unless one totally rejects the necessity of any human effort in its unfolding, sanctification calls the individual to some level or degree of partnership with God in the process of working toward self-transformation, though God is generally thought to have the vastly primary role. Reclaiming the *imagio dei*, in the sense of one becoming more godly, then could be stated as the purpose, goal, and ultimate end of the process and that toward which one is working, studying, and learning. To illustrate the aforementioned further complexity, what remains of the *imagio dei* (or that which still resides within them) also provides the means by which their share of the task can be accomplished by humans: their rational nature, creativity, etc.

Some Evangelical Protestants probably would choose to refer to the Bible itself as the well from which all should drink and, in many ways, this author would concur. However, for the purposes of this model it would be a better fit to see the Bible in the image of the water. Just as a well serves as the receptacle for water and the means by which water can be appropriated and used for nurture, to Evangelical Protestants so do the concepts outlined above motivate, guide, and enable them toward accessing the Bible in their respective journeys toward Christian spiritual formation.

DRINKING FROM THEIR OWN WELLS IN RELIGIOUS EDUCATION

To see how this gift is expressed within the confines of Evangelical Protestant religious education and in relationship to their core authority (the Bible), one can look to how they might respond to the catchphrase (popular within many circles): "God said it; I believe it; and that settles it." Utilized in reference to the Bible, this old saying is intended to speak to the issue of the finality of biblical teaching in whatever matter is at hand. Ironically, it actually stresses the authority of the interpretation alone rather than Scripture itself, or, at least, appears to hold the interpretation and the Bible as of equal in importance and authority. Individuals (such as Evangelical Protestants) who truly hold to scriptural authority would be more inclined to say: "God said it, and that settles it, whether one believes it or not."

Nevertheless, at this point neither would (or do) Evangelical Protestants throw up their hands in surrender. Rather, their challenge remains to become involved and to persevere in the study of the Bible (as curriculum and content and as a pedagogical informant) in order to find out what God is saying through it.

The Bible as their core authority states the parameters for the godliness they seek and is the measure by which they would evaluate what accomplishment of that goal they might realize. Hence, the great amount of energy, time, and other resources expended by Evangelical Protestants in religious education, especially that centered on the Bible.

Evangelical Protestant understanding of biblical teaching on godliness would not be limited to matters of morality or "orthopraxy" (i.e., right living) as some may think. Rather, both directly and indirectly, using the Bible as content and as curriculum also addresses issues of orthodoxy (right belief), including those related to *imagio dei*, sanctification, and priesthood of all believers. In both orthopraxy and orthodoxy Evangelical Protestants recognize the need for personal decision and commitment toward spiritual formation.

However, only in a few, most radical Evangelical Protestant faith groups would the Bible be the exclusive content or curriculum. The vast majority of Evangelical Protestants recognize that *imagio dei*, sanctification, and priesthood of all believers are not only doctrinal ends in themselves, but also the means for equipping and empowering the individual to find nurture toward Christian spiritual formation by drawing on various historical and traditional sources outside the Bible—particularly those of the Evangelical Protestant Christian tradition. For example, it is the norm and not unusual to find within printed curricula used by Evangelical Protestants allusions to or the broad use of biographical and devotional material of historical figures of faith as examples of spiritual formation. Often, these examples will stress the role played by Bible study in their growth.

Since they propose to center all they do and believe on biblical teaching, Evangelical Protestants will tend to use the Bible both as the foundational content in arriving at and in teaching those three doctrines. It will also serve as the apologia for the use of those doctrines in or their influence on pedagogy. Admittedly, many Bible teachers within Evangelical Protestant congregations rely primarily on the lecture, or expository methodology, though this would usually end with a challenge to the students or listeners to take responsibility and to commit in applying that which was taught to their own lives. On the other hand, most Evangelical Protestant Bible curricula will include materials and suggestions to assist teachers toward methodologies much more reflective of and informed by the three preceding theological concepts. That is, they are designed to call the student to creative personal engagement with the content and to personal application in living out biblical principles. The intent within this particularly educational or didactic moment is similar to that found in the time of "invitation" that characterizes the climax or conclusion of most Evangelical Protestant worship services. It is expected that, when one is confronted by and understands a biblical truth, one has the opportunity and duty (in keeping with the *imago dei*, priesthood of all believers, and the process toward sanctification) to respond to God in commitment and obedience. Alluding to the image of Isaac introduced in the first part of this chapter, the crux of the matter is equipping student for the task of re-digging the spiritual wells of those who have gone before, discovering and digging some new spiritual wells of their own, and—ultimately—pitching their own tents and finding their own spiritual homes by discovering and declaring their personal commitments toward Christian spiritual formation.

A GIFT TO RELIGIOUS EDUCATION

Though rising out of a distinctively Christian tradition, the concepts that compel Evangelical Protestants to understand that one's journey toward spiritual formation as a matter for which, ultimately, each individual must take responsibility, also speak to the religious education of any faith perspective. But, as a gift to religious education, the effect is even deeper, for the way these concepts positively influence the way Evangelical Protestants do religious education is a model for that of any religion.

Anthropologically, religion is simply defined as a system in which cultural and societal values, beliefs, and concepts are contained and by which they are transmitted. As related to the larger context in which it exists (i.e., the culture or society), the focus of the religion is often understood primarily in the corporate sense. Lost in this can be the very individual nature of religion and many of its implications. Even given the basic definition shared above, it must be understood that a culture is comprised of individual persons who serve not only as receptors, but also as the means by which cultural values are maintained and transmitted. One of the primary cultural concepts will appertain to how it views the transcendent and how that relates to personal existence, including the matter of, by some meaning, self-transcendence. The matter of spiritual formation, as described by Johnson, then applies to and is a concern of any religion and is a core issue for religious education. Therefore, regardless of faith orientation, any religious education must be structured so as to inculcate its adherents with traditions and dogma (redigging the wells of their forebears) and to equip and compel adherents to adopt those beliefs as their own (digging their own wells). It is by these means that, through its education, a religion's believers will be more spiritually formed by their faith (making their religion their soul's true home), so that their beliefs are characterized in their lives.

NOTE

[1] Susanne Johnson, *Christian Spiritual Formation in the Church and Classroom* (Nashville: Abingdon Press, 1989) 22.

GIFTS OF DIVERSITY

[CHAPTER 5]

DRINKING FROM OTHERS' WELLS

In the second chapter of *Christian Spiritual Formation in the Church and Classroom*, Susanne Johnson analyzes the role of psychology as a dominant influence on contemporary culture, especially as individuals work toward personal growth. Though affirming of psychology's potential as an empirical informant, Johnson is critical of its use as a well from which people draw in the more affective areas—especially those relating more directly to issues of spirituality. While psychology is often compatible and concurring with religious approaches to self-fulfillment, Johnson observes that, when it is made the *primary* determinant, one's quest for self-fulfillment will lose touch with the essence and centrality of spirituality.

At least to some degree and at some level, most Evangelical Protestants share Johnson's perspectives at this point. They would have similar concerns arise when considering how philosophy, management theory, and other disciplines are brought to bear in various sectors of parish and congregational ministry and religious education. There is much diversity among Evangelical Protestants regarding the quantity and quality of the interface and integration of sources outside with those inside their respective theological orientations. Also, it should be noted that, with many Evangelical Protestants, the further they perceive the source in question to be from their core authority (i.e., the Bible), the less apt they are to take it at face value. Though many accept the validity of using archaeology, various types of biblical criticism, psychology, and sociology (and other disciplines), they are more inclined to interpret outside sources in light of Scripture rather than the reverse.

Nevertheless, among Evangelical Protestants, the use of resources outside what may be called theological disciplines is and has been widespread. What have and continue to differ among them are the external subjects and disciplines employed and the means by and degree to which they are utilized by respective Evangelical Protestant individuals, groups, and institutions.

RESPONSES TO CULTURE

Consciously or otherwise, at this point Evangelical Protestants tend to reflect approaches observed by H. Richard Niebuhr in *Christ and Culture* or

E. Glenn Hinson in *The Integrity of the Church*.[2] In a more generalized approach (and one that, according to some, is too nebulous and repetitive), Niebuhr envisioned a spectrum of ways by which Christian communities tended to interact with their respective environments. One extreme was that of "Christ against Culture" which disclaimed culture and tended to be more isolationist. The other extreme, "Christ of Culture" seeks a relationship with culture as well as with the Christian community and what agreement and accommodation can be found between the two. It further recognizes and accepts (implicitly and explicitly) the inevitable role that culture, as the medium by and milieu in which religion is transmitted, plays in influencing religious content, forms, and structures. Between these two, "Christ above Culture" treats the Christ-culture tension as a separate issue from that of the personal relationship of grace and obedience that exists between Christ and the individual. It is this relationship that brings purpose to a person's life—that of effecting divine presence in the world. The perspective of "Christ and Culture in Paradox" is one that recognizes the legitimacy of the moral claims placed upon persons by both Christ and culture. Christians are seen as people with dual citizenship in the earthly and heavenly realms—the interests of which two are most often found in opposition. Also somewhat between the two extremes, but still conversionist, is "Christ Transforming Culture" in which a Christian community is motivated to fulfill the aims and commands of Jesus by becoming active in changing the culture and molding more in his image and design.

Hinson offers a more visual approach and one more directly based on Scripture. He discerns a series of four biblical images that express diverse—though not necessarily disparate—understandings of the individual and corporate purposes of Christians. "The New Humanity: the Body of Christ" is set within the context of God's creative activity. The image of God that was destroyed or damaged by sin gave way to the "old humanity" that was characterized by narcissism, immorality, and hate. The church as the new humanity (created and sustained by God through salvation and the continuing process of sanctification) serves as the means by which Jesus creatively continues a ministry of restoration in the world. To remain faithful to its nature and mission, the church must continually be on guard against corrupting influences and acceding to any authority other than that found in God as revealed in Scripture. The image of "The People of God" is rooted in that of Old Testament Israel. Bound to God by covenant, they are called by God to be participants in establishing God's ultimate earthly reign. In so doing, though living in the world, they are not characterized by it, but by

God's rule and by their being mediators of reconciliation. "The Servant" model rises from the servant motifs found in Isaiah, the Old Testament prophet, and in that claimed by Jesus for himself. This paradigm calls the church to a role other than that found in dominion or imposition. Instead, the church's mission is to be found in relating to the world with the ultimate goal being that of discovering and meeting the needs of the world. Hinson's last image, "The City of God," finds its origins somewhat in Genesis (in the covenant community begun in Abraham), but also in the New Testament book of Revelation (in the "new Jerusalem"). The emphasis here is on living so as to be distinguishable from the world, though unavoidably bearing some institutional and structural imprint of it.

It is this diversity among Evangelical Protestants that shows in numerous ways the means by which various dimensions and venues of religious education may utilize sources outside those of their immediate faith community and theological orientation to equip adherents and students toward spiritual formation and growth. Again borrowing from Johnson, this gift could be described as that of "drinking from other's wells."

PEDAGOGICAL PRINCIPLES

The value of "drinking from other's wells" is similar to that found in principles basic to various forms of liberal arts and democratic education. The historical and philosophical roots of these are found in Plato, Aristotle, Cicero, Quintillian, Martianus Capella, Erasmus, and Comenius, and more recently in John Dewey and many others.

Particularly important as a curricular approach, the original purpose of liberal arts education was understood to be that of enabling a free (hence the term "liberal") person to function in and to lead society so as to prevent that society's disintegration. The spectrum of the liberal arts was divided into two parts: the *trivium* (grammar, rhetoric, argumentation) and the *quadrivium* (geometry, arithmetic, astronomy, music). In the Middle Ages, an Augustinian cosmology prevailing, these were seen as something of a closed, static system. The trivium were seen as more basic to and equipping a person to study the advanced subjects of the quadrivium. Their collective value was seen in their interplay with and effect on the conduct of a society. In that context the end was to embody and embrace the Kingdom of God, so there was seen in them a relation to matters of spirituality and theology.

The necessary resources and environment would consist of—as one might expect—media and library. They also include, by many differing means, access to and discourse with a wide variety of traditional, current, and emerging disciplines. This demands that curriculum contain, teachers be conversant with, and students be led to familiarity with and use of immediately germane aspects of fields and subjects outside that of the prevailing discipline.

AN HISTORICAL MODEL AND PRECEDENT

A significant early precedent among Christians for "drinking from other's wells" is found in the example of the catechetical school that arose from the church in Alexandria, Egypt, in the third century CE Alexandria, founded, in 331 BCE by Alexander the Great on the site of a fishing village, quickly developed into a center for Jewish and Greco-Roman learning. There the Septuagint was translated, Philo (the Jewish philosopher) wrote and taught, and an extensive educational system (of libraries, lower level schools, and universities that would rival those of Athens and Rome) was developed.

The Christian church that would grow and thrive in Alexandria gave rise to a succession of three teachers in whom were vested responsibility for training and teaching the church's converts: Pantaenus (a converted Stoic), Clement, and Origen. These three, in order, expanded the church's curriculum to include subjects of a broad range of secular learning. Their perspective was that a student with solid grounding in their faith and doctrine had no need to feel threatened by the forthright exploration of intellectual and academic vistas beyond those of the church. Their respective purposes were manifold. They sought to enable their students to communicate with those outside the Christian community for both defense and explanation of the faith and for developing relationships through which non-Christians might be converted. Rather than seeing secular subjects as being necessarily antithetical to Christianity, they looked for ways by which they could be reconciled with the Christian faith and even used as tools that students could use in their own journeys toward spiritual formation. It was by these expanded means that Christians could better recapture and exercise the image of God in which they had been created.

Since Hellenistic educational structures were virtually all that the teachers of the Alexandrian catechetical school (as it is known) had experienced, it is natural that those structures formed not only much of the school's curriculum and structure, but also its pedagogy. The Alexandrians' methodologies were based on those employed by the Sophists, Socrates, Plato, Aristotle, and others and were utilized to equip the individual to determine truth whatever the source. The end was for the person to better comprehend God as revealed in Scripture. Additionally, the Alexandrian catechetical school can be seen as a precursor to and a model for medieval universities and ensuing Christian approaches to or applications of liberal arts education.

Taking similar approaches—and for like reasons—has enabled among contemporary Evangelical Protestants creativity in developing varying types and degrees of dialogue with disciplines outside those rooted in their core authority (i.e., the Bible). The extent to which these have formed and informed their religious education at all levels both varies widely and consistently provides the grist for debate and controversy among Evangelical Protestants. The contention usually focuses on either the nature of biblical authority or whether the Bible is actually remaining as the core authority or is being supplanted by the discipline(s) being employed.

EVANGELICAL PROTESTANT MODELS

Among Evangelical Protestants there is frequent and diverse use of psychology to inform their efforts toward spiritual formation. One area in which this is most apparent is that of pastoral care and counseling. Often described by Evangelical Protestants (in biblical terms) using the imagery of shepherding, this effort is seen as one that brings to confluence principles of psychology and theology to speak to people's needs as they confront the many manifestations of life crises. They see it as a matter of understanding people and the means by which to effect their continuing nurture as well as healing and recovery in the face of disease, injury, and grief in it many dimensions (i.e., differing kinds of loss and separation including death and divorce).

Evangelical Protestant efforts in connection with pastoral care and counseling are not limited to those on the parts of local parish ministers and in their training and education toward such. Rather, Evangelical Protestants often access and develop books, tapes, and other kinds of media in support of both formal and informal individual- and congregation-oriented programs and attempts to help persons deal with issues relevant to pastoral care and counseling. Whatever the means, the goal is to assist people toward understanding and appreciating their holistic nature and to help them discover ways to grow in wholeness. Integral to this is for all Evangelical Protestants (and virtually the exclusive emphasis for some) is the individual's learning and applying biblical principles for self-understanding and spiritual formation and growth.

Similarly, Evangelical Protestants frequently apply principles from psychology in their efforts in religious education. The most widespread example of this is their use of what they learn from developmental studies in designing age-appropriate content, curricula, and pedagogies. While this is not universal nor to be found in every instance of Evangelical Protestant religious education, it is regularly the case to find either implicit or explicit allusions to Piaget, Erickson, Kohlberg, Fowler, and others or, at least specific applications of some aspects of their theories.

Nor is psychology the only "well" from which Evangelical Protestants drink for informing spiritual formation. Deliberate engagement with and use of various philosophies and theories of education commonly mold Evangelical Protestant religious education at every level. As is the case with psychology, the tension Evangelical Protestants experience between their various respective theological positions and their diverse positions and responses to diverse educational theories and philosophies is often found at the heart of much of their research, dialogue, and debate regarding religious education. The disparity that exists among them, at this point also, closely correlates to and reflects their differing respective responses to culture as noted previously. Nevertheless, the conversation that rises from even this disparity (despite the rancor that can, and often does, characterize it) can be said to engender a richer and more kaleidoscopic tapestry of individual and corporate approaches to spiritual formation in general and religious education in particular.

Nowhere in Evangelical Protestant religious education are there many areas of disagreement more expressed or apparent than in the multifarious ways they approach the study or incorporation of liberal arts approach in elementary, secondary, and higher education. Their respective approaches to religious schooling consistently tends to be a continuation of that which they take to liberal arts education. One particular example concerns the interface of biblical authority with scientific theories and discoveries relating to cosmology—specifically on that of creation of the universe. Evangelical Protestants can be found at the polarities of both biblical and scientific/evolutionary creationism and at all points along the continuum that exists between the two. They often are on opposing sides of debates regarding the teaching of evolution and/or biblical creationism in public schools. Evangelical Protestants more acceding to and appreciative of the contributions of science point to the universality of truth—with God as the ultimate source, whether recognized as such or not—and maintain a similar perspective to other disciplines throughout all levels of education. They also are predisposed to take the approach that a solid foundation in religious faith will equip students to encounter any empirical discipline with little fear of apostasy, but with more potential for creative and informed holistic (and spiritual) growth.

However, Evangelical Protestants who favor exclusively or primarily teaching the latter see it as a matter of spiritual versus "worldly" growth. They also increasingly tend to support or establish parochial or independent "Christian" schools or advocate home schooling. Further, these same individuals and groups would be inclined to view with varying degrees of suspicion and caution sciences as taught in most secular universities and seek to constrain how sciences are taught or considered in their church-supported or -related institutions of higher education. Whichever of these two approaches one may take, the basic issue remains that of the nature of the connection between the core authority and those external to it and how that intersection affects spiritual relationships, wholeness, and growth.

A GIFT TO RELIGIOUS EDUCATION

The purpose of the religious education of any faith is, at least in part, to share, explain, and maintain its understanding of revealed truth. The more culturally or structurally institutionalized a religion, the greater its vested interests in maintaining faithfulness to its core. This would be relatively easy if that religion and its adherents existed in total isolation from the rest of the world—and if all concerned remained indifferent to all except the most narrowly understood concerns of the faith. Given human nature, however, this has never been the case. The reality is that humans are naturally inquisitive and they do not live in isolation. Also, it is inevitable that their sundry values and perceptions of truth will eventually conflict or come into confluence and tension. This has potential to affect humans' self-perceptions in general, ultimately how they view themselves as spiritual beings, and, so, their spiritual formation.

The difficulty, then, for religious education is to hold fast to truth as revealed in the basic tenets of the faith while conversing with truth as disclosed external to it. Further, the questions are whether or not it is possible for truths perceived as external to a faith can assist one toward spiritual formation within the context of that faith; if so, how; if not, how must or can one relate to truth outside the faith. In the terms of this paradigm the issues of the potential and/or methodology for spiritual formation by "drinking from other's wells."

What Evangelical Protestants offer religious education in this struggle are myriad models of how this can be attempted. While their expansive diversity often breeds the acrimony that marks their dialogue on these and related matters, it also provides a spectrum of paradigms from which the religious education of any faith may choose in leading its adherents to deal with truth whatever its source and to appropriate and incorporate that truth in their spiritual growth.

NOTES

[1] H. Richard Niebuhr, *Christ and Culture* (New York: Harper & Brothers Publishers, 1951).

[2] E. Glenn Hinson, *The Integrity of the Church* (Nashville: Broadman Press, 1978).

[CHAPTER 6]

ECUMENICITY FOR LEARNING

Taking similar approaches to that of "drinking from other's wells" has also enabled among Evangelical Protestants creativity in developing varying types and degrees of dialogue both within their respective fellowships and through expressions of ecumenicity and interdependence unmindful of denominational lines. For Evangelical Protestant individuals and groups, this ecumenicity has formed and informed their spiritual formation and religious education at all levels. What differs from "drinking from other's wells" at this point is that the "others" with which they relate are not contending perspectives in terms of disciplines quite distinct from theology or religion. Rather, in this case "others" are faith or religious perspectives that differ—and the degree of differentiation varies widely. Also significant is that diverse expressions of one's own spiritual growth and formation or that of other persons are the more explicit and deliberate purposes.

The nature of these mutual interests or values will differ widely among Evangelical Protestants and they will be sought out in multifarious arenas. These provide the criteria by which respective Evangelical Protestant individuals and groups will select the resources they will access and the others with which they will affiliate in whatever joint effort may be at hand or in question. Though they prefer to ally and/or draw on resources for fulfillment of perceived needs along the lines of what they hold to be the most foundational and crucial of theological tenets, Evangelical Protestants will and do often align with those with whom they may have serious basic doctrinal differences, but share ethical-political perspectives on an issue. Sometimes the formal or informal discourse will be with those with whom a particular Evangelical Protestant entity may differ on specific points of doctrine, but share a common view of spirituality or the devotional life. This makes for an interesting and sometimes puzzling assortment of cooperative efforts in which Evangelical Protestants participate and religious resources on which they will draw. An example of this may be found in the first chapter of this book in the references to the willingness of the National Association of Evangelicals and some Evangelical Protestant theologians to include and cooperate with—as valued members of the larger Christian family—Roman Catholics who share with them the common experience of having been "born again" and so claim and profess.

PEDAGOGICAL PRINCIPLES

The value Evangelical Protestants find in the ecumenicity they employ toward religious education is similar to that found in principles basic to various forms of democratic education. The historical and philosophical roots of democratic education are found in Plato, Aristotle, Cicero, Quintillian, and, more recently, in John Dewey and many others.

The ultimate end of the pedagogical processes proposed by democratic education is that of encountering and solving social problems. It was Teilhard de Chardin who wrote, "Since its birth, knowledge has made its greatest advances when stimulated by some particular problem of life needing a solution."[1] A situation with conditions ripe for education would be which learners communicate and collaborate with each other and with the teacher toward understanding and resolving a problem of common concern.

Both a means toward that end and an end in itself is the development of a social system engendered and characterized by democratic processes. This strategy requires participants to be able to negotiate with others from both similar and differing disciplines, circumstances, and perspectives. Learning, then, requires students to employ their past and present experiences along with those of others to apply what universals there might be in solving contemporary problems. This is a matter of mutuality in both self-revelation and responsibility for communication. The focus is on neither the differences that separate participants nor on narrowing those areas of disagreement. Instead, it is on the points of commonality and the nature of the communication and dialogue that exist among those involved. Such an approach requires of participants some level of awareness not only of the problem at hand, but also the commonality that exists and those with whom it is shared, and the skills necessary for effective communication. It also necessitates the availability of extensive formal and informal networks and a variety of resources and means for communication.

HISTORICAL MODELS

The Sunday School unions that rose in the late eighteenth and early nineteenth centuries serve as examples of how inter- and intra-denominational ecumenicity worked as a religious education response to a (social) problem and how such cooperative efforts facilitated both educational media and ends. The first Sunday School, established in 1780 by publisher and social crusader Robert Raikes, began in Gloucester, England, as a means for social reform through literacy training and character or values education. Sunday

School proved to be an agent of empowering the poor and the laity and, subsequently, also proved to be unpopular with the Church of England. However, it found supporters in England among such diverse persons as John Wesley and the William Fox. It was the relationship between Fox and Raikes that led to the 1785 founding of the first Sunday School Society for the purpose of propagating such efforts throughout England. Similar organizations rose—also across denominational lines—in England and in North America.

Of particular significance is that, in the United States, the burgeoning Sunday School movement for many years remained independent of and external to formal church and denominational structures. It grew through the efforts of the many Sunday School unions and societies that also proliferated. Rooted in a mission of teaching toward general Christian spirituality rather than that of narrowly-defined doctrine, most of these, though nondenominational, were comprised of various kinds of Protestants, and most published their own curricular materials. (The model given by these societies and unions for Sunday School curricula and publishing would later be adopted and followed by denominations.) The success of the various Sunday School unions, according to some, can be attributed to the nondenominational approach they established and maintained.

EVANGELICAL PROTESTANT MODELS

Whatever the desired commonality, it may be found in or out of the immediate congregation, denomination, faith orientation, or locale. In each case, what is being pursued is, by some definition, that which will provide both a cohesive force that draws and binds together those involved and a social lubricant to facilitate more rapid development of the affinity and trust so crucial to the educational process. The reality among Evangelical Protestants is one of tremendous variety among the resources or wells from which they drink and include those within and external to the larger body of Evangelical Protestantism.

Within the context of the immediate paradigm, however, resources either demanded by or accessible to persons involved in various respective venues of religious education include those that are increasingly available in digital or electronic form; publishing houses (and their many differing products including curricula, devotional material, and resources for congregational ministry); schools of all levels; and conferences, camps, and other opportunities for continuing education. Of importance is that many of these resources also provide the structure in which the interpersonal relationships necessary to the process can be negotiated.

One need give only a cursory look around in many communities, especially in the United States, to discover a wide range of spiritual resources on which individual Evangelical Protestants can and do draw to effect personal or individually directed religious learning. In fact, much has been made of the commercial marketing that is done to religiously-delimited target groups. Many differing products are sought out by Evangelical Protestants (and others) and published by older, more established publishers such as Zondervan and Eerdmans. as well as many newer companies. Among these are books, audio and video tapes, and computer software. The content of these various products run the gamut including fiction, inspirational/devotional, self-help of many types, topical materials, Bibles, commentaries, educational curricula, and other forms of nonfiction. Further, the commercial outlets for these products continue to proliferate.

Individual Evangelical Protestants are also often found among what we will call for our purposes "nondenominational interest groups." These would be religiously oriented (and often specifically Christian) organizations formed for the purpose of teaching, reinforcing, and propagating common religious values and bringing them to bear on particular spheres of individual, corporate, and social concerns. Among such organizations in which one will find significant numbers of Evangelical Protestants and from which they will draw spiritual nurture are diverse groups such as the Billy Graham Evangelistic Association, Yokefellows, Promise Keepers (for men) and Promise Helpers (their auxiliary for women), Habitat for Humanity, various Masonic orders, and Sojourners. Individual Evangelical Protestants are also among those allying with and learning from ministries and organizations borne by differing media such as James Dobson's *Focus on the Family*.

Many Evangelical Protestants also support, converse with, or access various explicitly sociopolitical organizations somewhat as expressions of their own spirituality, but more directly as tokens of their own values and ethical perspectives (rising out of their spirituality) and for materials for use in religious instruction. Again, the spectrum of these organizations among whose memberships and/or supporters will be found significant numbers of Evangelical Protestants is broad and would include the Christian Coalition on one end and People for the American Way or the American Civil Liberties Union on the other. Interesting to observe is not only their diversity, but also the way in which any one of these organizations can be so warmly embraced by some Evangelical Protestants while being so excoriated and denounced by others.

Seeking spiritual nurture for themselves and their families, many individual Evangelical Protestants are proponents of differing types of nonpublic primary and secondary education. Those attempting to take more direct responsibility will often opt for homeschooling while relying on various resources available from not only their respective states or jurisdictions, but also "Christian" publishers (usually those identified as more theologically, socially, and politically conservative—or at least more mainline Evangelical Protestant) for their curricula. Others choose by varying means to support parochial schools. Sometimes such schools could be those of another denomination or church (even Roman Catholic in some instances), those sponsored by the congregation of which the person is a part, or a school simply identified as private or "Christian" and owned and operated either by a specific person or organization other than a local congregation.

On the other hand, many Evangelical Protestants elect to uphold the public school systems. These find opportunities for spiritual nurture in student-led Bible clubs or organizations such as Young Life, Youth for Christ, Fellowship of Christian Athletes, and prayer clubs.

The ways in which Evangelical Protestants approach higher education reflect the dissimilarity found in their respective means of dealing with primary and secondary schooling. Common among denominations identified as Evangelical Protestant are colleges and universities established as part of a strategy to provide access to liberal arts education with a particular emphasis on spiritual values and spiritual formation as integral elements. Such schools will enroll students not only from their own respective faith communities, but also from a broad range of faith orientations from closely-aligned Evangelical Protestant, mainline Protestant, Roman Catholic, and Jewish bodies. These colleges often will include in their curricula required religion courses and chapel services. Conversely, Evangelical Protestants may seek enrollment to such universities and schools—and those from other faith traditions—for varying possible reasons including the general educational quality of the school, majors available, and shared general spiritual values.

Evangelical Protestant students enrolled in a religiously-oriented or -founded college or university, but one of a faith tradition other than their own tend to take one of several options that are or may be available to them. Of course, one often taken (usually to the dismay of parents and their faith family of origin) is to no make no affiliation with any means of spiritual nurture. A second is to join in with the religious activities sponsored by the host school and colored by its faith traditions. Another is to become active in a nondenominational or parachurch Christian organization such as Navigators, Intervarsity Christian Fellowship, or Campus Crusade for Christ. Additional opportunities for spiritual nurture are campus organizations supported by the faith tradition of the individual, but not of the host institution(e.g., Wesley Foundation and Baptist Collegiate Ministries). Evangelical Protestant students enrolled in public colleges and universities may take similar approaches. Evangelical Protestant college students enrolled in schools—whether denominational or state—away from their homes are often encouraged by their "home" churches and denominations to affiliate with a local church that is as close to their faith perspective as possible, whether or not it is of the same denomination.

This multifarious means by which Evangelical Protestants pursue higher education is also reflected in the way they do theological higher education. There are some Evangelical Protestant seminaries that are either nondenominational or are supported by more than one denomination. Though many Evangelical Protestant denominations have their own, distinct seminaries, it is not unusual for their student bodies to include those from their own and other Evangelical Protestant bodies. Likewise, Evangelical Protestant students sometimes enroll in seminaries or divinity schools of mainline denominations and churches.

Many Evangelical Protestant scholars, researchers, and teachers read, study with, or otherwise are formally or informally involved in discourse with those outside their faith community. For example, though there are professional and academic groups organized specifically for and by Evangelical Protestant religious educators (e.g., National Association of Christian Educators), many of them join with and contribute to more ecumenical and diverse professional organizations (e.g., Association of Professors and Researchers in Religious Education or the Religious Education Association). All the above rise from and contribute to the continuing diversity and tensions within the Evangelical Protestant fellowship.

Through their congregations Evangelical Protestant continue the diversity they exhibit as individuals and through their approaches to education external to the congregation. Primarily of the free church tradition—i.e., governance is vested in the local congregation—Evangelical Protestant congregations have potentially great latitude in selecting curricula and other resources in support of their sundry ministries and work. Though some may feel bound by a sense of loyalty or tradition to access only materials produced by their denominational publishing house, most are free to do otherwise and are increasingly acting on this freedom. As a result, this has enabled and empowered the local congregation to seek out and apply educational resources that reflect the needs and perspectives of their particular context. This aspect of the gift of ecumenicity for learning will be further explored in the following chapter.

A GIFT TO RELIGIOUS EDUCATION

The gift of Evangelical Protestants, then, is a model of how a wide spectrum of resources and associations can be utilized on every level of religious education by those of a multiplicity of perspectives within the same and differing general faith communities—and still toward the same ultimate end. Admittedly, there are pitfalls in following the model of this gift. Many of them are realized and manifested in the general fellowship of Evangelical Protestantism as well as in many of its distinct denominations. Accessing such diverse resources will inevitably lead to disparate perspectives on some matters and the tension that rises from those differences. Suspicion of those at variance can be nurtured and accusations of apostasy thrown at them by those of their faith who desire more uniformity. And there is the potential for some to fall away from at least certain aspects of the faith and find themselves moving toward, if not into, other faith orientations.

One the other hand, the many dimensions of dialogue required by and rising from this paradigm enables and engenders relevance, growth, vitality, and discovery in and through religious education. A faith that refuses to accept these and seek them out is doomed to empty ritual and eventual irrelevance, because it is no longer nurturing its adherents toward discourse and interaction with the society (in the form of other religions or faith perspectives) around them. In fact, it can be (as exemplified by some Evangelical Protestants) that such discourse, rising from a firm grounding in the faith, can enrich and strengthen one's basic faith orientation. If the primary purpose of religious education is indeed the nurture of people toward spiritual formation and growth, every resource available should be employed and made available to learners.

NOTE

[1] Teilhard de Chardin, *The Phenomenon of Man*, trans. Bernard Wall, Torchbook ed. (New York: Harper & Row, 1961) 249.

[CHAPTER 7]

VARIETY OF RESOURCES FOR THE CHURCH

Among Evangelical Protestant churches, the most dominant form of governance is that in which the local congregation has at least the majority of, if not total, control over its own affairs—especially those internal to it. Though commonly rooted in discernment of biblical principles, the theological foundations for church governance as understood among Evangelical Protestants has some variation and holds in tension the doctrine of the priesthood of all believers with that related to authority vested in pastors and/or other church offices. The means by which this tension is resolved or expressed can be found in both explicit and implicit structures. For example, one historical distinctive of most churches of most Baptist denominations and fellowships has been that of stressing local church autonomy and congregational governance closely related to emphasis on the priesthood of all believers. It is not unusual, however, for individual Baptist churches (from the more fundamentalist to the more liberal, but more often among the former) by design or by default to relegate ruling authority in any number of matters to their pastor or to a denominational structure.

Nevertheless, since there seems to be many interpretations of the variety of models for how New Testament churches were organized, one should not be surprised to find among Evangelical Protestants myriad ways of structuring, planning, and otherwise carrying out the work and ministries of a local congregation. This diversity is particularly apparent in the wide range of Evangelical Protestant approaches to the structures, curricula, and content of religious education.

This freedom and diversity have not only required, but also enabled and empowered the local congregation to seek out and apply educational resources that reflect the needs and perspectives of their particular context.

PEDAGOGICAL PRINCIPLES

A body of water whose water remains undisturbed stagnates. To remain vital, its water must be stirred up by wind, tides, or currents—or augmented and filtered through the various dynamics of the hydrological cycle. Likewise, and as with any practice or discipline, education is in constant need of renewal. Without replenishment and refreshment—and stirring up from time to time—it becomes stale. Whether individually or corporately exercised, any educational form or curriculum focused simply on self-replication easily falls into rote practice and soon loses vitality.

Findley B. Edge, himself by some definitions an Evangelical Protestant, once wrote that the two most important goals for Bible study and teaching in a church are "Better Bible Knowledge" and "Better Christian Living." He saw the latter as the primary goal because it was the ultimate purpose of the former.[1] Toward that end, Edge observed that students will be more open to learning and accepting the reality of the Bible lesson when they see in it relevance to their lives.

Edge suggested that all levels of planning for Bible teaching have specific "Conduct Response Aim[s]" and noted that, although awareness of generalized concepts is important as a step toward learning, "teaching in general terms is inadequate for securing conduct response" [his emphasis] and that "a person's need lies in those specific areas where he or she needs to practice those ideals."[2]

In his earlier work, *A Quest for Vitality in Religion*, Edge wrote out of a concern for the debilitating effect that institutionalization has had on the life of the church. As part of the solution, he suggested that a major part of the task of religious education within the church should be to assist Christians in relating biblical knowledge to areas of interest, concern, and decision making within the context of their lives and their worlds. Further, he seemed to understand the limitations of the church in providing a full spectrum of the wide-ranging resources potentially needed for such an enterprise and suggests that study groups use "all available resources."[3] The point for Edge is not that the church encourage its members to abandon the Bible as the core authority. Rather, whatever means are available should be employed to enhance biblical knowledge and understanding, inform regarding areas of life concerns, and help one learn how thus to apply biblical principles to life. Similarly, Timothy A. Lines wrote that "to be a genuine religious educator means to be aware and open to the resources available and not limited to the small pieces or fragments of truth each individual's faith tradition may have to offer."[4] In sharing his model of "The Religious Educator as Coach," Lines describes the role of the religious educator as one that nurtures learners toward competent implementation of all resources toward self-directed spiritual maturity. In so doing, Lines writes, one "does not sacrifice individuality . . ., but instead discovers resources to become an even stronger individual as a result of walking with others on a shared path."[5]

Arguably taking Edge one step further, Lines also implies that using a variety of resources can strengthen ties to one's faith community of origin. "The more we learn about others, the more we learn about ourselves.... This means building bridges to reaching others rather than erecting walls to keep them away."[6] It also is part of and integral to the process that Reuel Howe called "the miracle of dialogue," which "is the calling forth of persons who have found their own unique relation to truth and who serve that truth with creative expectancy."[7]

RESOURCES USED BY EVANGELICAL PROTESTANTS

One area of resources in which there is great variety and in which Evangelical Protestants continuously access is that of publishers to which they look for various kinds of materials for support of differing areas of individual and congregational spiritual development and religious education. Of course, there are many different Evangelical Protestant denominationally- sponsored or -affiliated publishing houses that have as one of their primary foci production of curriculum and materials in particular support of religious education programs peculiar to churches of that denomination. Most also offer some variety of other dated and undated materials to be used for instructional purposes not directly related to a specific program. Some publish differing types of media containing devotional, inspirational, and forms of self-improvement content—all with a particular doctrinal bent reflective of that of their denomination. It is these resources to which Evangelical Protestant churches and individuals are more apt to look first, immediately, and more consistently. (And it will be the churches of the sponsoring denomination that will provide the core customer base for the publishing house.) This loyalty is sometimes deliberate and founded on a relationship of experience and trust. However, it often can be simply due to habit and a level of ignorance of other resources that are available. In such instances the churches tend to be either complacent or content with the level of unrest, tension, or dissatisfaction that will exist.

Dissatisfaction can arise for a plethora of reasons. Sometimes it will be due to specific doctrinal differences between the particular individual or church and the writer(s), or editorial staff, or majority of other churches that participate in the denomination. On the other hand, often the matter is one of the individual or church needing a specific type of material for reasons of purpose, theme, content, or their particular parish context that are simply not available from their own denomination. Of course, sometimes the divergence may be related to issues of quality of either the pedagogy or the physical product, cost, or convenience.

Whatever the reason, Evangelical Protestant churches frequently (and increasingly do) look beyond their own respective denominational publishing. In these situations they may look to publishers of denominations with some affinity to their theological perspective or to one that is non- or transdenominational. (There are many nondenominational Evangelical Protestant churches. These rely on any number of the numerous resources available—and often individually utilize an assortment of them.)

One way to categorize the nondenominational resources on which Evangelical Protestant churches often rely are those that are program-oriented or -originated. These differ from nondenominational publishers in that they develop curricula and materials around a specific concept or approach—or for a specific target group. Examples of these are youth- and student-oriented parachurch organizations such as Campus Crusade for Christ, Young Life, Campus Life, and Navigators. Others, such as the Bible-memorization-centered Awana (for "Approved Workmen [sic] Are Not Ashamed" from 2 Tim 2:15) and the Child Evangelism Fellowship are aimed toward children and youth. Examples of adult-targeted programs include those such as Precept Ministries (an inductive approach to Bible study) and Weigh Down Workshops ("Biblically-based" and "Christ-centered" workshops dealing with weight loss and/or substance, emotional, and sexual addictions).

Nondenominational noncurricular publications on which laity and clergy of Evangelical Protestant churches often draw as resources for spiritual nurture and/or religious education are various kinds of journals and periodicals. These range from general theological interest pieces such as *Christianity Today* to those of more narrow topical concern such as *Leadership, Christian History*, or *Biblical Archaeology Review* along with those published by nondenominational groups with which they may align or affiliate.

Nor should one overlook the digital or electronic resources available to and utilized by Evangelical Protestant churches. Some may arguably be described as simply digitalized formats of what has been traditionally published (i.e., books, journals, periodicals). On the other hand, Evangelical Protestant churches are increasingly using newer media such as the Internet not only for promotion and publicity of local parish and congregational activities (through organizations' and churches' web sites and home pages), but also for more specifically educational purposes. Just a little time spent "surfing the 'net'" will reveal many Evangelical Protestant churches, organizations, and resources mutually linked and pointing to many different kinds of documents and materials that can be and—it may be assumed—are used by individuals and churches for purposes of spiritual nurture and religious education. (Most of the resources specifically named above have their own web sites that offer not only information such as their respective purposes, missions, and products, but also doctrinal statements. Many can also be found to have "pointers" or links from local church web sites.)

Evangelical Protestant churches also access a number of differing types of conferences for varying purposes from spiritual growth and nurture to more specific training for clergy and/or laity toward fulfilling particular tasks and functions within the church. These opportunities and resources find their roots in the Chautaqua movement that was begun by Methodists in the late 1800s and became a model for the spread of popular studies in the Bible and in lay education. Their origins are also to be found, especially among Evangelical Protestants, somewhat in the camp meetings (or encampments) and revivalism of the Second and Third Great Awakenings of the late nineteenth and early twentieth centuries. Born out of the fire and frontier model of the evangelistic efforts of the First Great awakening, these gatherings of the devout together for an intensive and extended time of worship, encouragement, exhortation, and conversion began to include didactic purposes for persons of all ages. (Significantly, it was out of the Second and Third Great Awakenings that there rose some of the more prominent figures in the pantheon of Evangelical Protestant heroes such as Charles G. Finney, Dwight L. Moody, and R. A. Torrey. These movements were also vital to the establishment of Moody Press, Fleming H. Revell Company, and many other publishers to whom Evangelical Protestants look for diverse religious education curricula, media, and materials.)

As is true regarding publishers, Evangelical Protestant churches most often tend to look first to conferences and training sponsored and supported by their respective denominational entities, if any. These may take place at encampments or assemblies owned and operated by a denomination for that purpose. However, they may also be held at similar sites owned by other organizations (public and private), but structured and led by denominational institutions. In either case, it is not unusual to find Evangelical Protestant churches of those other than the sponsoring denomination in attendance.

Otherwise, Evangelical Protestant churches regularly may utilize conferences and other training events and opportunities sponsored and led by non- and trans-denominational groups. Denominationally-aligned Evangelical

Protestant churches will seek these for reasons similar to those that move them toward publishers outside their denomination as noted above.

Whether denominationally oriented or not, these conferences and assemblies have myriad themes, goals, and purposes. They are usually geared for a specific age group and, within particular purposes, designed with the developmental needs and abilities of that age group in mind. Conference content may be centered on the development of Bible knowledge, but it often will focus on training in some church-oriented skill area such as evangelism, teaching, organization, leadership, and administration. Content may also be focused on various life-skills including (as appropriate) parenting, marriage enrichment, and personal finances. For most Evangelical Protestant churches, it would be vital for training in either of these two skill areas to be either explicitly or implicitly (preferably the latter) biblically-based.

The processes by which Evangelical Protestant churches choose among possible resources—again due to their freedom and diversity—vary widely. Generally, what deliberate choices there are may be made either by the congregation at large, a group or committee within the church, or specific persons in leadership positions (most often the pastor or some other director/minister of religious education if there be one). The means by which this is decided will reflect how the individual church, by design or by default, resolves the tensions that exist naturally among local congregational governance, pastoral authority, and relationships within and to denominational structures.

There can be any number of reasons for the choices Evangelical Protestant churches make regarding which they access and utilize within each area of resources. Though these may include the relatively mundane, such as cost and convenience, the reasons can be more significant. The more revealing reasons are related to matters of theology—usually more specifically a church's perspective (or that of whomever it is that chooses for the church) regarding the Bible as its core. That will drive both what is perceived to be the content that is needed as well as the structure and curriculum by which the content should be delivered. Further, this may reasonably be assumed to be the purpose for which so many resources that cater to Evangelical Protestant churches provide clear, simple statements of the doctrinal perspectives reflected in their curricula, materials, and products.

Nevertheless, it is the freedom of each believer as a priest that, in turn, frees a church to determine by whatever means it chooses or allows to access those resources it deems appropriate toward the religious education of its congregants. Beyond the specific pedagogical principles alluded to previously, this enables all churches—whether or not they so choose—to tailor their programs and ministries of religious education to their particular local needs, perspectives, and desires.

A GIFT TO RELIGIOUS EDUCATION

As was the case regarding the gift of Evangelical Protestants, there are pitfalls in following the model of this gift. One relates especially to those churches belonging to specific denominations. Accessing a variety of resources can easily disrupt what unity can exist or uniformity desired within such associations of churches even though they commonly recognize the freedom of all those within their fellowship. These, in turn (and as noted in the previous chapter), offer the risk of alienation among those churches.

However, the reality is that any religious education must be sensitive to the specific needs of local congregations. Another reality is that no single source of religious education curricula or materials—whatever the faith community—can be informed or equipped well enough to be capable of meeting *every* situation faced by adhering congregations. People and congregations in those specific contexts *can* be aware of specific local needs, pedagogies through which they are more apt to learn, and faith perspectives that can be understood and appreciated by their local adherents. What a wonderful gift to be free to select from a variety of resources with which they can identify and will feel comfortable—and to adapt and adopt them to develop more effective approaches to religious education for their communities.

NOTES

[1] Findley B. Edge, *Teaching for Results*, rev. ed. (Nashville: Broadman & Holman, 1995) 4.

[2] Ibid., 63.

[3] Findley B. Edge, *A Quest for Vitality in Religion: A Theological Approach to Religious Education*, rev. ed. (Macon GA: Smyth & Helwys, 1994) 83.

[4] Timothy Arthur Lines, *Functional Images of the Religious Educator* (Birmingham AL: Religious Education Press, 1992) 44.

[5] Ibid., 115.

[6] Ibid., 515.

[7] Reuel L. Howe, *The Miracle of Dialogue* (New York: The Seabury Press, 1963) 17.

[CHAPTER 8]

VARIETY OF RESOURCES FOR THEOLOGICAL HIGHER EDUCATION

Also a gift to religious education, one area that demonstrates the diversity among Evangelical Protestants and is among the concerns that provides not only wide-ranging variety but also the most heated contention and competition among them, is the assortment of resources they provide for theological higher education. An earlier chapter has already mentioned theological higher education as an arena in which Evangelical Protestants themselves draw on many different resources. Here, the issue is that of the resources they provide for themselves and whomever else might choose primarily through schooling and training in theology as an academic discipline for its own sake and—probably more important to the majority of Evangelical Protestants—theology for the sake of practice in ministry.

Those factors that have enabled—and compelled—Evangelical Protestants to establish and develop so many seminaries and divinity schools that differ so widely in perspectives of theology, pedagogy, and mission are the freedom and diversity they enjoy—again based on a confluence of their belief in the authority of Scripture, the priesthood of all believers, and evangelism as the primary mission and task of the church.[1]

EVANGELICAL PROTESTANT RESOURCES

There are many differences and similarities among the variety of resources Evangelical Protestants make available to religious education and their individual distinctiveness. Certainly the most obvious and easily described differences would relate to size, degree programs offered,[2] and whether or not an institution is denominationally run or funded. However, their distinguishing marks and the differences that exist even among those schools very similar in those ways that can be described above can be demonstrated in terms of five concerns:

- the agencies to which they look for accreditation of their schools and standards for their degree programs
- their approaches to scholarship as it relates to ministry
- their relationships to churches
- their approaches to culture and the broader academic community
- their approaches to pedagogy

Most Evangelical Protestant seminaries seek some form of accreditation. Many will hold accreditation from a "regional" body that also accredits public schools and universities and is recognized by the Commission on Recognition of Postsecondary Accreditation. Some will obtain recognition by more narrowly defined agencies with fewer "secular" ties and more accommodating and acceptable to the conservatives or separationists among them. The accrediting agency that is most influential in theological education and to which most Evangelical Protestant seminaries and theology schools look for educational criteria and in which they seek membership is the Association of Theological Schools in the United States and Canada (ATS). Most Evangelical Protestant seminaries will seek or hold accreditation in more than one of the above. An individual school's decision regarding to which accrediting agency it will apply is often related to the variability available to them as related to a particular agency's standards. Funding can also be a factor, for some philanthropic foundations, churches, and denominations to which a school may appeal for monetary support (or to which their faculty may apply for grants) often favor schools holding accreditation by particular or specific agencies.

Regardless of the accrediting agency's standards, Evangelical resources often can and do differ in their approaches to scholarship as it relates to ministry. An example of how this is possible is found with the Master of Divinity (M.Div.) degree, recognized by ATS as the degree program most generally awarded and most expressly designed for ministry preparation and ordination. The goals of an M.Div. program, according to ATS, would be illustrated by a list (not to be "seen as exhaustive or mandatory") that includes for a person the following:

- familiarity with and the ability to discuss the basic documents and the traditions of the faith family in which ministry will take place
- knowledge of ministry theory and the ability to adapt and adopt such to one's particular area of ministry
- competency in ministry skills
- ability to work with and lead people in various avenues of local ministry
- awareness of ministry resources[3]

Even a casual reading of these purposes and goals reveals their general nature and the latitude possible in working toward their accomplishment. Not surprising, then, is that, within the constraints of that one accrediting agency, Evangelical Protestant schools will differ significantly on emphases and the means by which they deal with the tension between theory and practice. On one hand, some focus heavily on the former, stressing scholarly research and study and, therefore, being quite competitive academically—sometimes, arguably, to the neglect of the practical. Detractors of these schools decry what they variously call conforming to a worldly model, emphasizing mind over heart, loss of spiritual zeal, or being caught up in an "ivory tower" mentality and losing touch with practical matters and the real world of congregational ministry. On the other end of the spectrum would be those that center on training in practical skills with relatively little attention given to basic issues of the scholarly concerns of theory and backgrounds. Critics of these point to the dangers of oversimplification of issues, ministry as technology rather than profession, and zeal without knowledge. Most Evangelical Protestant schools—perhaps somewhat due to the influence of ATS—are to be found somewhere between these two extremes. Though often found *toward* one end or the other of this continuum and/or being particularly strong in one area or the other (sometimes both), they find more balance.

The role faculty are expected to play as related to the above regard also varies. However, it is not unusual with most Evangelical Protestant seminaries to have some written statement or unwritten understanding (usually the former) of expectations of faculty membership and involvement in a local church. These and other provisos can be variously devised, developed, understood, and enforced, but their common design is to tie their faculty—and, so, their academic enterprise—more firmly to the practice of ministry within the local congregation.

Problems arise, however, between what Fisher Humphreys has called a "folk theology" that can be highly internalized, but poorly expressed and an "academic theology" that may be well-expressed, "but not necessarily internalized."[4] Many schools, therefore, will also have formal or informal declarations of principles or statements of faith to which faculty must adhere and within which they are required to teach. Similar in purpose to the expectations of faculty as mentioned above, the purposes of these is to demonstrate and maintain loyalty to a faith tradition and the supporting constituencies.

The interplay of these two differing kinds of parameters with the freedom offered in the usually held (at least within the fellowship of Evangelical Protestants) doctrine of priesthood of all believers obviates the complexity of the doctrine, for that tenet also intimates accountability. For these schools and their faculty, this complexity can be simply stated as an issue of leadership and how the school and faculty relate to churches and/or the sponsoring faith community (i.e., faith community as either a formal denomination or as an informal constituency). Simply expressed, the question is one of whether the theological academia of a faith orientation should take the role of change agent in leading and motivating the churches toward qualitative growth or innovation or the role of a follower—as a direct arm of the churches, vested with responsibility for preparing future ministers through inculcation and indoctrination.

In their various approaches to theological higher education, Evangelical Protestants evidence many differing answers to this question and many different applications and expressions of whatever answers they may have. There are Evangelical Protestant individuals and groups that welcome varying types and degrees of diversity, expecting their respective academic resources to lead and, even, to be a prophetic voice within the fellowship. However, there are also those that expect of their "academia" strict and narrow compliance to closely confined interpretations not only of Scripture, but also of what faith statements there might be from the denomination or school. The latter rarely accept anything from their resources for theological higher education anything remotely resembling the prophetic or that which might, by some measure, threaten existing faith structures and traditionally understood.

Evangelical Protestant perspectives at these preceding points not only reflect their respective views of relating to culture, but also they directly influence how their seminaries, as resources for theological higher education, differ in their respective and individual approaches to culture and the rest of academia. Michael Peterson, in *Reason & Religious Belief: An Introduction to the Philosophy of Religion*, examined ways in which the tension between science and religion may be addressed. These ways reflect and can help one understand the variety of modes by which Evangelical Protestant theological higher education relates to and deals with the surrounding culture and that of the general scholarly world and other academic disciplines.

Philosophically, the struggle is one of bringing into congruence contrasting epistemologies. In a chapter titled with the query, "Religion and Science: Compatible of Incompatible?" Peterson stated the varying ways of addressing the tensions at hand in the form of three questions:

- "Do Religion and Science Conflict?"
- "Are Religion and Science Compartmentalized?"
- "The Question of Complementarity"[5]

According to Peterson, the type struggle realized in the evolution-creationist Scopes trial of the 1920s is inevitable when one assumes that religion and science (or any other academic discipline, for that matter) conflict. This results from each area being similarly defined in terms of objects, aims, and methods.[6] On the other hand, the differing academic areas can be perceived as being compartmentalized or simply having to do with separate and distinct concerns. Finding roots in Karl Barth and neo-orthodoxy, this perception sees—because of the wide differences—no conflict or interaction between religion and science.[7] Complementarity sees the two areas as sharing like objects, but differing as to aim and method. This suggests the possibility—and, for some, the desirability—of meaningful dialogue not in the sense of mutual completion, but toward mutually understanding, accepting, and respecting not only the differences in perspective, but also the value of having those differing viewpoints.[8] Again, one can find in Evangelical Protestant seminaries and faculties myriad examples of each way described by Peterson.

Dan O. Aleshire expressed the tension in other terms. Referring to David Kelsey's *To Understand God Truly: What's Theological about Theological Education* (1992) and *Between Athens and Berlin: The Theological Education Debate* (1993), Aleshire observed that two "schooling traditions" have permeated theological higher education, and it is their merger that evokes the struggle. One of those traditions is that which is "particular and confessional and reflects the religious affections of an ecclesial tradition." The other "is general and reflects academic virtues such as academic freedom and critical inquiry."[9] Though referring to the state of theological higher education in general, his description succinctly states a tension that particularly characterizes that found within Evangelical Protestantism.

One would assume that those factors would effect curricula. Nor is it startling that, with all the foregoing influences, viewpoints, and determinants, the resources within Evangelical Protestant theological higher education would evince such a variety of approaches to pedagogy. Of course, there is the long-standing (and long-running) debate and tension between what can be described as "traditional" versus contemporary teaching methodologies. And among Evangelical Protestants—regardless of position along the theological spectrum within that fellowship—there are both those steeped in and committed to the classical, long-standing approaches to teaching as well as those others very willing to experiment with new and innovative educational methods and media. However, an even deeper pedagogical question, whatever the specific methodology employed, relates to their varying understandings of the role of teaching as an event and not just as a curriculum or a set of policies.

A reflection of the role tension mentioned above, this crucial question is whether the purposes of theological higher education are to educate, equip, and train by helping to learn or by indoctrination. Those individuals and entities at or toward one of the two extremes—even with Evangelical Protestantism—often point to those at the other with accusations and in pejoratively stated terms of cloning versus apostasy. One of the expressions of both the variety of resources among Evangelical Protestants and the benefits of that diversity is that examples of these differing pedagogical philosophies are to be found not only at the two extremes, but also all along the continuum between them.

A GIFT TO RELIGIOUS EDUCATION

There is some measure of uniformity among Evangelical Protestant resources for theological higher education. Generally, as one might expect, regarding some of the foundational issues surfaced in this chapter, the tendency is for more uniformity to be found among those resources within a given denomination. This will be particularly true with denominations having fundamentalist leanings or commitments. However, even among those there will be some measure of differences at other points.

With so little uniformity across there are many opportunities for controversy and fractiousness. As one whose teaching ministry—mostly in theological higher education—has been within the context of a faith community mired in political and theological controversy for the entire span of that ministry, this writer is well aware of the personal, denominational, and institutional costs and damage of such conflict as well as the way in which it detracts from the mission of the church and its efforts in religious education.

Differences need not inevitably lead to contentiousness, however. And there are numerous examples of the benefits of honestly and openly held differences and the variety of resources that rise from those dissimilarities. This is especially possible when those who differ share significant and basic similarities such as found among Evangelical Protestants (i.e., the core issues as previously stated) and when those affinities are appreciated and affirmed and given priority.

Similar to the advantages found for the churches, a variety of resources for theological higher education offers creativity in selection. A student preparing for ministry either within or external to Evangelical Protestantism has the advantage of being able to choose among seminaries that differ in many ways, certainly finding one that will offer the kind of ministerial education she/he desires—from simply confirmation in what is already known to challenging toward growth in any number of areas.

Again due to the commonality provided by the core principles, the diversity among Evangelical Protestants in theological higher education compels most, if not all, toward some form of academic and scholarly reconsideration of their respective positions regarding the numerous areas of disagreement. For some, the issue will be a matter of apologetics and preparation for argumentation. Others will see it as a means toward dialogue for growth and understanding not only of themselves, but also of others—and, perhaps, as a step toward what reconciliation may be necessary. Whatever the motivation, the result can be the enrichment of not only academia, but also, as a result, the students and eventually the churches and congregations the students will serve. In this sense, then, theological higher education should be seen not only arguably as a subdiscipline to religious education or as the venue through which religious educators are taught and prepare for their respective vocations, but also as a resource for religious education in the church.

In summary, the variety of resources Evangelical Protestants offer for theological higher education is a gift to religious education in three ways. It enriches the broader fabric of that discipline by its contributing numerous and diverse approaches to the study and teaching of the theological perspective represented. It offers differing paradigms for holding in tension the confessional claims of faith with various understandings of scholarship and learning. It also demonstrates how assorted frames of reference, though fertile ground for dissension, can enrich religious education for the congregations and individuals within the same general faith family.

NOTES

[1] It should be noted at this point that the resources alluded to in this chapter are those that may legitimately lay claim to being educational institutions. Unfortunately, among the fellowship of Evangelical Protestants, there have sprung up over the years "seminaries" and "universities" that are not truly educational, but provide little more than mail-order degrees. These should not be considered as part of the gift described in this chapter, but are a blight on both religious education and Evangelical Protestantism.

²Bulletin 41 (1994) of ATS (The Association of Theological Schools in the United States and Canada) lists standards for ten doctoral and eleven masters degrees.
³Ibid., part 3, 35-36.
⁴Fisher Humphreys, "Teaching Theology to Ministers," *The Theological Educator* 57 (Spring 1998): 54.
⁵Michael Peterson et. al., *Reason & Religious Belief: An Introduction to the Philosophy of Religion* (New York: Oxford University Press, 1991) 196 ff.
⁶Ibid, 198-200.
⁷Ibid., 200-202.
⁸Ibid., 202-204.
⁹Daniel O. Aleshire, "Southern Baptist Theological Education," *Baptist History and Heritage* XXIX, no. 2 (April 1994) 14-15.

[CHAPTER 9]

CHOICE IN EXPRESSION OF SPIRITUALITY

Among the many areas of diversity to be found among Evangelical Protestants is their sundry different forms and understandings of spirituality. This is true not only of what will be found in their working definitions, but also in the many distinctive means by which religious education is done in their churches.

Spirituality has many definitions. Susanne Johnson has noted, in fact, that spirituality has become such a "popular" concept in our culture that "the word ["spirituality"] is used so loosely in literature that it is difficult to discern what it means" and that it "has become cluttered with meanings."[1] Laurence Scheindlin observed that spirituality is often vaguely linked to an amorphous concept somehow related to values, but, trying to coalesce the idea, chose to describe it as "an act of reaching beyond the self" and found that "the development of a rich inner life is a prerequisite for spirituality."[2]

Writing nearly a century ago, William James stated, "There thus seems to be no one elementary religious emotion, but only a common storehouse of emotions upon which religious objects may draw."[3] Though, according to Parker J. Palmer, "There is no such thing as 'spirituality in general,' " he does allow that "every spiritual search is and must be guided by a particular literature, practice, and community of faith."[4] David S. Dockery and David P. Gushee suggest that spirituality (more narrowly and accurately Christian spirituality) refers to "the overall quality and nature of the Christian's spiritual life" or one of many differing historical traditions regarding spiritual development "some corresponding with classic denominational and theological categories (e.g., Catholic, Wesleyan, Reformed, and Anabaptist spirituality, etc.), and others crossing such lines."[5] For John R. Tyson, " 'Christian spirituality' describes the relationship, union, and conformity with God that a Christian experiences through his or her reception of the grace of God, and a corresponding willingness to turn from sin and (to use a Pauline phrase) 'to walk according to the Spirit.' "[6]

VARIETIES AMONG EVANGELICAL PROTESTANTS

Richard J. Foster, in *Streams of Living Water*, identified and described six differing traditions of spiritual life or spirituality:

- the Contemplative
- the Holiness
- the Charismatic
- the Social Justice
- the Evangelical
- the Incarnational[7]

Though one of these might safely be said, by both those outside the Evangelical Protestant family and those within it, to be particularly characteristic of that faith group, each one finds expression somewhere in the broad spectrum of Evangelical Protestant life. Separately and together they serve to illustrate the diversity, variety, and choices for spirituality to be found in Evangelical Protestantism.

The first expression of spirituality among Evangelical Protestants to consider is that which might be considered stereotypical of them. Foster calls this the Evangelical Tradition, the primary goal of which is "discovering the Word-centered life" and succinctly defines it as "a life founded upon the living Word of God, the written Word of God, and the proclaimed Word of God."[8] Foster traces the historical lineage of this spiritual tradition from such early figures as Athanasius, Chrysostom, and Augustine and through later persons such as Thomas Aquinas, Wycliffe, the Protestant Reformers, George Whitfield, William Carey, Charles Spurgeon, and Dwight L. Moody to the most significant contemporary embodiment of the tradition, Billy Graham. He also links the tradition to historical movements and groups including the Dominicans, the Reformation, the Roman Catholic and Protestant missionary movements, and the Great Awakenings and the student volunteer movements.

Foster defines the Evangelical Tradition in terms similar to the description of the gifts of common core and common purpose as discussed in earlier chapters of this book. Significantly helpful is that Foster outlines "three great themes" in depicting the relationship between these two issues and the spirituality of the Evangelical Tradition:

- "the faithful proclamation of the gospel"
- "the centrality of Scripture as a faithful repository of the gospel"
- "the confessional witness of the early Christian community as a faithful interpretation of the gospel"[9]

He further notes four strengths of this type of spirituality:

- the call to conversion
- the stress on discipling the nations
- faithfulness to the Bible
- faithfulness to right doctrine[10]

Attendant dangers or pitfalls are, among others he admittedly chose not to list or discuss: "the tendency to fixate on peripheral and nonessential matters," "the tendency toward a sectarian mentality," "too limited a view of the salvation that is found in Jesus Christ," and "the tendency toward bibliolatry."[11]

Obvious from the description of the dimensions of Evangelical Protestantism described in the opening chapter of this book (as well as the previously mentioned gifts) and Foster's definition of the tradition, is why Foster so labeled this tradition "Evangelical" and why it would be most widely accepted as a relatively safe generalization regarding this faith group—however one might agree or disagree with Foster's outline of strengths and weaknesses. Surely it would also be safe to say that the spirituality of anyone claiming to be an Evangelical Protestant would at least be significantly or primarily colored by this spiritual tradition as described by Foster. However, given the freedom and diversity already observed within and among their fellowship, one should not be surprised to find other traditions also influencing and finding expression in the spirituality of Evangelical Protestant individuals and congregations.

Not unusual is for there to be found among Evangelical Protestants what Foster calls the "Contemplative Tradition." Foster defines the contemplative life as "the steady gaze of the soul upon the God who loves us"[12] and as "a life of loving attention to God."[13] He includes among the earlier historical figures of this movement and tradition Gregory of Nyssa, Benedict of Nursia, and Clare of Assis. These were succeeded by Brother Lawrence, Nikolas von Zinzendorf, and Theresia of Lisieux and, more recently, Thomas Merton and Henri Nouwen. Groups and movements that have followed, practiced, and carried the tradition range from the early Desert Fathers and Mothers through the Benedictines and Poor Clares and, from the sixteenth and seventeenth centuries to the present, through Moravians and Pietists.[14] Many of these latter two groups find adherents today among Evangelical Protestants.

Foster objectively evaluates the positive and negative aspects of the Contemplative Tradition.[15] He lists the following as contributions:

- It stresses and engenders basic issues such as the love of God.
- It compels one beyond a solely intellectual approach to religion.
- It emphasizes prayer as essential.
- It underscores the "solitariness of our life with God."

Likewise, Foster names the "perils" of the Contemplative Tradition:

- It can separate one from the "ordinary life."
- Its exercises can consume one to the point of "spiritual gluttony."
- It can engender tendencies to "devalue intellectual efforts to articulate our faith."
- It can incline one toward disregard for the communal aspect of faith.

The Holiness Tradition finds Tertullian, Gregory of Nazianus, Bernard of Clairvaux, Thomas a Kempis, Ignatius of Loyola, Menno Simons, Teresa of Avila, John Wesley, Francis Asbury, E. Stanley Jones, and Dietrich Bonhoeffer among its forebears and Cistercians, Roman Catholic Reformers, Anabaptists, Puritans, and those of the Holiness and Keswick movements among its historical precedents.[16] As with the Contemplative Tradition, these also are the progenitors and champions of the faith for numerous Evangelical Protestant individuals, congregations, and denominations.

The Holiness Tradition "focuses upon the inward reformation of the heart and the development of 'holy habits' "[17] and can be simply defined as "a life that functions as it should."[18] Again, Foster notes both the strengths and weaknesses of this tradition.[19] Among its strengths are:

- Its consistent focus on the greatest objective for Christians (i.e., that of reflecting the glory of God)
- Its fixing on the heart as the source from which all conduct flows
- Its offer of the possibility of real transformation in the life of a person
- "Its tough-minded, down-to-earth, practical understanding of how we 'grow in the grace and knowledge of our Lord and Savior Jesus Christ' (2 Pet. 3:18)"

On the other hand, Foster notes that the Holiness Tradition can lead to:

- legalism
- a drift away from understanding salvation as by grace alone
- losing touch with the implications of one's humanity while holding oneself up as an example of perfect behavior.

One would expect to find Foster pointing to certain more recent Pentecostal and Charismatic movements (e.g., the Azusa Street revival in California) and twentieth-century personalities and leaders such as Aimee Semple McPherson, Kathryn Kuhlman, C. H. Mason, Demos Shakarian, and Oral Roberts as precedents in the Charismatic Tradition. However, he also includes Perpetua, Gregory Thaumaturgus, Alcuin of York, Hildegard of Bingen, Francis of Assis, Joan of Arc, George Fox, and John Wesley among its progenitors. He describes the goal of the Charismatic Tradition in terms as "a life immersed in, empowered by, and under the direction of the Spirit of God."[20]

Not only are there expressly and particularly Charismatic or Pentecostal denominations (e.g., Assemblies of God) and congregations numbered among Evangelical Protestants, but also there are significant numbers of persons and churches who would be identified by themselves and others as part of the Charismatic Tradition to be found within the fellowship of most—if not all—Evangelical Protestant denominations and faith groups. Despite the freedom they enjoy and their common focus on Scripture, it is this tradition and its practices (e.g., *glossalalia*) that can be the most divisive among Evangelical Protestants and within denominations so identified. Further, the tradition is also influencing among Evangelical Protestant churches many aspects of worship that are still not strictly charismatic in practice. Further, Evangelical Protestants who have been more recently attracted to or influenced by this tradition often allude to experiences very similar to those of historical heroes of Evangelical Protestantism such as John Wesley and Charles Finney.

Foster observes that the Charismatic Tradition does not try to tame God, empowers and energizes the practice of the Christian life and ministry beyond simple words, and it makes spiritual growth central. However, it also can shift one's attention from God and the use and effect of spiritual gifts to the gifts themselves, decry and denigrate the cognitive, and attend too much to unfounded or theologically weak eschatological issues.[21]

To Foster, the parentage of the Social Justice Tradition includes several individuals of the early church, but many from the Middle Ages on and with particular proliferation in the eighteenth and succeeding centuries. A few of the latter are Catherine of Genoa, Vincent de Paul, Roger Williams, John Woolman, William Wilberforce, Sojourner Truth, William Booth, Mother Teresa, and Martin Luther King Jr. Some of the movements that have reflected this tradition or found root in it are the Vincentians, the Sunday School movement, the Salvation Army, abolition and suffrage, and the

American Civil Rights movement.[22] Many of these persons and movements find either direct or indirect, but substantial, legacy among contemporary Evangelical Protestants—especially Williams and King among Baptists, Booth with the Salvation Army, and Sunday School among the vast majority of Evangelical Protestants.

Foster defines the aim of this tradition as "a life committed to compassion and justice for all peoples."[23] He notes that, despite its idealism, the Social Justice Tradition (with Christian love as the vital point and motivating factor) evokes political activism (not simply in the secular or popular sense of the term, but with the connotation of effort), challenges churches to relevancy and not just theoretical faith, advocates peace in social relationships, stresses the importance of bringing that same peace to human relationships with the environment. Unfortunately, within the Social Justice Tradition, its basic purpose and ultimate can be lost and the tradition slip into political secularism (i.e., overidentification with partisan political agendas) and its own kind of legalism.[24]

The final stream of spirituality identified by Foster, the Incarnational Tradition, is that which "focuses upon making present and visible the realm of the invisible spirit" and "addresses the crying need to experience God as truly manifest and notoriously active in daily life." Some of those figures and movements that have expressed and/or contributed to it include early Christians Origin and Monica, an assortment of scientists and artists of the Renaissance and subsequent cultural periods, and such twentieth-century personalities as Dag Hammarskjold and Aleksander Solzhenitsyn.[25]

Though numerous Evangelical Protestants would appreciate particular contributions of many of these leaders to their respective fields and make allusions to them in appropriate circumstances, it is doubtful that more than a few might claim any of these individuals or movements as being of primary importance in arriving at their own spirituality. Three exceptions should be noted, however. Ironically, the significance of Dante Alighieri and John Milton to the development of doctrine and perspectives related to eschatology, evil, and Satan. among many Evangelical Protestants (whether or not they realize it) probably exceeds that of the Bible itself. Also, and in a more positive and biblically faithful way, the spirituality of almost all Evangelical Protestants would resonate with Hammarskjold's notations such as "Not I, but God in me," "We act in faith—and miracles occur,"[26] which strike important chords for them, because they speak to both the inner and daily nature of the spiritual life.

Nevertheless, the influence or presence of the Incarnational Tradition among Evangelical Protestants is to be found in particular emphases on living lives of daily sacrifice as a means to relate to and identify oneself in relationship with God. It points to God's interest in and God's indwelling presence with people in their daily lives and blesses the physical world (of work, ecology, etc.). However, people so inclined can fall prey to confusing a religious image with that which it represents and to falling into ritualism or, as Foster puts it, seeking "to manage God through externals."[27]

SPIRITUALITY IN RELIGIOUS EDUCATION

One could easily become overwhelmed when considering the many possible forms of spirituality offered by the traditions outlined above and found among Evangelical Protestants—and others composed of the multitudinous possible combinations of those traditions. Adding to the complexity is that spirituality can be expressed in many differing ways and arguably in every area of a person's or congregation's life. Further, as discussed in earlier chapters, it may be said that everything a congregation does is, by some definition, religious education.

For the majority of people, the most obvious expression of spirituality is in worship. From the structure of a worship service itself and the respective involvements of the various persons who lead and participate, to the thematic content of the worship and the very architecture of the worship site itself, worship not only reflects spirituality, but also teaches (by design or default) about doctrine and practice. As with other faith communities, Evangelical Protestants struggle with the tensions that rise from generational and cultural differences regarding worship forms. For example, the struggle between "traditional" and "contemporary" worship is common. There is tremendous diversity among Evangelical Protestants as to how they resolve these issues and, so their worship forms. Explicitly or implicitly, consciously or subconsciously, intentionally or unintentionally, the individual and corporate spirituality is one of the dominant factors influencing decisions regarding worship. Likewise and as a result, spirituality is also one of the most significant content areas taught by worship.

Further, the way people and communities of faith state and carry out what they understand to be their core purpose and mission both rises from and teaches their respective and shared spiritualities. Obviously, for Evangelical Protestants this will relate to their various views and perspectives particularly on salvation and the gospel—and not only how it is attained but also its purpose and how it is expressed in the life of the individual and the church. At this point specific differences regarding soteriology can and do result in differences in expression. For example, how they view the process of salvation and the respective roles of people and God in it, will form not only what they say about it, but also how they share it with others. These patterns themselves also teach by reinforcement for some and by precept and example for others.

The role of service or ministry in individual and corporate life varies among differing traditions of spirituality. It is a more integral aspect of the redeemed life for some Evangelical Protestants than for others and, certainly the areas of service and ministry toward which they are compelled will differ—sometimes as a result of their respective spirituality, but also (and, perhaps, more often) by the needs as perceived in and by their surrounding communities. As a mode of religious education, service and ministry among Evangelical Protestants have the dual effect of reflecting and teaching their doctrine and spirituality.

However, is should not be overlooked that spirituality also finds significant expression in schooling within Evangelical Protestant congregations including the curricula, content, and methodologies they employ. As with the above areas by which religious education occurs, these various aspects of schooling rise from and instruct in respective approaches to spirituality as well as specific doctrine. Spirituality is often that which will incline Evangelical Protestants toward the previously noted diversity in resources of all types and at all levels of religious education. One notable example is that of the "Experiencing God" curricula originally developed and written by Henry T. Blackaby and Claude V. King, at the time of the curriculum's development, two employees of Southern Baptist Convention agencies. The original study was titled *Experiencing God: Knowing and Doing the Will of God* and reflects an amorphous or mixed spirituality and has been both accepted and denigrated within the family of Evangelical Protestants and for reasons related to spirituality as well as doctrine, hermeneutics, and pedagogy.

A GIFT TO RELIGIOUS EDUCATION

Any faith that has among its ends cultivating the inner life and developing the relationship of that inner life to the transcendent by its very nature and definition is concerned with spirituality. The religious education of any faith that seeks to be alive and relevant among differing people and diverse cultures and generations must, within certain parameters, allow for diversity in expression of spirituality. This is similar to Hans Küng's call for Christianity to discover what the power of God makes possible: newness of awareness, motivations, attitudes, actions, and aims.[28] Thomas P. Williamsen put it this way: "The challenge for the church is to herald a vision of service that grows out of a person's deep spiritual connectedness to God and a sense of oneness with humankind."[29] The urgency is underscored when one recalls that spirituality touches every internal and external area of an individual life from vocation to sexuality.

For those reasons the religious education of Christianity or any faith is enriched through attention to and expression by and via the differing personalities of its adherents. In the same way, that of Evangelical Protestants is both nurtured and nurturing due to the many diverse expressions of spirituality found among them. Their gift is a paradigm—with all its weaknesses and strengths as well as those among their various traditions of spirituality—for how this occurs.

NOTES

[1] Susanne Johnson, *Christian Spiritual Formation in the Church and Classroom* (Nashville: Abingdon Press, 1989) 11-12.

[2] Laurence Scheindlin, "Preparing Children for Spirituality," Religious Education 94, no. 2 (Spring 1999): 191-98.

[3] William James, *The Varieties of Religious Experience: A Study in Human Nature* (New York: Random House, 1902) 29.

[4] Parker J. Palmer, *To Know as We Are Known: A Spirituality of Education* (San Francisco: Harper & Row, 1983) 14.

[5] David S. Dockery and David P. Gushee, "Spirituality and Spiritual Growth," *Preparing for Christian Ministry: An Evangelical Approach*, David S. Dockery and David P. Gushee, eds. (Wheaton IL: Victor Books, 1997) 83-84.

[6] John R. Tyson, "Introduction: Invitation to Christian Spirituality," *Invitation to Christian Spirituality: An Ecumenical Anthology*, ed. John R. Tyson (New York: Oxford University Press, 1999) 1.

[7] Richard J. Foster, *Streams of Living Water* (San Francisco: HarperSanFrancisco, 1998) xvi.

[8] Ibid., 233.

[9] Ibid., 219.

[10] Ibid., 225-28.

[11] Ibid., 228-30.

[12] Ibid., 4.

[13] Ibid., 58.

[14] Ibid., 24.
[15] Ibid., 51-55.
[16] Ibid., 60.
[17] Ibid., 61.
[18] Ibid., 96.
[19] Ibid., 84-94.
[20] Ibid., 132.
[21] Ibid., 128-31.
[22] Ibid., 136.
[23] Ibid., 182.
[24] Ibid., 176-81.
[25] Ibid., 236-37.
[26] Ibid., 257, 259.
[27] Ibid., 266-68.

[28] Hans Küng, *Why I Am Still a Christian*, trans. David Smith et. al., ed. E. C. Hughes (Nashville: Abingdon Pressm 1987) 60-62.

[29] Thomas P. Williamsen, *Attending Parishioners' Spiritual Growth* (Bethesda MD: The Alban Institute, 1997) 9.

[CHAPTER 10]

DEMANDING DEVELOPMENTAL SENSITIVITY

Almost universally, educators of all persuasions realize—perhaps assume—the importance of developmental studies to informing pedagogy. However, to some it may seem that the religious education of any faith group with such closely defined parameters as those that define Evangelical Protestantism would leave little room for consideration of the particular demands raised by studies in and theories of developmental psychology.

While certain aspects of psychological studies may be suspect to some of the most conservative or fundamentalist Evangelical Protestants, there are features or dimensions of Evangelical Protestant theology that seemingly demand sensitivity to and application of issues surfaced by developmental studies. This is not to naively believe or claim that all Evangelical Protestants everywhere, because of their theology, consistently apply developmental principles to all they do—including their efforts in religious education and schooling. Rather, the point is that, despite blind spots and sometimes being oblivious to the many implications of their own doctrines, Evangelical Protestant emphases on the authority of Scripture, the various aspects of salvation, and the priesthood of all believers—as examples—challenge them and the religious education of all faiths to concern for and application of what is revealed through developmental studies.

PARADIGMS THAT INFORM RELIGIOUS EDUCATION

An important contribution of developmental studies is to sort out and to make clear the tasks people face at various ages in their lives. Of course, there are myriad theories and paradigms for understanding the ways and areas in which people are equipped to deal with and accomplish those tasks at their respective ages. Most, if not all, developmental models or theories have something to offer one toward understanding education in general and religious education in particular. However, space and time do not allow for a thorough review of all of these. For our purposes here, the paradigms offered by four major developmental theorists will serve as examples and—later in this chapter—how particular Evangelical Protestant doctrines at some level require attention to them. Even the four theorists covered (Piaget, Erikson, Kohlberg, and Fowler) will each be given only cursory overviews with some specific mention of aspects to which this chapter will subsequently allude and connect a specific Evangelical Protestant belief.

[PIAGET]

Though they have their critics, Jean Piaget and Erik Erikson are accepted as among the most important developmental psychologists and informants bringing developmental studies to bear on education. Piaget's theories could be said to have the most obvious connection to education because they deal with the psychomotor, intellectual, or cognitive aspects of learning that are vital to any area or type of education. The issue for Piaget was not one of mental ability (i.e., intelligence per se), but the way that persons are capable of thinking logically or processing information at particular stages, points, or ages in their lives. As with most developmental theories, Piaget sees the need for solidifying the cognitive development of which one—especially a child— is capable at a specific level before being able to process at the next level. Piaget outlines four basic stages of cognitive development:

- sensorimotor development (ages 0-2)
- preoperational thought (ages 2-7)
- concrete operations (ages 7-11)
- formal operations (ages 11-15)

In the sensorimotor level, the infant is learning through her elemental senses and reflexive motor functions to distinguish between her self and her surroundings. Early on the infant does not understand object permanence (i.e., that objects exist even when not in view), but the concept is grasped late in this stage as a part of normal learning and maturation. In preoperational thought, though the child remains largely egocentric, normally there is growth in language and conceptual development and complexity. The cognitive processes tend to be more intuitive and impulsive, and differentiation is based more on visual perception. By early in the concrete operational stage a child, moving beyond simple visual perception, understands the principle of conservation (i.e., objects can maintain the same mass though in a different shape or configuration). He also is becoming less egocentric, allowing him to understand basic objective relational concepts and to contemplate perspectives different from his—though abstraction is still difficult. The formal operational stage is the one in which the child begins to think and reason more scientifically and becomes more able to deal with abstract reasoning. By this she is able to work toward problem solving by developing and determining hypotheses and ways by which these may be tested.

[ERIKSON]

Erikson's theory has to do with a person's psychosocial development. He described this as occurring through a progression of eight crises that deal with particular ever-expanding arenas of human relationships and with the desired consequence of each crisis being an aspect of a healthy personality. These eight stages or crises are:

- trust vs. mistrust (ages 0-1)
- autonomy vs. shame and doubt (ages 1-3)
- initiative vs. guilt (ages 3-5)
- industry vs. inferiority (ages 6-11)
- identity vs. role confusion (adolescence)
- intimacy vs. isolation (young adulthood)
- generativity vs. stagnation (middle adulthood)
- integrity vs. despair and disgust (older adulthood)

The first two crises, basic trust vs. basic mistrust and autonomy vs. shame and doubt, focus on the relationships between the child and the primary caregivers or parents and have as their respective goals the cultivation of hope and will. The third stage, initiative vs. guilt involves the family and should lead to the development of a sense of purpose and goal-orientation. The crisis of industry vs. inferiority centers on the relationship of the child with his neighborhood and/or school, and it is out of this crisis that he should have acquired perception of himself as basically competent. Adolescence, for Erikson, is the time for the crisis of identity vs. role confusion in which the person is focused primarily on her peer group and, though developing a greater awareness of her singularity as a person while maintaining appropriate relationships with other distinctive individuals, thus giving rise to a sense of genuine fidelity both to herself and to others. The crisis of intimacy vs. isolation occurs within young adults as they sort out their relationships with their friends and, if married, with their spouses. It is through this crisis—and based on what one has learned in earlier crises and especially in that immediately preceding—that he can relate to others in a genuinely loving (not just in the romantic sense) and mature manner. Middle adulthood finds one in a crisis of generativity vs. stagnation. Though one at this stage cannot help but be concerned with deteriorating faculties, the challenge is to move, through relationships found in family and co-workers, beyond oneself to caring for others—both known and unknown to them. In the crisis of integrity vs. despair and disgust, a senior adult seeks to resolve her own life journey with her opportunities and find a healthy acceptance of those areas and times of failure or missed opportunity on her part or that of anyone with whom she has had a relationship.

[KOHLBERG]

Somewhat different than Piaget and Erikson but related to them and arguably more closely related to the immediate or obvious issues of religious faith and education, Lawrence Kohlberg offers a theory of a person's development in the way by which moral reasoning is done. Kohlberg's model is divided into three levels. Each level is comprised of two stages, each of which describes a particular orientation that drives the decision-making process in that phase. The three major levels are:

- preconventional
- conventional
- postconventional

At the preconventional level a child's moral reasoning is limited to obedience or other means by which reward can be obtained and/or punishment avoided. At the conventional level the child's concern is the approval of others (i.e., being seen as a "good boy" or "nice girl") or the meeting of others' expectations by adherence to rules and obedience of authority. The postconventional level sees moral reasoning based on more internalized values derived either from social contracts and/or consensus or, in the highest stage, from individually accepted and developed universal ethical principles that take into account various and varying perspectives while respecting the dignity and rights of other persons.

[FOWLER]

The developmental theory most obviously connected to and reflective of the concerns of religious education is that of faith development advanced by James Fowler in his 1981 book, *Stages of Faith: The Psychology of Human Development and the Quest for Meaning*. Fowler sees faith as a universal (as do developmentalists Piaget, Erikson, and Kohlberg with the areas of concern of their respective theories and with whom Fowler relates his theory and engages in a sort of dialogue) and takes an approach to faith similar to those of Paul Tillich and Richard Niebuhr. That is, everyone has *something* in which they have faith and, therefore, on which they center their lives and that gives meaning to their lives. In this way faith is not necessarily to be understood as a "salvific faith" in the sense that Evangelical Protestants would understand it.

Fowler's stages, like those of Erikson and dissimilar to Piaget's and Kohlberg's, are not hierarchical. The first experiences of faith begin with birth, and one's faith is lived out in relationship and shapes the imagination. Further, each individual learns to process his/her faith by experiencing seven successive stages related to his/her respective developmental abilities. These seven stages of faith are:

- primal (ages 0-3)
- intuitive/projective (ages 4-8)
- mythic/literal (7/8-11/12)
- synthetic/conventional (from 11/12-young adulthood)
- individuating/reflexive (17/18-30s/40s)
- conjunctive (mid-life)
- universalizing (older adulthood)

The first of these stages is the preconventional or primal stage in which rudimentary faith is bound up in the meeting of the basic physical and security needs of the infant. Intuitive/projective faith (ages 4-8) is the stage in which meaning is made of faith and trust established intuitively and by imitation. Faith is experienced more episodically and symbols taken literally. In the mythic/literal stage (7 or 8-11 or 12) the person comes more consciously to join and belong to his immediate group or faith community, using the reasoning and thought beyond intuition that is now possible, though the child still tends to think concretely. At the synthetic/conventional stage (from 11 or 12 and can last long into adulthood) the person begins to make meaning out of life according to the directions and criteria of popular convention and begins to experience life as distinct and separate areas of concern. While one's own judgment is increasingly trusted, there also is an awareness that values often come into conflict. Therefore, judgment is used more to choose between authorities. An individuating/reflexive faith (usually not before 17 or 18 and often does not emerge until the mid-30s or 40s) is one of transition that recognizes a lack of congruence between one's self and the various groups of which one may be a part and, so, takes more personal responsibility for commitments and attitudes. A conjunctive faith is unusual before mid-life. It is a stage in which one not only recognizes but also embraces the many tensions and ambiguities resulting from their faith. Further, many of the old truths (i.e., those they have held from an earlier age and stage) are reappropriated but with more of a sense of personal ownership and expressed in more personal terms. For Fowler, the final stage, that of universalizing faith is rare. In it the self ceases to be the centering reference point. Life is still valued, loved, and taken seriously, but the person comes to grips with its transitory nature and, so, it is held more loosely.

DEVELOPMENT AND THE AUTHORITY OF SCRIPTURE

As the central and foundational tenet of Evangelical Protestants, the authority of Scripture requires of them particular attention to developmental issues for many reasons—and usually finds them faithful at least in the attempt. First, it seems logical that, if the authority of Scripture extends to every area of moral, ethical, and spiritual life, it applies to persons' dealing with their respective developmental tasks at whatever stage in which they find themselves. If this be true, it is important—vital, even—that the truths and precepts of Scripture be taught not only to meets a person's needs, but also in ways and with vocabulary and concepts that are understandable to them.

Second, the Bible is replete with directives and examples of individualized preceptual teaching that has direct and indirect implications for developmental sensitivity. The Old Testament is very clear in including the entire family—and, so, all those throughout the life span—in the covenant community. Of particular significance is that, though children are only infrequently referred to otherwise, in the passage flowing out of the *Shema* (the foundational statement of the Hebrew faith) in Deut 6, one of the most important responsibilities of parents and the rest of the faith community was to instill in their children the teachings of the Law. This is also made clear from Exod 13:14ff and various passages from Proverbs and narratives throughout the historical literature. Though the New Testament makes frequent use of children as a metaphor, it mentions them little as objects of teaching. However, great importance is vested by Evangelical Protestants and others in Jesus' call for his disciples to allow children access to him (cf. Matt 19:14) and in his pattern of accepting people "where they were" and conversing with them and teaching them precepts in terms with which they were acquainted (e.g., in parables involving familiar figures and images). The symbolic nature of religious language and literature poses special problems for teaching at the younger developmental levels, which makes the concrete character of biblical stories so integral to drawing young children into and under the Bible and its authority.

Related to its explicit principles and precepts, the Bible's narratives demand sensitivity to developmental characteristics. This goes beyond the individual's capacity for understanding and otherwise dealing with hermeneutical matters related to historicity versus the mythical nature of biblical narrative. Even assuming a literalist perspective, one's ability to understand and accept paradox will influence how they will read, comprehend, and apply the contrasting stories of King David as "a man after God's own heart" with those of his serious spiritual, personal, and moral failures. At this point the respective developmental capacities may explain why children appreciate the heroics of the David-Goliath story and middle adults can not only identify with but also grow and learn from the humanity and tragedy revealed in the sordid stories of David's family and court. In each situation the narrative as simply tales of either heroism or family drama can overwhelm their potential toward spiritual growth if developmental levels are not taken into account when teaching them.

DEVELOPMENT AND SALVATION

Perhaps nowhere is the need for sensitivity to such a broad range of developmental issues, areas, and theories more vital among Evangelical Protestants than in teaching and conversation related to salvation. Only those Evangelical Protestants who see salvation in the most simplistic and ritualistic way will deny the importance of attention to the individual's developmental capacity to helping a person, regardless of age, understand and be able to make a responsible decision regarding and, so, have a genuine experience of, salvation. The issue includes that concern most often referred to as "the age of accountability" (that age at which a person—the term is usually used in reference to a child or children—has the capacity for making a profession of faith or commitment to Jesus Christ that marks the initial step or event in personal salvation, i.e., one's conversion). At the very least this requires capacities for some basic comprehension of personal responsibility and accountability and individuation. Further, a more holistic, mature , and complete perspective of the biblical teaching of conversion would require attention, if developmental theories are to be believed and incorporated at this point, that the emphasis shift—as people have capacity to comprehend—from reward/punishment (the realities of heaven and of hell) to more universal principles such as looking beyond oneself.

Also, mature biblical teaching on salvation goes beyond nurturing or redirecting faith at the initial conversion experience and, as reflected in Fowler's paradigm, includes understanding faith development as pilgrimage. Of course, this is consistent with the aspect of salvation known as sanctification and that finds special emphasis among many Evangelical Protestants.

Here, directly related to and the outgrowth of learning and application of biblical principles as described above, there must be a direct and immediate correlation of whatever principles are at stake to the general and specific developmental and personal needs and capacities of the individual that must also be addressed if the Bible is to be deemed relevant.

DEVELOPMENT AND THE PRIESTHOOD OF ALL BELIEVERS

To be consistent with their treasured doctrine of the priesthood of all believers demands that Evangelical Protestants relate to each member of their fellowship as a functioning "priest" regardless of their respective ages. This requires that each individual be not only allowed, but also challenged, equipped, nurtured, and enabled to perform as such—again, for many obvious reasons, all with an awareness of and sensitivity to the innate and developmental abilities of the student. Only in so doing can a child, for instance, truly be seen and experience belonging to the fellowship not only through heritage, lifestyle, and personal experience, but also in mission and ministry and an appropriate level of theological reflection as shared with the community of faith.

A GIFT TO RELIGIOUS EDUCATION

The most apparent contributions of Evangelical Protestants related to the demand for developmental sensitivity are those made by scholars, theorists, and writers of religious education within that fellowship whose work rise out of those concerns discussed above and the many others not mentioned. The immediacy of their concern that rises out of their theological perspective engenders relevance and urgency to what they have produced and, so, enhances the quality and adds to the body of research to the benefit of all concerned with religious education.

Theirs is a gift also in the sense of demonstrating how sensitivity to developmental needs not replace or detract from core tenets of one's faith. Rather, such awareness can, indeed, emerge from a deep understanding and appreciation for and faithfulness to those beliefs.

The implications for this kind of sensitivity to developmental issues touch all areas of religious education: content, curricula, pedagogy, and so on.. Ultimately, it provides a framework by which the religious education of any faith can ensure its future by reaching out and being relevant to all generations and at all ages throughout the human lifespan.

[CHAPTER 11]

PERSONALIZED APPROACH TO RESPONSE AND EXPRESSION

The tremendous freedom and diversity among Evangelical Protestants is already evident from the discussions and descriptions at several previous points and in most of the preceding chapters. This variability has been part and parcel of the Evangelical Protestant witness both due to and throughout the many differing histories of the faith groups that comprise that fellowship. That diversity, however, is also intertwined with the value and centrality of the individual and the individual and personal nature of faith—especially in its salvific expression—found in the core tenets and doctrines of Evangelical Protestantism. This creates an atmosphere and environment of freedom and individuality that precipitates not only differing denominational and congregational faith idioms and paradigms, but also a personalized approach to the inner, qualitative concern of spirituality and to the outwardly oriented, practical nature of expressing faith and responding to its challenges.

The immediacy of the personal relationship with God as believed and articulated by all Evangelical Protestants bespeaks an experiential religion and the very personal and individual nature of faith and freedom. This has obvious affective implications as already discussed regarding the inner life of spiritual formation. However, it is significant how diverse—indeed, virtually individualized within the general fellowship of Evangelical Protestantism and, so, within even the denominations so oriented—the overt faith or religious lifestyles this engenders. Without becoming mired in the albeit important systematic theology (or soteriology) of this conviction of Evangelical Protestants, a simple image, parable, or metaphor may suffice to understand its construct and consequences. The image is of a parent with many children. That parent, ideally, loves all those children at the same quantitative level. Also, each child bears basically (or exactly) the same genetic imprint of that parent. However, due to that parent's recognizing the individuality of each child, the relationship of that parent with each child will be qualitatively different, though each would be similarly labeled as parent-child. Each parent-child bond, though sharing certain congruence with all or some of the others, will nevertheless, be unique. In the same way, the general Evangelical Protestant perspective of God is that the "plan of salvation" is the same for all. Though there remain significant disagreements among them regarding the respective roles of Providence or the person in making the choice (i.e., the tension between the more Calvinistic and those more Armenian), they agree that the salvation experience is mediated and experienced individually.

Nonetheless, as the heavenly (and ideal) parent, God recognizes the unique makeup of each child (and created them as such) and, so, each God-Christian relationship, though sharing certain similarities with all others, is free to emerge or mature within whatever constraints may rise from an understanding of Scripture. Of course, as previously stated, though most, if not all, Evangelical Protestants would hold to this epistemologically, those toward the Fundamentalist end of the Evangelical Protestant spectrum are less inclined to hold to it ethically or in practice.

Further implications and support for this personalized approach to expression is found in the doctrine of the priesthood of all believers. Though this doctrine has its corporate ramifications that cannot be overlooked nor should they be lost, the central issue and focus remain that of and on the individual. The connection here is related to that of direct access to God, but expressed in terms of no need for a human advocate other than oneself. With Jesus as the "High Priest" (cf. Heb 5:6, 10; 6:20; 7:7), each believer is free to develop a personalized and individual approach to her/his ministry as a priest. This, in turn, must take into account the particular and specific giftedness (i.e., for Evangelical Protestants especially in terms of spiritual gifts) of each person in discerning, understanding, planning, and working toward accomplishing each person's respective expression of ministry. If, then, it is God's Spirit that engenders and empowers the individual ministry, each person's ministry cannot or should not be constrained by the walls and chains of convention or tradition.

Moreover, this freedom of response and expression must be accompanied with a sense of equality, acceptance, and inclusiveness for all members and in all areas of congregational life, for it is a call to shared power—power in individual determination and corporate leadership. This is a significant shift away from a hierarchical mode of governance and away from a focus on creeds as human determinants of expected or required responses to and expressions of faith. It is in this sense that the responsibility of each believer as priest and the freedom found in it is to be balanced with accountability in relationship with a congregation of other "priests." This is the root of the concept of local church governance and, so, why individual local churches or congregations, too, share in the freedom to a very overt and—for each church—individualized and personal expression of and response to their faith and its demands as perceived by each congregation or body.

The focus for each believer as a priest must, then, shift back to the core authority—that of Scripture—as the source not only from which one derives sustenance and direction for spiritual formation and growth, but also as the wellhead from which one derives a personal call to faith and service and the standard by which should be measured conduct in every area of one's life. Simply stated, the authority of scripture—as opposed to any other potential source of control—frees, requires, and enables each person to respond to what they individually find God, through the Bible, calling them to be and to do.

EXPRESSION, RESPONSE, AND RITUAL

Ritual is certainly one of the most visible and discernible aspects of what is shared in the corporate life of a congregation. Intriguing is that, despite what general uniformity of doctrine might be found among Evangelical Protestants, there is also great variety in the types and methods of various rituals to be found among them as individuals and as bodies.

Though by definition Evangelical Protestants would agree on the need for a person to be "born again" through accepting and professing faith in Jesus as Lord, some would disagree as to the role, method, and role of baptism related to that experience. Most would see baptism as an act of obedience to the command of Jesus on the part of the believer, but some differ as to the necessity of the ritual. The mode—i.e., immersion, pouring, sprinkling, etc.—is an important issue for others (especially Baptists), and many of those make such an issue or test of fellowship. Even the words said (the formula) in the ritual are significant to some, especially in terms of various Trinitarian references. For many, the ritual of baptism has overtones of initiation into and identification with the family of the congregation.

Regardless of the particular and specific traditions of the respective Evangelical Protestant denominations and congregations regarding baptism, it is not unusual for personalized variations to be allowed that take into account the context and heritage of the congregation or, even, a particular baptismal candidate. For instance, it would not be unusual for a Baptist church, though equipped with a baptistery in its sanctuary, to observe baptism in a lake, pond, creek, or river nearby in connection with a celebration of the heritage of the church such as its centennial. Nor would it be uncommon for a baptismal service, regardless of the mode and in conformity to general traditions of the church otherwise, for the candidate to be given an opportunity for input regarding the development and design of his baptism.

An example would be a parent/layperson taking part, perhaps even as the primary administrant, in the baptism of her child. Another would be the candidate being given various kinds of occasions for sharing a short confession of faith or a personal testimony of his conversion experience as part of the ritual.

Though infant baptism—in the truest sense of the term—would be unknown among Evangelical Protestants, many observe some form of ritual that, at some level, welcomes a child into the life and community of the congregation. Some would refer to this as a "christening," but most would choose to call it either a baby, parent, or family dedication. This is becoming increasingly employed among Evangelical Protestant congregations as they grow in understanding the vital role the immediate family, the family of faith, and the cooperation between the two plays in the nurture of the child. Here, too, there is great variability in terms of how these rituals are constructed and carried out.

Another ritual, variously known as the Lord's Supper or communion, which has always been seen as having certain pedagogical value, also has various expressions among Evangelical Protestants. Here, too, the physical makeup of the elements, the formula, the mode, and the method may differ from one instance to the next, but almost all Evangelical Protestants will agree that this particular ritual is not, in the strictest sense, a sacrament. Rather, the elements are understood as symbolic of the body and blood of Jesus and the obvious emphasis that is shared and which remains the central point of the ritual is that of his sacrifice in atonement for sin. However, the expression of this and the individual response elicited will vary and will almost always be based on an understanding of Scriptural teaching and references to the Passover meal or the Last Supper and that perhaps indirectly as an expression of a local tradition or the doctrinal heritage of the faith community. Important to stress is that, though the corporate nature of this ritual is arguably one of its major emphases (and the method of delivery of the elements often will be from a *common* cup or *common* loaf), individuals often are urged to reflect on their personal responses to the meaning of the ritual to them in their lives.

EXPRESSION, RESPONSE, AND WORSHIP

Separate from the issue of specific rituals, there also exist among Evangelical Protestants the tremendous diversity of worship that rises from personalized overt expressions and responses to their faith. Among Evangelical

Protestants, as with so many faith groups and, somewhat, throughout history, there is a certain tension regarding worship forms that can be described as intergenerational. Much of this is due to the personal nature of even corporate worship. Regarding corporate worship, this tension is most commonly discussed today in terms of "traditional" versus "contemporary." In many cases it could be described as somewhere along the spectrum between "high church" and "low church," but among Evangelical Protestants it would almost always be skewed toward the latter of these two alternatives. Individual Evangelical Protestant congregations will often organize their worship in reference to one of those forms (or, perhaps, as "blended"—i.e., varying kinds of mixtures of the two polarities). When done deliberately and explicitly, it is usually with the intent to develop a worship style that reflects the social context in which it takes place or meets the needs and would intentionally attract a specific group. This is seen as an outward expression and response of the congregation to their shared faith—and an invitation to those outside to join in it.

Further, among Evangelical Protestants, one may find varying levels and types of use of liturgical calendars in planning for worship, regardless of the style. A liturgical calendar that might be employed is that correlated with what is normally understood as the church year or Christian calendar. Though it would not be wittingly called such, the planning calendars developed by various Evangelical Protestant denominations often become a *de facto* liturgical calendar for participating congregations wishing to include different denominational emphases in their worship.

Evangelical Protestants, however, also have a strong emphasis on personal worship beyond that which the individual experiences as part of the congregation. Most Evangelical Protestant churches encourage members to practice the discipline of daily personal worship. Those will often provide literature to assist in and training for the practice of personal worship. In fact, this area provides one of the greatest needs addressed by the diversity of resources for spiritual formation mentioned in an earlier chapter. Programs and curricula developed may range from the highly structured (with specific required time frames, Bible passages, questions for reflection, prayer topics, etc.) to the more informal (e.g., "Read through the Bible in a Year" outlines to those that offer Bible passages to be read along with a devotional thought and suggested prayer theme.) However, frequently emphasized among Evangelical Protestants at this point is the importance that persons discern the time, structure, method, and approach to personal worship that best suit their respective needs, schedules, and contexts. The issue is for each individual to take responsibility for their growth especially, as they understand it, as experienced through expression and response to personal faith and spirituality.

This individualized nature of and approach to personal worship provides the grist for debate among Evangelical Protestants as well as others in the U.S. related to the matter of prayer and Bible reading in the public schools even beyond issues related to the ethical and constitutional. Some would argue that to ban mandated prayer and Bible reading restricts not only free exercise (i.e., expression) of religion, but also free speech. Others observe that to allow it contradicts personal responsibility, is actually establishment of religion, and violates one's freedom to refuse participation in the exercise.

EXPRESSION, RESPONSE, AND SERVICE

The various perceptions of the Christian gospel held even among Evangelical Protestants also finds diverse overt expression in the ways they respond to perceived calls to service through missions and ministry. In circumstances too many to number and too multifarious to discuss at any significant length here, the respective cultural contexts, personal and congregational and /or denominational resources and gifts, and awareness of issues and needs interact with what Evangelical Protestants understand through their study of Scripture and their personal worship of and relationship with God, to engender very personal and individualized strategies for service. Such finds immediate expression through churches and individuals serving the realized needs of congregants and the surrounding community through programs and local service emphases. Not only does this impact missions and ministry strategy, but also it is at the root of the growing cadre of short-term and volunteer missionaries among the laity of Evangelical Protestants.

For example, in 1972, Henlee Barnette wrote *The Church and the Ecological Crisis* in which he called the church to a holistic eco-theology and to a theological agenda in which the doctrine of stewardship would extend beyond "giving a tithe faithfully and sees a responsibility to the whole earth."[1] Five years later, in *Rich Christians in an Age of Hunger: A Biblical Study*, Ron Sider linked Christians' responses to world hunger to the larger issue of the environment. These and similar attitudes regarding respective understandings of the Christian gospel and faith have resulted, among Evangelical Protestants, in a confluence of modern missions with ecological issues that has been expressed mostly in terms of agricultural missions. More specifically, there are examples of Evangelical Protestant missionaries (both as lay volunteers and "career" missionaries) who have training or skill in agricultural sciences (or, perhaps, civil engineering) as individuals and—most often—with significant support from their churches, denominations, or missions agencies, helping farmers dig wells, develop irrigation systems, and practice innovative farming methods. On the other hand, it is this same concern and perspective that finds many Evangelical Protestants responding through support of and participation in differing types of environmental activism and/or organizations such as the Au Sable Institute, the Evangelical Environmental Network, and the Christian Environmental Association.

EXPRESSION, RESPONSE, AND EDUCATION

Much of what has been discussed previously regarding sensitivity to developmental concerns relates to the personalized approach of education among Evangelical Protestants. However, the diversity of overt expression of and response to faith through education is expressed for other reasons and in other ways also.

The freedom Evangelical Protestants enjoy enable them, and their doctrinal emphases (especially those alluded to earlier in this chapter) compel them, to contextualize learning in terms of pedagogy, content, curriculum, and the educational outcomes that are expected. One will find in most of the curricula employed by Evangelical Protestants (and particularly in the teaching helps that will typically be included) differing means of encouraging teachers to consider the specific context, abilities, and needs. of the students in their respective classes in developing and carrying out lesson plans. Moreover, it is typical that in and through such curricula, students are invited to offer their own particular responses to what has been learned both through discussion and through "living out" the lesson. In addition, the variety of educational resources available to and utilized by Evangelical Protestant churches allow them to develop educational strategies, programs, and ministries that, in and of themselves, are conspicuous manifestations of their churches' views of faith and their answers to the questions posed by their respective faith and spirituality.

A GIFT TO RELIGIOUS EDUCATION

This gift to religious education in general is one of freedom—freedom of the individual and freedom of a congregation and to design an approach to religious education that is a unique expression of their personal faith as lived out within the immediate context. The witness of Evangelical Protestants at this point is how this does not necessarily detract, but rise from the core issues of a religious perspective.

The gift is also one of challenge. The challenge of any religious education that seeks to elicit personalized expressions of and responses to faith on the part of either individuals or congregations (or both), is to develop not only an awareness of the implications of core tenets, but also an atmosphere of freedom within the parameters those doctrines allow.

The task then is that of equipping and enabling teachers to further equip and enable students to discover, develop, and act on what they find to be the responsibilities of their personal faith. The emphasis is one not of restriction, as is often the case regarding orthodoxy in any religion, but of finding choices for living and bringing one's faith to bear on those decisions and, so, on one's life.

NOTE

[1] Henlee H. Barnette, *The Church and the Ecological Crisis* (Grand Rapids: Eerdmans, 1972) 83.

GIFTS OF FUNCTION

[CHAPTER 12]

PURPOSEFUL BIBLE STUDY

Having a commonly understood reason for learning has value beyond that of uniformity or conformity. Because any human enterprise has some implicit or explicit purpose, pragmatism (in the popularly understood sense of the term) is not so much the issue. Rather, it seems to offer at least the additional advantage of impetus and motivation. In *Contemporary Approaches to Christian Education* (1982), Jack L. Seymour, Donald E. Miller, et. al. described five differing but related perspectives related to theory and practice of Christian education: religious instruction, faith community, spiritual development, liberation, and interpretation. One of the most helpful aspects of the book was the way it demonstrated the influence of the perceived goals or purposes of Christian education on respective views of content, setting, curriculum, the teacher, and the learner. Of course, in any instance, congruence of the identified goals of respective participants in an educational enterprise is important not only to harmony but also to efficient and effective teaching and learning.

The core tenets of Evangelical Protestants and especially that of authority of Scripture cut across the approaches offered by Seymour particularly as related to their respective goals, namely,

- The goal of *religious instruction* is "to transmit Christian religion (understandings and practice)."
- The goal of the *faith community* is "to build the congregation into a community where persons can encounter the faith and learn its lifestyle."
- The goal of *spiritual development* is "to enable persons to grow in faith and spiritual maturity."
- The goal of *liberation* is "to transform the church and persons for liberation and humanization."
- The goal of *interpretation* is "to connect Christian perspectives and practices to contemporary experiences."[1]

Each of these goals could describe an approach taken by various Evangelical Protestant individuals, congregations, denominations, and organizations. However, most Evangelical Protestants would probably choose differing means or terms with which to describe their purposes for Bible study and the emphasis on it that permeates virtually all that they do.

Though there is disagreement among Evangelical Protestants as to the means by which the Bible developed (i.e., dates, authorship), there would be unanimity that the Bible—by whatever divinely-guided means or method—did not develop haphazardly and by chance. Rather, they would agree that each part of the Bible was written with certain, definite purposes in the minds of God and the human authors. Therefore, not surprising is that their approaches to Bible study would reflect such intentionality and would have as a specific goal the discovery of those divine purposes.

Those Evangelical Protestants aware of the concept would probably agree that the point and purpose of Bible study would include movements toward "shared praxis" as shared by Thomas Groome in *Christian Religious Education: Sharing Our Story and Vision* (1980). However, the two focal references for Evangelical Protestants when speaking of purposeful Bible study would almost certainly and universally be accepted as 2 Tim 3:16-17 and Matt 28:19-20. The former passage reads,

> All Scripture is inspired by God and is useful for teaching, for reproof, for correction and for training in righteousness, so that the man of God may be thoroughly equipped for every good work.

In the latter, Jesus challenges his disciples with these words:

> Go therefore and make disciples of all nations, baptizing them in the name of the Father and of the Son and of the Holy Spirit, and teaching them to obey everything that I have commanded you. And remember, I am with you always, to the end of the age.

In this vein, whether referring to the study of the historical, didactic, poetic, or even apocalyptic literature of the Bible, the preferred Evangelical Protestant idiom would keep in mind what has already been described as their common mission and speak of, among other possible terms, salvation (especially in terms of conversion), spiritual growth (or, as some would choose to express it, sanctification, at least in the spiritual dimension of the term), vision, and service.

After a brief review of the role of purpose in educational theory and pedagogy, each of the terms offered above will be discussed and described in terms of its role in giving purpose to Bible study and its implications for religious education theory.

THE PEDAGOGY OF PURPOSE

The issue of purpose brings into focus the relationship (and the tension) between educational theory and educational practice. Though philosophical perspectives regarding metaphysics, epistemology, ethics, and aesthetics certainly influence and drive an educational theory, it is the eye toward practice that contextualizes it and, so, more directly affects the respective roles of the teacher, student, content, curricula, and methodology. Therefore, it is important—even vital—that a more thoroughly though-out and developed educational theory or approach will seriously consider the goal or purpose of education at the point in question. In this sense, purpose is not only a determinant of educational theory but also a control mechanism enabling more effective and efficient development of educational components (i.e., content, curricula, methodology) and adequate assessment and evaluation. Moreover, to speak of or plan and work toward one particular purpose or goal does not necessarily preclude the realization of others either as further ends or as additional means toward other ends. Nor does it preclude concurrently working and planning with other purposes in mind. In fact, in the following discussion, one can see that, though these various purposes for Bible study can be specified individually, there is a strong correlation among them all and between each one and each of the others. They need not (this writer believes—as, probably would most Evangelical Protestants—that they cannot) be compartmentalized or isolated from each other.

SALVATION AS THE PURPOSE

For Evangelical Protestants, Bible study aimed toward conversion is seen as an obviously basic point for beginning. Though in reading the "focal references" mentioned above one could center on the allusions to obedience and correction, the most vital step in such a pilgrimage, as Evangelical Protestants understand it, is that of establishing a personal relationship between the individual and God. To use the metaphor for conversion introduced by Jesus in John 3:3 and most popular among Evangelical Protestants as a self-descriptor, one cannot grow as a child of God unless one has been "born again." As Findley Edge, writing out of a concern that Christian education in general and Bible study in particular become more purposeful and results-oriented, put it, "A personal experience of conversion is the only adequate foundation and the only sufficient motivation for Christian growth."[2] For Edge it is conversion that impels the person beyond a rigid, institutionalized, ritualized, or perfunctory approach to religion or faith to a longing and motivation for learning of the faith as well as the direction and strength to follow its teachings and demands. This is the crux of what Harold Burgess described as the traditional Protestant theological approach to religious or Christian education in which is found "the facilitation of a direct, experiential, present, and continuing encounter between the student and God."[3] It is the desire to understand the nature of conversion as this human-divine encounter that drives Evangelical Protestants to study the Bible. Many of them would agree that God is revealed in some ways and to some degree by nature and that nature not only demonstrates the glory of God (cf. Ps 19:1, et. al.) but also, through many of its processes, reflects and serves as metaphors for God's work in redeeming humanity. However, it is the Bible that, as their core authority, for them is the most reliable source of knowledge regarding one's need for and how one can experience God's redemption and grace. through the experience of conversion. For Evangelical Protestants, this is the whole (or, at least, the initial) purpose or point of the gospel in the New Testament and of what is referred to in the literary and theological study of the Bible (especially in reference to the Old Testament) as *heilsgeschichte* (salvation or redemption history). For this reason, if for no other, Evangelical Protestants center so much of their evangelistic efforts and their religious education on the Bible and the study of it.

GROWTH AS THE PURPOSE

Thomas Groome once observed, "If Christians are to live as a redeemed people, we must live in opposition to sin, both personal and social.... Far from reducing us to passivity, the gift of salvation places a mandate on us to be involved within history in such a struggle."[4] It is this kind of struggle, engagement, and growth that Evangelical Protestants have in mind when thinking of sanctification. Though they would certainly see it as both a supernatural act and the work of God's grace, they would also acknowledge a significant role of Bible study toward that end, especially stressing God's activity and role of self-revelation through and inspiration of Scripture as well as illuminating Scripture so that a person can discover, appropriate, and apply the truths contained therein.

Woven throughout the narrative fabric of the Bible in stories of individuals' and nations' respective and various interface with God, along with the more directly instructive biblical literature, one can see and learn how God's righteousness and God's grace have been revealed, shared with, and brought to bear sometimes triumphant, but always flawed and eventually failing humanity in direct and personal ways and in "real life" situations. For

Evangelical Protestants, the issue is not whether the Bible applies to life. That is assumed. Rather, it is a matter of hermeneutics, i.e., how it applies and what it has to say regarding directions for one's life today. As previously noted, there remains great diversity (that is often acrimonious) among Evangelical Protestants regarding respective interpretations and applications of biblical teaching. This variance could be said to be most apparent at the point of bringing biblical truths—which originated and were written in ancient cultures vastly different than those found in most settings today—to bear on the spiritual, emotional, social, and moral lives of the late twentieth and early twenty-first centuries. On one end of the Evangelical Protestant spectrum, the biblical literalists among them approach that issue very differently than do those on the other end who recognize and whose hermeneutical approach takes into account respective cultural milieus. Of course, there also are many Evangelical Protestants who are either consistently at some specific point between those two extremes or who find themselves moving from one extreme to the other depending on the biblical passage or social situation in question. The particular hermeneutical approach will, in turn, directly affect their respective strategies for Bible study toward the purpose of personal and spiritual growth. Nevertheless, whatever the hermeneutical or educational approach, the intent remains the same and the intensity can be great as they study and teach the Bible for the purpose of applying its truths to daily living and growth.

THE PURPOSE OF VISION

The concept of vision can be understood in differing contexts. It can be interpreted in the more mystical sense such as found when a biblical prophet was functioning in the role of a *ro'eh* (or seer) or in such instances as that found in Isa 6:1-8, regarding that prophet's call. On the other hand, visions could also be understood as coming in the form of dreams, such as Paul's dream recorded in Acts 16:9-10. Though both are related to a supernatural revelation regarding divine mysteries or, at least, what is not otherwise available to or through human perception, the primary difference between dreams and visions has been described this way: "Dreams often lend themselves to allegorical interpretation, while visions focus more on the message disclosed."[5] Nevertheless, the basic inference of each is normally related to God's revelation of individual or corporate purpose or direction and usually above and beyond, but not exclusive of, concern for day-to-day human activity and growth as described above. Rather, the emphasis is on and refers to the larger, more strategic scale and is often seen either in connection with or expressed in a personal or corporate sense of vocation or calling. In this sense, Evangelical Protestants study the Bible for the dual purposes of measuring human "vision" and discerning God's strategic direction.

First, though obviously accepting of the concept of supernatural (and more explicitly, divine) intervention, revelation, or vocation, most Evangelical Protestants understand that not all impulses or "visions" experienced by individuals are of or from God, no matter how well-intentioned that person may be. Rather, most understand that biblical teaching requires it. For instance, 1 Thess 5:19-21, speaking to this issue directs, "Do not quench the Spirit. Do not despise the words of prophets, but test everything; hold fast to what is good." Given the Bible as their core authority, it is natural that for this reason alone Evangelical Protestants would be inclined to use it as the standard by which they would measure prophecies and visions—as well as their responses to such. However, the Bible is often interpreted by Evangelical Protestants as directing its use as that measure: "Indeed the word of God is living and active, sharper than any double-edged sword, piercing until it divides soul from spirit, joints from marrow; it is able to judge the thoughts and intentions of the heart"(Heb 4:12). This demands Bible study for the purpose of such testing and discernment.

Second, Evangelical Protestants also proactively seek personal or corporate vision from God in that they aspire to finding God's direction for them in the same sense that God may take the initiative in intervening with a direct revelation. This is somewhat akin to the issue of sanctification, but more specifically deals with matters of vocation—and not exclusively with career connotations. The end in mind is to ascertain God's will, however narrowly that may be interpreted. Many Evangelical Protestants would find the impetus for this search in Rom 12:2: "Do not be conformed to this world, but be transformed by the renewing of your minds, so that you may discern what is the will of God—what is good and acceptable and perfect." Here, too, they would assume that the place to begin is in the Bible. Much of the didactic biblical material provides grist for their searches, but they would also find of special interest the patterns that characterize stories of various biblical personalities' dealing with finding God's way for them.

SERVICE AS THE PURPOSE

Flowing out of their respective visions, Evangelical Protestants' strong senses of their core authority and their core mission have significant mutual impact at the point of service as a purpose for Bible study. The great majority of them would agree that, as expressed through the Bible, God's will (or vision) for all Christians is some sort of service as expressed through evangelism, missions, or ministry. (These terms carry various connotations and implications for differing persons and fellowships among Evangelical Protestants and are sometimes seen as synonymous within certain contexts, but always related.) Obvious though this may be to most of them, they would still insist that the Bible be studied and taught not only to share this truth with those new to the faith, but also that all might learn appropriate (i.e., the biblical) strategies, content, and shapes for different areas of service and for each to be equipped for such.

Though it certainly has other dimensions (esp. those related to social ministry), the most generally understood and accepted definition of evangelism has to do with sharing or disseminating knowledge of the salvific aspect of the gospel. This service is variously expressed in terms or expressions such as "leading people to the Lord" and "winning the lost for Christ." Among Evangelical Protestants it is assumed that a solid foundation in and of Bible study is vital to effective evangelism because it helps one learn (at least in a basic way) not only the biblical doctrine and processes related to salvation, but also patterns for evangelism lived out in the lives of persons in the Bible. It is believed that by studying the Bible toward that end one relies more on the authority of Scripture for forming their evangelistic efforts than on their own human frailties and limitations. Significant is that most programs of or curricula developed by Evangelical Protestants for evangelism are strongly rooted in Bible study and many focus on extensive memorization of Scripture.

Related to evangelism is service through missions. For Evangelical Protestants, the primary thrust of missions is evangelism as discussed above, but is apt to have more social ministry implications regardless of setting. However, though most of them would acknowledge that missions begins "across the street," the term is normally construed to mean moving further out geographically and typically has more crosscultural connotations. Here, too, Evangelical Protestants are wary of wandering far afield from parameters given in Scripture, but consciously look to Bible study to discover both missiological doctrine and biblical paradigms after which they can pattern their own missions efforts and appropriate authority for that service.

Likewise, ministry has multifarious definitions, connotations, and dimensions. Whether through evangelism or missions or through service on committees, or as teachers or leaders, or through more explicit social action, or whatever form it may take, Evangelical Protestants are compelled to study the Bible for discovering principles and paradigms for ministry. Further, whatever the area of service, Bible study in and of itself is understood as being at the very least the single most important method for equipping individuals and congregations. Because most Evangelical Protestants accept that a part of any service will result in spiritual warfare of some sort, the issue is not only (or even so much) that of cognitive learning, but also of the affective and, more precisely the spiritual or devotional learning.

A GIFT TO RELIGIOUS EDUCATION

The components of religious education of any faith can easily drift into empty ritualism and, so, lose any significant purpose other than exiting for its own sake. On the other hand, having a purpose that matters is an important component for engendering relevance and vitality and for maintaining the care of faith as the focal point of the religion. The many dimensions of the purposeful Bible study that characterizes so much of what Evangelical Protestants do, demonstrate how religious education plays a part in keeping faith consequential in the lives of adherents.

NOTES

[1] Jack L. Seymour, Donald E. Miller, et al, *Contemporary Approaches to Christian Education* (Nashville: Abingdon Press, 1982) 32.

[2] Findley B. Edge, *Teaching for Results*, rev. ed. (Nashville: Broadman & Holman, 1995) 10.

[3] Harold William Burgess, *An Invitation to Religious Education* (Birmingham AL: Religious Education Press, 1975) 31.

[4] Thomas H. Groome, *Christian Religious Education: Sharing Our Story and Vision* (San Francisco: Harper & Row, 1980) 94.

[5] Walter Harrelson, "Vision," *Mercer Dictionary of the Bible*, Watson Mills, ed. (Macon GA: Mercer University Press, 1990) 949.

[CHAPTER 13]

FOCUS ON RELATIONSHIPS

Vital to understanding the common essence of the Jewish and Christian faiths is found in the covenant-making nature of God. The importance relates both to the legal and personal structures of covenant. The point is similar to that found in laws regarding incorporation almost universally in jurisprudence and, specifically, in that of England, the United States, Germany, and other countries That is, in those jurisdictions a "thing" cannot be party to a contract or covenant. Such must be between to persons. Therefore, when an organization incorporates, it becomes a legal entity and, in a sense, a legal "person."

Much of what Martin Buber, the great twentieth-century Jewish philosopher and theologian, wrote related to the basic issue and nature of relationship and dialogue and one's attitude toward them. Buber stated that neither dialogue nor personal relationship is possible between a person and an object, which he referred to in terms of "I-It." Rather, personal relationship and discourse take place only when persons regard the personhood of the other, which he expressed in terms of I-Thou," the latter term underscoring the reverence and respect one holds for the personhood of the other. In his book, *I and Thou*, Buber wrote that it is within the context of an "I-Thou" encounter that one person truly comprehends relating to another as subject to subject (i.e., truly as persons) and not object to object. It is through this sort of relationship that the personhood of both the "Thou" and the "I" becomes more clear. Indeed, this is the meaning of relationship and, to Buber, basic to existence.[1] So, for Buber, relationship cannot be either aloof or apathetic.[2] Further, such also must involve the whole person.

It is important to note Buber's recognition of the reality that no person can relate to every other person in every instance in the sense of "I-Thou." For instance, an anthropologist doing a field study must maintain some degree of objectivity (i.e., an "I-It" perspective) in observing the people who are subjects of the study, because the task at hand is not to identify with the subjects of the study but to observe them. The significance of Buber at this point is not only in the parameters and definitions he provides by which to comprehend the personal nature of relationships, but also in his observations that such an association is not superficial but has to do with the innermost parts of the individuals involved and affects all that they are.

Among the gifts of Evangelical Protestants is their emphasis on the personal nature of relationships. Virtually all of their theological dimensions, by many definitions, have to do in some way with the relationship(s) that do or can exist among and between persons and God, the community, and churches. However, Evangelical Protestant theology also holds that the purpose of the gospel can be described in terms of one discovering or recovering one's true personhood as created by God, but corrupted by sin—a right relationship with one's self. Further, many of the emphases on, approaches to, and resources for spiritual growth previously discussed (in reference to Evangelical Protestants' accessing them) relate one's spiritual pilgrimage with that of self-discovery and connect one's mental and emotional health with spiritual issues in ways that could be said to enrich one's relationship with one's self.

What follows is a brief examination of how the concept of relationship is viewed by various philosophies and approaches to education and how it has been approached through the history of education. This will provide a helpful framework for an ensuing description of how Evangelical Protestant theology and practices focus on the four relationships mentioned above: God, self, community, and church. The conclusion of this chapter will set in context these elements and demonstrate how and why this focus on relationships is a particularly significant gift of Evangelical Protestants to contemporary religious education.

THE PEDAGOGY OF RELATIONSHIP

Though developmentalists have contributed much to understanding how humans are capable of learning, as individuals, at certain stages in the lives, there have been and are assorted educational theorists such as John Dewey, Lev Vygotsky, and James Michael Lee who emphasize the social or relational nature of learning. Vygotsky, in contrast to Piaget's concentration on respective levels of ability, focused on a child's potential and "what the child might accomplish with the guidance of adults or peers."[3] Quite opposite to Jean-Jacques Rousseau who seemed to view relationship as an influence more apt to corrupt, Vygostsky further and more positively "stressed that much of what we learn we learn from others."[4]

In some ways all education can be expressed as movement toward bettering, developing, enriching, and equipping individual persons. However, the more relationally-oriented theorists have recognized that people are social creatures. Human groups could be spoken of as simply collections of individuals. But this would be to overlook the innately synergistic nature of any group of persons—that group is more than simply the sum of its parts.

Awareness or emphasis on the relational nature of pedagogy is nothing new. Even in Plato's allegory of the cave, entering into human relationship is seen as necessary. For Plato, those who have attained knowledge "must be made to descend again among the prisoners in the den, and partake of their labours and honours, whether they are worth having or not" to the end that citizens of the state are held "together by persuasion and necessity, making them benefactors of the state, and therefore benefactors of one another."[5]

Of course, in Hebrew/Jewish education the essence of learning and knowledge had to do somewhat with relationship. The home was the central place of education in the Old Testament culture and family of faith. In relationships experienced through the home, children were trained for what would be their adult gender roles. The sons were trained by their fathers in farming, a craft, an art, or some other means to make a living. Daughters were taught various household duties and skills by their mothers.

As a part of the above cited parent-child relationship and the parental responsibility for leading the family in faithfulness to God, the *Shema* calls for religious training and education to be a natural and integral part of everyday family relationships. This sense of integration or intimacy is at the heart of the Hebrew word *yada*, "to know." The general instructions given in the *Shema* and the many more specific ones given in much of the Mosaic Law clearly are driven by, among other reasons, this educational purpose and from this estimation of what is meant by "knowing."

That the Old Testament book of Proverbs contains so many passages addressed to "my son" or concerning a wise (or foolish) son, underscores the emphasis placed on parental religious instruction. Josephus wrote,

> Our principle [sic] care of all this is this, to educate our children well; and we think it to be the most necessary business of our whole life, to observe the laws that have been given us, and to keep those rules of piety that have been delivered down to us.[6]

Nor can the role of rituals, feasts, and festivals be underestimated in equipping and affording opportunities for religious instruction to take place through home and family relationships. Each of the religious observances of the Mosaic Law had educational value. Passover, the Day of Atonement, the Feast of Booths (Tabernacles), or the various forms of Sabbath observances (day, year, Jubilee), and the many others—all were rich not only in educational content (through their respective themes), but also in methodology.

For instance, the theme (educational content) of Passover was to remind the people and teach the children about the work of God in delivering the children of Israel from bondage in Egypt. The various elements of the Passover celebration served both as object lessons/symbols and as cues for the children to ask questions of the parents. Even the "routine" sacrifices, religious observances (e.g., dietary laws), and the actions and offices of the priests, Levites, and prophets would function as similar mechanisms to set in motion family discussions. Such participation in discussion with the parents and others would be, for the children, of immediate instructional value and model the question/answer pattern that would characterize study of the Law from formal rabbinic dialogues to informal conversations among the "laity." It would also serve the purpose of signifying to the child the importance of one's engagement (i.e., becoming intimate) with the story of the covenant people and to realizing their relationship with the larger family of faith, even that of past generations. The point remained that of both establishing and learning from relationship.

Various early Christian writers and theologians (e.g., Clement of Alexandria, Origen, Gregory of Nyssa, John Chrysostom) had views of the relational nature of education similar to those of Judaism. One who particularly stressed various aspects of relationship as vital to learning was Augustine of Hippo. He urged teachers to discover and/or establish common relationships with their students and to become familiar enough with their students so as to appreciate their respective uniqueness as individuals and especially as a means to affect the individual student's relationship with God. Ensuing figures and groups in the history of religious education that accentuated intimacy and relationships in education were Gerhard Groote and the Brethren and Sisters of the Common Life, the Pleasant House (of Vittorino da Feltre), Pestalozzi, Froebel, Zinzendorf, and Friedrich Schliermacher. Of course, this is also at the heart of much of the theory of more recent educational theorists such as John Dewey and religious educators such as Horace Bushnell, George Albert Coe, and William Clayton Bower.

RELATIONSHIP WITH GOD

The Evangelical Protestant focus on relationship with God is of a decidedly Trinitarian character. As has already been noted, at the heart of the core mission and core experience of Evangelical Protestants is what they prefer to call "a personal relationship" with God through Jesus Christ. For Evangelical Protestants, the significance of this has several different and interrelated dimensions. Referred to in Jas 2:23, the first is the salvific, which is to be found in connection with the personal, covenantal, and faith relationship that Abraham had with God: "And the scripture was fulfilled that says, 'Abraham believed God, and it was credited to him as righteousness,' and he was called God's friend" (NIV).

The writer of the New Testament book, Hebrews, in offering examples of the kind of relationship with God that was available through faith, in several verses expounded on the relationship shared by Abraham (cf. Heb 11: 8-19). Paul, the Apostle, in his letter to Christians in Ephesus, pointed out that those who had once been estranged from God had, through faith in the atoning work of Jesus, found that broken relationship restored—and through implication, those who had not could (Eph 2:11-22). Further, the intimate nature of this relationship was alluded to in Paul's letter to the church in Rom 8:15-17 (NIV):

> For you did not receive a spirit that makes you a slave again to fear, but you received the Spirit of sonship. And by him we cry, "Abba, Father." The Spirit himself testifies with our spirit that we are God's children. Now if we are children, then we are heirs—heirs of God and co-heirs with Christ, if indeed we share in his sufferings in order that we may also share in his glory.

God's role in relationship, especially to the redeemed, is also seen to be that of teacher. The instruction of God is seen as having to do with guiding and equipping toward particular tasks—similar to what God told Moses in Exod 4:12: "Now go; I will help you speak and will teach you what to say" (NIV). As King David wrote, however, God would also teach a person in and through their daily lives (cf. Ps 25, especially vv. 4-5, 8-9).

Most significant to Evangelical Protestants, however, is the instruction Christians find in their relationships with God through Jesus. They note that, in the Gospels, Jesus was most often referred to as "Rabbi" or "Teacher." They further observe that it was not only the miracles of Jesus that attracted many (and disturbed the religious establishment), but also his teaching. Like those aspects of teaching by God as noted above, Jesus' teaching as recorded in the Gospels had to do with both the salvific and the ethical or behavioral. Much of the teaching of Jesus had to do with how persons can become citizens of God's Kingdom (i.e., recover personal relationship with God). The remainder revolved around how those citizens should live. It is interesting that the single largest body of the teachings of Jesus in the New Testament (the "Sermon on the Mount" found in Matt 5–7) had focused almost exclusively on this latter aspect.

Evangelical Protestants often refer to Jesus as the "Master" or "Model" Teacher. In describing and discussing the pedagogy of Jesus, frequent mention is made of his relationship not only with his disciples, but also anyone whom he was trying to teach. In identifying teaching principles embodied by Jesus, Kenneth Gangel and Christy Sullivan list first "the teacher must know the students well in order to approach them on the basis of their self-perceptions."[7]

In the relationship of the individual with God, the Holy Spirit has numerous implications for Evangelical Protestants and not only those of the more Pentecostal or Charismatic orientation. First, by the definition of the term "inspiration," it was God's activity through the Holy Spirit by which the Bible—the core authority for Evangelical Protestants—was written and collected. It should also be said that it is for this reason that the Bible *is* authoritative for them. Second, even as creation occurred at the movement of God's Spirit (cf. Gen 1:1-2), so it is the Holy Spirit that, by various understandings among Evangelical Protestants, draws people to relationship with God and, through the process of regeneration, makes of one a new creation. However, one's relationship with the Holy Spirit also makes available to them gifts, power, and encouragement for daily living and service along with illumination toward understanding God's teaching and leadership whether revealed through Scripture or in some other way.

RELATIONSHIP WITH THE SELF

Jesus' parable of the "Prodigal Son" (cf. Luke 15:11-32) is among the most favorite and most often cited among Evangelical Protestants. The parable was shared by Jesus in response to those who questioned his friendly relationships with "sinners" (as in Matthew 11: 19) and has as its basic premise the relationships among a father and his two sons. However, many find significant the passage that sets the stage for the restored relationship between the father and the son who had left and wasted his inheritance in profligate living. According to Luke 15:17, it was when the young man "came to his senses" (NIV) or, "came to himself" (NRSV) that he realized his depraved condition was not that for which he had been born. For Evangelical Protestants, the point of the parable at this juncture is that the corruption of sin (both as cause and effect) are far from God's intended purpose for humankind, the zenith of creation. Therefore salvation, first as conversion, can be described as one's finding their true, God-intended selves as created in God's image that had been destroyed by sin.

For Evangelical Protestants, continuing salvation as experienced through spiritual maturity or sanctification is also a matter of self-discovery or growing in relationship with one's rediscovered, recovered, or new self. As described and discussed previously, this, too, has many and various spiritual implications. However, of particular significance here, especially as of late and as a part of a larger cultural or social movement, is that in many Evangelical Protestant fellowships, congregations, and curricula, this spiritual aspect of self-discovery and relating effectively to one's self is being frequently connected to issues of pastoral counseling and self-improvement.

RELATIONSHIP WITH THE COMMUNITY

Evangelical Protestants also have a strong focus on the relationship of the individual or the congregation with the community in which they find themselves and that the biblical mandate is that God's people meet the needs of their communities. Whether stated in terms of common purpose or as personalized approaches to expression and response, relationship is seen as a key element or strategy in evangelism, ministry, and service. Regarding evangelism, Delos Miles once wrote:

> God gives most lay Christians more opportunities to evangelize lost persons in the natural, normal course of their day-today lives than he gives ordained ministers. He expects us to utilize our relationships in a manner which will reflect our relationship with him.[8]

Findley Edge put it this way:

> Humans are able to find the solution to the problems that are involved in their horizontal relationships [i.e., in their communities] only when they find a transforming relationship with the eternal God. But the Christian has a witness to give, a mission to fulfill, a ministry to perform that must be carried out in the social order of which he or she is a part.[9]

RELATIONSHIP WITH THE CHURCH

The long-standing and pervasive Evangelical Protestant emphasis on the priesthood of all believers is often misunderstood by overlooking the corporate dimension of that seminal doctrine. Although appreciation of soul competency (i.e., of the individual) is integral to comprehending it, priesthood of all believers does have its corporate dimension and, so, is not exclusively individualistic. Rather, it should be seen more as a model for relationships of interdependence among believers. Of course, the quality of the relationship among members of a congregation reflects that of its members with Jesus. This focus underscores the importance of the church as the body of Jesus. That is, each separate part has a function, not as an exact replication of every other, but certainly in connection with all. Though certainly Evangelical Protestants realize the many different functions of a church, the relational has to do with *koinonia*, or fellowship (i.e., in the sense of commonality or community). Often referred to as the "family of faith," most view the church as having relational purposes similar to that of a human family. Though some have expressed them in terms of psychological, emotional, and material support. Diana Garland holds that these functions may relate to the meeting of "needs for intimacy, sharing of resources, help, commitment, and sharing of life purposes."[10]

A GIFT TO RELIGIOUS EDUCATION

Despite the incredible variety of means for communication available among people today, they continue to crave intimacy in relationship. Increasing numbers of people feel isolated and lonely even in the midst of multitudes and crowded conditions. Though seldom the only factor, the results of such are reflected in tragic newspaper headlines and untold stories of human misery every day. Many people today desperately need a rediscovery relationship. Meeting this need was at the heart of what Parker Palmer was calling for when he summarized the importance of relationship in learning this way: "The truth we are seeking, the truth that seeks us, lies ultimately in the community of being where we not only know but are known."[11] The religious education of any faith that overlooks this can become dysfunctional and exacerbate the problem of isolation rather than working toward its eradication. The consistent and continuous focus of Evangelical Protestants on relationships is a move toward helping people understand their own needs and ways they may be countered through synergistic relationships and responsibilities. It is also a model and a challenge for religious education—no matter the faith orientation—to meet this contemporary challenge.

NOTES

[1] Martin Buber, *I and Thou*, 2d ed., trans. Ronald Gregor Smith (New York: MacMillan, 1958) 11.

[2] Ibid., 15.

[3] D. C. Phillips and Jonas F. Soltis, *Perspectives on Learning*, 2d ed. (New York: Teachers College Press, 1991) 53.

[4] Ibid., 54.

[5] Plato, *Republic*, Book VII, in *Dialogues of Plato*, vol. 7 in Great Books, trans. Benjamin Jowett (Chicago: Encyclopedia Brittanica, Inc., 1952) 390.

[6] Jospehus, *Against Apion* 1:12, in *Jospehus: Complete Works* (Grand Rapids: Kregel Publications, 1960) 610.

[7] Kenneth O. Gangel and Christy Sullivan, "Evangelical *Theology and Religious Education*," Theologies of Religious Education, ed. Randolph Crump Miller (Birmingham AL: Religious Education Press, 1995) 81.

[8] Delos Miles, *Introduction to Evangelism* (Nashville: Broadman Press, 1983) 104.

[9] Findley B. Edge, *A Quest for Vitality in Religion: A Theological Approach to Religious Education*, rev. ed. (Macon GA: Smyth & Helwys, 1994) 106.

[10] Diana S. Richmond Garland, "An Ecosystemic Perspective for Family Ministry," *Review & Expositor* (Spring 1989) 86.

[11] Parker J. Palmer, *To Know as We Are Known: A Spirituality of Education* (San Francisco: Harper & Row, 1983) 90.

[CHAPTER 14]

A BALANCE OF THE INWARD AND OUTWARD NATURE OF SPIRITUALITY

Evangelical Protestant scholar and theologian, Stanley J. Grenz, once described three "pillars" of contemporary theology:

- fundamentalism that seeks to be faithful to the message of the Bible,
- progressivism that is determined to address cultural issues
- confessionalism that focuses on remaining faithful to heritage

In depicting Evangelicalism (i.e., Evangelical Protestantism), Grenz suggested "that evangelicalism offers the best context in which to accomplish theological balance [among the three pillars]." He also wrote that "although it has often wandered from the mark, the evangelical movement, seen in its best light, attempts to work toward this ideal."[1]

Likewise, the essence, foundation, and core of Evangelical Protestant theology seem to afford tremendous opportunity for balance also of the inward and outward nature of spirituality. This does not mean that such balance is to be found consistently across the Evangelical Protestant spectrum. Nor is even proportionality of these two aspects always seen in any one Evangelical Protestant individual or group. That is, to borrow from Grenz, many often "wander from the mark." However, the diversity and variety that characterize the family of Evangelical Protestants, coupled with the ultimate demands of their theology, produce an overall balance among them.

Some may wonder why this gift of Evangelical Protestants is being presented as one of function. The issue of function is related more directly to that of religious education. That is, among the primary and most basic functions of religious education is leading, teaching, and/or directing persons toward spiritual formation or a spirituality seems to be best described in terms of a balance of the inward and outward life of a person.

BALANCE IN PEDAGOGY

Any indepth consideration of or approach to pedagogy will be based on a balanced educational philosophy. This means that the educational philosophy will have attended to the three basic philosophical questions or determinants: metaphysics, epistemology, and axiology. As one bears in mind these three issues, there arises a certain symmetry and balance among them, for they are interrelated and, indeed, evenly interdependent because no one of them can stand without consistency with the other two nor can any two hold apart from agreement with the remaining one. Further, one finds a similar pattern evident within each determinant as a unit.

Metaphysics is arguably the most speculative aspect of philosophy because it deals asks questions regarding the nature of reality. Whether these questions are couched in terms of the nature of existence (ontology), or the origins of or what order can be found in the universe of reality (cosmology), or the connection between the mind and the body (anthropology), or the existence and nature of the Divine (theology), one cannot escape either the inner, more reflective or contemplative aspects of metaphysics. However, nor can one ignore that which is experienced through the interaction of one's senses with that reality however it might be inwardly or reflectively considered.

Epistemology, rather than dealing with conjecture about the nature of reality, examines how truth can be known in whatever reality—if it can be known at all—for instance, in epistemological issues of truth as either *a priori* (i.e., basic to and dependent on reality as it exists) or *a posteriori* (i.e., contingent on persons' comprehension of it). Whatever one's response to these queries, it remains the task of human experience to verify or substantiate whatever ultimate truths there are. Further, epistemological questions may be posed as to the nature of truth as either subjective (i.e., residing within the individual and/or liable to change) or objective (i.e., absolute and/or immutable). Still, the issue is one of balance and looking to both the inner and outer aspects of the relationship between human beings and truth.

Philosophical questions of axiology relate to issues of the good or values as residing in or reflective of truth and reality, thereby drawing on and balancing the contemplative nature of metaphysics and epistemology. Axiology itself is comprised of the two fields of aesthetics and ethics. These, too, can be understood as having to do with inward and outward dimensions that are to be held in balance. Aesthetics is the part of axiology that deals with artistic beauty—which is outwardly expressed but inwardly construed in connection with individual imagination, though, admittedly, one's personal perception of beauty is significantly influenced—at least initially—by prevailing cultural norms. Nevertheless, aesthetics remains considerably subjective. Ethics, on the other hand, deals with questions of good or right action. In some sense, the process or direction of ethics is one of inward perception giving rise to outward action. Axiology can, then, be said to be the end toward which pedagogy, and especially that of religious education, strives.

Over the history of educational theory one can find tension between the inner versus the outward nature of learning. Where the classical idealism of Plato and atomism of Locke were inwardly directed and focused and variously understood innate abilities and how such were achieved or appropriated, those of behaviorism were concerned with learning—though grounded in something innate—as expressed by outward action and conduct. In contrast to these two general historical approaches, Gestalt theory and those of developmentalists such as Piaget and others sought to relate the cultivation of certain specifically understood inborn human psychological and physiological capacities to behaviorally-expressed learning. It was then the democratic or social orientation of Dewey and others that draws on both a balance of the inner nature of the individual with the esoteric character of social relationships to effect heuristic learning toward solving commonly-experienced problems.

It was the balance of these historical philosophical emphases that found expression by Findley B. Edge's call for more deliberately seeking results in religious education and, most specifically, in Bible study and teaching. Edge suggested that the particular results for which Christian religious education should be designed and working is that of "Better Bible Knowledge" and "Better Christian Living"—a balance between inner, mental (or cognitive) learning and that which is outwardly expressed in the lives of persons.[2] Edge was well aware that even this balance can be susceptible to the pitfalls of simple verbalization and emotional catharsis. He did not deny the need for verbalization or the reality that spiritual experience is often accompanied by emotion. However, he did stress that "*Christian teaching is complete when it results in Christian action—only then*" [his emphasis].[3]

THE INWARD NATURE OF SPIRITUALITY

Evangelical Protestants perceive the scriptural mandate regarding the inward nature of spirituality as being rooted in various biblical passages and principles. It is the consistency and the pervasive character of the call by their core authority (i.e., the Bible) to attend to the inward nature of one's spirituality that compels Evangelical Protestants to do so (albeit never ideally either as individuals or as groups). Donald S. Whitney expressed it this way: "No spiritual discipline is more important than the intake of God's Word. Nothing can substitute for it. There is simply no healthy Christian life apart from a diet of the milk and meat of Scripture."[4]

First, the *Shema* of Deut 6:4-6 commanded Israel, specifically in vv. 5-6, "You shall love the Lord your God with all your heart, and with all your soul, and with all your might" and to keep God's commands "in your heart." In commenting on these verses, John D. W. Watts called attention to the inward nature of this by noting, "In Hebrew thinking the heart was the center of consciousness, intellect, and will" and that Israel's devotion to God must "be characterized by singleness of purpose, undivided allegiance, [and] unique concentration."[5] The *Shema*, then, was beyond a basic doctrinal statement. It called for commitment of one's feelings, thoughts, and motives to God.

Additional importance is placed on the *Shema* by Evangelical Protestants as it was echoed by Jesus responding to a question as to what was the "greatest commandment" in Matt 22:37. Also, in Luke 10:27, Jesus similarly affirmed that passage's importance toward one's finding eternal life. However, it is also significant to Evangelical Protestants that even Jesus' ethical teaching focused on the inward nature of spirituality. To see this, one only need note the many places in the "Sermon on the Mount" (cf. Matt 5–7) where Jesus stressed the importance of right attitudes and emotions in human relationships as necessary to holy living and, by implication and by most definitions, a healthy spirituality. In fact, the clear mandate of Jesus in Matt 5:20, "For I tell you, unless your righteousness exceeds that of the scribes and Pharisees, you will never enter the kingdom of heaven," is one that requires attention to the inward nature of one's spirituality.

The same theme can be found in much of what was written in other books of both the Old New Testaments. Many of the Psalms—especially many of those of David—seek God's comfort, guidance, and redemption of the inner person. This is especially clear in Ps 51:10.

The Old Testament prophets spoke out resoundingly against both the evident sins (idolatry, etc.) and empty religious practices superficially exercised in the name of God and often focused on the inward nature of individual and corporate spirituality in the hope of effecting change in outward expressions of it (e.g., Amos 5:21, 24). In the New Testament the Apostle Paul emphasized the significance of the inward nature of spirituality in passages such as that found in Rom 12:2.

Obviously, for Evangelical Protestants, this inward or inner nature of spirituality is focused on conversion. That is, they do not deny spirituality as a universal among humans, but characteristic of Evangelical Protestants is that their greatest desire is that people experience and develop *Christian* spirituality. Moreover, their most basic understandings of the concept and nature of the term requires that this particular form of spirituality begin with conversion—i.e., the common experience of being "born again." Evangelical Protestant writer Henry T. Blackaby, though not using the terms "spirituality" or "Christian spirituality," noted that growth in such is possible only if one is "willing to respond to God's invitation to an intimate love relationship with Him."[6] Paul demonstrates the significance of the redemptive relationship of faith in Jesus with the inward nature of spirituality in Eph 3:16-17: "I pray that, according to the riches of his glory, he may grant that you may be strengthened in your inner being with power through his Spirit, and that Christ may dwell in your hearts through faith."

Nor should it be overlooked that most Evangelical Protestants would note that an inherent part of their common mission, based on Jesus' mandate to his followers in the "Great Commission" of Matt 28:19-20, is attention to the conversion of the inward nature of one's spiritual life. Two of the basic calls in that passage are to "make disciples" and to "baptize." Evangelical Protestant theology requires that the first step toward being or becoming a disciple (i.e., understood either as a "follower" in terms of a fellow traveler or pilgrim or as a "student") is a change or conversion in one's attitude, mind, and heart. Simply stated and using the metaphor of human development, prerequisite to one's growing and maturing in Jesus Christ would be the experience of being "born again." Though many Evangelical Protestants may disagree on some of the other points of baptism, there is virtually universal agreement that baptism is also an outward symbol of the inward conversion that has occurred in the life of the one being baptized and, so, an expression of that person's commitment to both further obedience to Jesus Christ and to the fellowship of believers that share that common experience. Whatever the understandings of these two basic calls, inward Christian conversion remains the genesis of authentic Christian spirituality.

Implicit in the two basic calls of the Great Commission and their respective understandings as described above is commitment to sanctification—that aspect of the salvation as understood by Evangelical Protestants that both begins with inward conversion and ensues from it. This, in turn, is given additional impetus by understandings of and emphasis on the doctrine of the priesthood of all believers. A Scripture passage to which Evangelical Protestants would point in support of attention to the inward nature of sanctification is Rom 12:2 in which Christians are urged by Paul not to "be conformed to this world, but be transformed by the renewing of your minds." Regarding this passage, D. Stuart Briscoe observed, "The inward power of this transforming experience is the renewed mind."[7] Dale Moody understood this passage as having a double meaning regarding the two aspects of salvation, both conversion and sanctification. Regarding the latter he wrote that Paul's challenge was to "a new man who is to go on being renewed in the spirit of his mind."[8]

The kind of inward change and growth is enabled from drawing on a number of differing sources, but all ultimately from God. Blackaby particularly stresses the roles of scriptural authority and of the Holy Spirit in engendering inward Christian spiritual formation: "The Bible is God's Word to you. The Holy Spirit honors and uses God's Word in speaking to you. The Scriptures will be your source of authority for faith and practice."[9]

That the inward nature of spirituality is of significant interest to Evangelical Protestants is attested to by the popularity among them of such writers as Henry Blackaby. Blackaby's *Experiencing God* study has been a widely-used curricula for Evangelical Protestants and has been revised into various editions tailored for wider audiences. It also has provided a "template" for an edition of a study Bible.

Further, Evangelical Protestant concern for the inward nature of spirituality is also verified by their increasing attention to the entire spectrum of spiritual disciplines (including those inwardly and outwardly directed). Writers and speakers about spiritual disciplines who have found audiences among Evangelical Protestants include those more distinctly and narrowly of that fellowship (such as Donald S. Whitney) and others who appeal to a more ecumenical audience. An example of the latter is Richard J. Foster, a Quaker and the author of *Celebration of Discipline: The Path to Spiritual Growth* (HarperCollins, 1978).

THE OUTWARD NATURE OF SPIRITUALITY

Crucial for many Evangelical Protestants—and toward introducing the balancing effect of a stress on the outward nature of spirituality—are passages and scriptural themes such as those especially characteristic of the New Testament book of James. Prime examples are verses 22 and 17, respectively, "But be doers of the word, and not merely hearers who deceive themselves," and "So faith by itself, if it has no works, is dead." Though certainly agreeing with Martin Luther that salvation is by grace alone, most Evangelical Protestants would find it difficult to agree with him that the book of James is a "right strawy epistle." Rather they understand that the biblical mandate is that one cannot divorce the inward nature of one's spirituality from the outward. Or, as Jas 2:18ff clearly teaches, a genuine faith will give rise to outward manifestation in faith-generated action.

However, the scriptural call to remember the outward nature of spirituality does not begin with James. To begin with, there was much more to the *Shema* of Deut 6 than just doctrine. Indeed, from its basic charge rises the Mosaic Law most of which deals with outward manifestations of the inward spirituality involved in covenant with God. Other parts of the Law, such as Lev 19:18, are representative of this principle and are clearly consistent with the premise that one cannot separate love for God from love for others. Moreover, these two passages (i.e., from Deut 6 and Lev 19) and axioms are specifically linked by Jesus as recorded in Matt 22:37-39 and Mark 12:30-31 and affirmed by him in dialogue with a lawyer as recorded in Luke 10:26-28. The point of these passages (especially the latter passage as implied by its context) is that one cannot satisfy God simply with correct answers to doctrinal questions or other attitudes. that remain inwardly directed with no outward expression. Simply stated, love for and faith in God is to be lived.

This is the reason that consistency with their theological dimensions—both especially and specifically their core authority—demands of Evangelical Protestantism balancing the inward aspect of salvation with the outward manifestation in terms of both conversion and sanctification. One significant expression or manifestation of the outward nature of spirituality is found in the primary understanding Evangelical Protestants have of their common mission and that which is central to their identity—evangelism. Donald S. Whitney, in fact, identifies evangelism as a spiritual discipline, describing a sort of balance between the inward nature of spirituality as experienced in worship and the outward nature of it expressed and experienced through evangelism: "Only the sheer rapture of being lost in the worship of God is as exhilarating and intoxicating as telling someone about Jesus Christ."[10] Rebecca Manley Pippert, in *Out of the Salt Shaker & into the World* (InterVarsity Press, 1979) described the problem of finding this balance between one's inner and outer lives (i.e., as expressed through evangelism) as one of compartmentalization. She encouraged an approach to evangelism that, though rooted in one's inwardly experienced personal relationship with Jesus Christ, was "more concerned with how our lives reflect his love, his holiness, his obedience, than the latest witnessing techniques."[11]

John R. W. Stott described an additional facet of this balance that relates not directly to evangelism, but to the outward nature of spirituality as expressed through one's obedience to Jesus through living ethical lives consistent with his commands as given in the Sermon on the Mount. Regarding this body of Jesus' teachings, Stott wrote: "Here is a Christian value-system, ethical standard, religious devotion, attitude to money, ambition, life-style and network of relationships."[12] Stott's summary statement also is an excellent concise image calling for a balance between the inward and outward natures of spirituality that would resonate with most Evangelical Protestants. He wrote, "Only when the Christian community lives by Christ's manifesto will the world be attracted and God be glorified."[13]

A GIFT TO RELIGIOUS EDUCATION

This gift of Evangelical Protestants to religious education is in its intersection (albeit unwittingly and unintentionally) with what educational philosophy gives to pedagogy. Though based on and originating in theology rather than philosophy, most of that which characterizes Evangelical Protestants address the gamut of concerns historically held and spoken to by philosophies and their resulting pedagogies. Certainly one can see among Evangelical Protestants frequent examples of failure to live up to the ideals toward which their various dimensions and earmarks point. Among these ideals is the balance between the inward and outward nature of spirituality. This reflects the best that the philosophical and pedagogical approaches of idealism, realism, behaviorism, and so on have to offer religious education—especially when taken as a group. That is, the pedagogy of religious education must be concerned with both the inner world of ideas and with working toward bringing what truth is found in that realm to bear in the world in which people live.

It might be said that, in contrast with philosophy, Evangelical Protestantism holds certain *assumptions* regarding truth and how it is known. However, what it shares due to its fiber can be a healthy balance regarding the genesis of the inward world of truth finding expression in the outer world even when that truth originates in a specific religion—and even when that religion and its truths are more narrowly understood.

NOTES

[1] Stanley J. Grenz, "Theology and Piety among Baptists and Evangelicals," *Southern Baptists & American Evangelicals: The Conversation Continues*, ed. David S. Dockery (Nashville Broadman & Holman, 1993) 151.

[2] Findley B. Edge, *Teaching for Results*, rev. ed. (Nashville: Broadman & Holman, 1995) 4-5.

[3] Ibid., 7.

⁴Donald S. Whitney, *Spiritual Disciplines for the Christian Life* (Colorado Springs CO: NavPress, 1991) 24-25.

⁵John D. W. Watts, "Deuteronomy," in *The Broadman Bible Commentary*, vol. 2, Clifton J. Allen, ed. (Nashville: Broadman Press, 1970) 215.

⁶Henry T. Blackaby and Claude V. King, *Experiencing God: Knowing and Doing the Will of God* (Nashville: The Sunday School Board of the Southern Baptist Convention, 1990) 8.

⁷D. Stuart Briscoe, *Romans*, vol. 6 in *Mastering the New Testament*, Lloyd J. Ogilvie, ed.(Dallas: Word Publishing, 1982) 216.

⁸Dale Moody, *Romans*, in *The Broadman Bible Commentary*, vol. 6, Clifton J. Allen, ed. (Nashville: Broadman Press, 1970).

⁹Blackaby, 9.

¹⁰Whitney, 93.

¹¹Rebecca Manley Pippert, *Out of the Salt Shaker & into the World* (Downers Grove IL: InterVarsity Press,1979) 102.

¹²John R. W. Stott, *Christian Counterculture: The Message of the Sermon on the Mount* (Downers GroveIL: InterVarsity Press, 1978) 19.

¹³Ibid., 222.

[CHAPTER 15]

PURPOSEFUL STUDY OF MORAL AND ETHICAL ISSUES

Evangelical Protestants, in various ways, for varying reasons, and from (often vastly) differing perspectives are compelled by the foundations of their theology and as expressions of their spirituality to address moral and ethical issues. Unfortunately, the perception of Evangelical Protestants of many outside that fellowship is often limited to stereotypes and generalizations that, admittedly, do find some basis in fact. That is, some assume that all Evangelical Protestants are of the far-right-wing bent in terms of personal, moral, and partisan politics. Moreover (and this, too, is lamentable), numerous Evangelical Protestants make this same mistake and mindlessly assume positions for reasons of equating Evangelical Protestantism (or Christianity, even) with particular political parties, positions, or perspectives. This, however, is far from accurate. Rather, the historical and theological development of Evangelical Protestantism gives ample witness to the diversity and the general agreement that both often can characterize "Evangelical Protestant positions" on ethical issues confronting respective generations.

A conspicuous example is that of the tremendous disparity that has historically existed across the Evangelical Protestant spectrum over issues regarding race and biblical teachings about aspects of race-related matters. Early on, the progenitors of today's Evangelical Protestants found themselves at odds over slavery. Many of those who were pro-slavery found—in their study of the Bible—what they felt to be compelling evidence of God's not only condoning, but also instituting slavery (cf. the story of Noah's curse on his son Ham in Gen 9:18ff and Paul's failure to condemn slavery in various of his letters, but especially in that to Philemon). Of course, most of these were from the southern plantation culture so dependent on slavery for economic viability or prosperity. However, other antecedents—particularly those from northern, non-slavery-dependent economies—found in their studies of the issue (especially those of the Bible, but also drawing on the writings and examples of such Christians as William Wilberforce), biblical commands not only to stand against slavery but also to become active abolitionists. Spiritual and hermeneutical descendants of both of these streams continue among contemporary Evangelical Protestants, but the issues have more currently related not to slavery itself, but to matters related to civil rights. Many Evangelical Protestants, driven by what they learned from studying the issue, were and continue to be on the cutting edge of the civil rights movement. Likewise, there remain others whose contexts and hermeneutics restrain them from having similar perspectives, but rather maintain God's blessings on and command for racial segregation.

Of course, the stands on moral and ethical issues that Evangelical Protestants have taken, often resulting in division, have—for good or ill—been characterized by at least a nominal attention to the study of the biblical and extrabiblical aspects and resources concerning them. Further, these issues have been and continue to be numerous and over a wide spectrum.

That which gives rise to this diversity are the Evangelical Protestant core values and the variety of hermeneutical approaches and conclusions at which they arrive. One is tempted to compare and contrast purposeful study of the Bible with that of moral and ethical issues in terms of deductive versus inductive. There is a strong deductive emphasis in the purposeful Bible study that characterizes Evangelical Protestants, for it is through their study of the Bible that they deliberately and intentionally look for universal, guiding, and authoritative principles they can apply to life in its many dimensions. Likewise, among Evangelical Protestants attention to moral and ethical issues can be described as inductive in that they may start from the position of a particular matter of personal, social, or political importance, surmising various principles that may apply and search Scripture for truths that may speak to and/or support those principles or, at least, one or more among them.

However, these generalizations are, paradoxically, too limiting for a sound description of either purposeful study of either the Bible or specific moral issues. Among Evangelical Protestants this is especially true of the latter. This chapter will examine the effect of Evangelical Protestant theology on their study of moral and ethical issues and how the theological variability that exists among Evangelical Protestants influences their respective approaches to their study of those issues. The corresponding influence of the social context of the individuals involved in the study also will be appraised in terms of determining how that, in turn, impacts their theology. The analysis will then focus on descriptions and examples of both deductive and inductive paradigms by which Evangelical Protestants model their study of moral and ethical issues and how these paradigms affect and are impacted by their pedagogical theory and practice.

THEOLOGY AND THE STUDY OF MORAL AND ETHICAL ISSUES

That which compels Evangelical Protestants to study moral and ethical issues is also that which results in their diversity of approaches not only to the content, curricula, methodology, and results of that study: their theology. The differences begin somewhat with images of and strategies for the church as held and understood by respective interpreters of the Bible and students of the issues. These are similar to Christian ethical approaches described by H. Richard Niebuhr in *Christ and Culture* (1951). Some see the church ideally as more separate from the world and, thus, take a relatively isolationist perspective, sometimes suggesting that the church withdraw from the world and exercise its prophetic function from a distance. Others, though certainly not accommodationists, are concerned that the church become integrally involved in and identify with the world, challenging the world's norms through relationships that develop. These would remind others that the Old Testament prophets were for the greater part not only voices for God, but also fellow citizens of Israel and Judah, the nations to whom they were speaking. There are also some others who see the world and the church as speaking to such different and distinct issues and arenas that one has little to do with the other. However, in theory at least (perhaps not in practice), this position is virtually nonexistent among Evangelical Protestants.

Despite their universal high regard for Scripture as their core authority, there is some disagreement among them on application of hermeneutical principles and dimensions. The basic issues relate to the nature of Scripture itself. There are those that are thoroughgoing inerrantists and others that would rather not use the term. In either instance, however, one need not necessarily take a literalist approach to understanding the truths of Scripture. Moreover, an individual's theological presuppositions cannot help but flavor one's hermeneutical tendencies no matter how objective one is trying to be.

Another important factor that influences the diversity that exists among Evangelical Protestants regarding purposeful study of moral and ethical issues is that of the respective contexts in which they live and function. Because they span the entire demographic, socioeconomic, and geographical spectrum, there are examples of Evangelical Protestants functioning in almost any profession or occupation. Understandable is that they, as is true with most people, find much of their inclinations and perspectives being formed or significantly influenced by their individual settings and situations. Likewise, they find it easy to make pronouncements about or toward the "ideal" when not themselves living in a setting that in which that ideal is more difficult to follow. This has been this writer's experience having lived in many different areas of the United States and the world and having been born in 1949 and about to enter the year 2000. For example, in the southern United States in the 1950s and 1960s it was perilous for a minister to preach or to teach the clear biblical mandate regarding racial justice, but quite safe (except in tobacco-growing areas) to preach or teach about smoking and other forms of tobacco. In like manner, many Evangelical Protestants who farmed tobacco (and/or still do), though taking positions in line with the Bible on race, found it difficult to see how tobacco production is morally problematical. Similarly, given the petroleum-based economy that dominates those of us who live in west Texas, it is not surprising that people here—and the Evangelical Protestants among them—are inclined to see the hydrocarbon emissions of automobiles as less of a contributor to air pollution than the emissions of factories and plants. that burn coal. Similar disparity of and tensions among immediate perspectives deriving from one's context can be seen in any moral or ethical issue including those of war and peace, the entire gamut of environmental concerns, biomedical issues, justice, race relations, gender equity, and so on. Moreover, this diversity of perspective that rises from differing contexts is further amplified by the many differing pedagogical approaches that are employed among Evangelical Protestants.

Though differences may divide Evangelical Protestants (and deeply) on various moral and ethical issues in terms of the assumptions, prejudices, and perspectives they bring to the consideration as well as the conclusions at which they arrive, still they remain compelled to study them for the purpose of learning and applying to life. As in their approach to purposeful Bible study, Evangelical Protestants (again, ideally) are keenly aware that the Bible, as their core authority mandates right living, speaking to some moral and ethical issues explicitly and to others by principle or implication. They recognize that the Mosaic law, for instance, though grounded in both general declarations of principle as expressed in the *Shema* and in covenant declarations as that in Exod 19:5-6, is predominantly practical. Though it certainly guides regarding cultic and ritual activity, the major portion of it deals with right ways to conduct corporate and individual lives and proper relationships among people and those of people with the rest of creation. They also know that throughout the entire Bible there is the charge not to let one's faith become merely a reflective, speculative, and introspective matter, but one of activity. This is best summarized by Jas 1:22-25:

> But be doers of the word, and not merely hearers who deceive themselves. For if any are hearers of the word and not doers, they are like those who look at themselves in a mirror; for they look at themselves and, on going away, immediately forget what they were like. But those who look intently into the perfect law, the law of liberty, and persevere, being not hearers who forget but doers who act—they will be blessed in their doing.

Evangelical Protestants also know that the priesthood of all believers requires their attention to the moral and ethical dimensions of life. It is in this role that they serve as mediators in the sense of both teaching and learning regarding God's moral and ethical requirements. Indeed, these two aspects build on and require each other. In terms of their internal relationships (i.e., those within the context of the fellowship of believers however broadly or narrowly that may be understood) as well as the external, this implies dialogue, instruction, accountability, and—sometimes—the prophetic voice. Most Evangelical Protestants, however, recognize that the internal or external character of the relational setting will dictate certain nuances of differences in the methods and means by which these are accomplished or manifested. Problems arise, however, when, despite the determination of Evangelical Protestants to be a "people" of the Book" (i.e., the Bible), their specific life situations can so influence and/or predispose them to particular conclusions from their topical or Bible studies that they unwittingly either vest more authority in their culture than in the Scripture itself or they confuse one with the other. It is the task of discriminating between these two influences that provides a great deal of the purpose for their study of moral and ethical issues whether that study be deductive or inductive in approach.

DEDUCTIVE PARADIGMS OF THE STUDY OF MORAL AND ETHICAL ISSUES

For Evangelical Protestants, Bible study is the primary setting in which they do deductive study of moral and ethical issues. The paradigms by which this is accomplished vary, but understandably are most often found in the form of purposeful Bible study. By this approach, they study the biblical text to find universal axioms. The significance at this point is that Evangelical Protestants, for the reasons described above, are ideally compelled to take these principles or precepts and apply them their moral and ethical lives—especially in terms of seeking the holiness and spiritual maturity that is the continuing mark of sanctification.

Typically, this would mean that after arriving at the premises (as understood in the scripture), the question would be asked as to its application in a contemporary context. The particulars of this context (i.e., its specificity) may be determined by the teacher or left open to suggestions and discussion on the part of the students.

Naturally, such an approach would incline those involved to apply the principles at stake to those issues of immediate concern or awareness. These may relate to matters affecting the broader or more narrowly understood community of individuals. However, the strength of such an approach is that it is more likely to have immediate individual and corporate importance for the teacher and/or the students. By this, not only is the Bible's relevancy demonstrated, but also its authority in all areas of life is reinforced.

Of course, this approach is not without its pitfalls. Most obvious seems to be those of the dangers of eisegesis or isogesis. Eisegesis occurs when one reads into the Bible one's predispositions or more than what is there rather than the legitimate intent of the text (though, admittedly, even that can be debatable). Those factors that can easily precipitate eisegesis are the theological and cultural contexts or presuppositions of those studying the text. Simply stated or applied, we tend to see what we want to see or already believe. Isogesis, on the other hand, is when one does not read enough into the text. Though it may be unwitting, due to personal discomfort with what the text could be saying at a deeper level, one focuses on the most superficial and avoids or glosses over the more profound truth.

Attending to matters of biblical backgrounds and other means by which solid interpretations are derived can help one avoid these pitfalls. For Evangelical Protestants, the struggle is to keep the Bible as the authority. However, given the powerful influence of one's culture on the conscious and subconscious, it is difficult to escape these biases affecting one's interpretation and application of biblical principles.

INDUCTIVE PARADIGMS OF THE STUDY OF MORAL AND ETHICAL ISSUES

Among Evangelical Protestants inductive paradigms for the study of moral and ethical issues rise from the need to deal with those matters with which they are concerned and confronted. Even the ethical issues that may not directly impact their lives may be studied out of awareness that it one day might, an appreciation of the interconnectedness of all creation and their desire to be good stewards of it, or with an eye toward missions or ministry (or some form of activism) toward fulfillment of the needs surrounding or surfaced by that moral or ethical issue.

Thematic studies are the most prevalent form of inductive studies of moral and ethical issues found among Evangelical Protestants. Many of the curricular resources published by the various resources accessed by Evangelical Protestants—and especially those that are denominationally-supported—provide among their offerings such studies. These studies typically approach an issue by first exploring the importance of the matter, how it impacts people or the rest of creation, and various data and other information to "get the facts." Not surprising is that, from this point, Evangelical Protestants inevitably then introduce biblical passages that may speak to or shed light on the issue as understood from the foregoing part of the study. It is from this total set of extrabiblical data and biblical passages that they draw a conclusion regarding either moral choices in the matter or what should be done in response to it.

The strengths and weaknesses of this paradigm are similar to those of the deductive. However, one distinctive advantage is that it requires at least some measure of attention to physical, cultural, psychological, and political realities. At the same time it allows—or could be said to even culminate in—application of the core authority. An additional weakness is that, given human frailty, it is easy to be compelled to be concerned with and study only those moral and ethical issues that require change in others and avoid those that may require one's personal growth and metamorphosis through self-analysis and criticism.

A GIFT TO RELIGIOUS EDUCATION

The theological dimensions of Evangelical Protestants compel their study of moral and ethical issues. These same dimensions require that such study not be simply an academic exercise, but for the purposes of understanding and of action. Life is seen somewhat as a lab by both inductive and deductive paradigms (though, arguably the former more so than the latter). This demands that religious education be not only knowledgeable regarding the theological dimensions of the faith community, but also aware of and informed respecting contemporary moral and ethical issues. The gift is one of challenge and relevance. Any religious education can unwittingly fall prey to engendering a type of gnosticism whereby what occurs is simply an inwardly-driven knowledge of and commitment to a certain set of precepts. Religious education can be more than that. Rather, through the study of moral and ethical issues, religious education can be a relevant and prophetic voice, making a difference in the world and lives of its adherents and faith communities.

[CHAPTER 16]

VISION FOR GROWING THE KINGDOM OF GOD

Of all the Evangelical Protestant gifts that relate to function (and, perhaps, of all their gifts to religious education), their vision for growing the kingdom of God may be the most multidimensional, misapplied, and misunderstood. The most basic issues are obvious in the three basic elements of the phrase by which the gift is defined: vision, growing, kingdom of God. Each of these can be described or defined in various ways and has given witness to its own misappropriation as well as its correct use.

Historically and biblically, the concept of vision evokes images of prophets and other people of God being granted a type of foresight or insight generally not available or perceived, but supernaturally (i.e., divinely) given. Sometimes the vision would be a matter of God's self-disclosure (cf. Dan 1:28). Many of the Old Testament prophets received (or perceived) their calling through a vision (cf. Isa 6). Similar to that of dreams, the common purpose of vision was to enable the one involved to look and see beyond the existent physical reality. Whether it took the form of an allegory or a clear, straightforward command or statement, the vision served to enable the visionary to see what was needed, possible, probable, or inevitable. Misappropriation of this concept sometimes comes in the more sensationalized form in which, for less than honorable apparent ulterior motives, one purports to have a "God-sent" vision of the biblical, explicitly supernatural type. More often, however, misuse of the concept relates to the commonly understood meaning of the term.

The current understandings of vision relates to a less spectacularly-expressed mode (but, as understood among most Evangelical Protestants, possibly still divinely-originating) that relates to the future. Ray S. Anderson, professor at Fuller Theological Seminary, an Evangelical Protestant institution, once explained that "mission must be perceived as the 'vision' that informs the goals and strategy of the people [i.e., the church]."[1] Though Anderson was, at that point, referring to the role of ministers as leaders and connecting that role to vision, the confluence of priesthood of all believers and the authority of Scripture demands recognition of that vision—particularly in this sense, but, by implication by any definition—is not a purview limited solely to the clergy, but open to all Christians.

The second element, growing, also has various understandings, definitions, and implications. Most Evangelical Protestants would express growth as having both qualitative and quantitative dimensions. In the qualitative, they see vested those matters related to depth or maturity of corporate or individual spirituality. Not unrelated to this dimension would be that growth found in sanctification. Due to its subjective nature, this dimension of growth is almost certainly the most difficult to evaluate. There exists wide disagreement as to the criteria by which such would be measured. The means is equally debatable, and the agent (i.e., whether the ultimate responsibility for the assessment of spiritual growth resides in God or in human beings—or a combination of the two) is an additional matter of dispute. This debate is most obvious in the tension that exists between the Armenian and Calvinists among Evangelical Protestants.

The quantitative dimension of growth deals with more concrete, objective terms and, so, is more easily grasped. As a result, it is this dimension that receives more attention and, by default, often is the only one considered. Focusing on the quantitative dimension growth, the numbers involved, and (more altruistically) the salvific aspect of the gospel serves to concentrate much of Evangelical Protestant effort, worship, training, education, and financial expenditure on evangelistic techniques and events.

Whether rising from a qualitative or quantitative understanding of growth, there remains the possibility—and instances—of misapplication of the concept. Of course, however it may be understood, one's perspective as to misappropriation depends on one's various presuppositions regarding that dimension. Some of the more sensational methods toward numerical growth are disdained by many, though applied by many others. Further, even some of the more theoretical approaches to church growth are often debated. An example would be the "homogenous unit principle" advanced by Donald A. McGavran in *Understanding Church Growth* (rev. ed., 1980). McGavran proposed that because people tend to convert in groups (even if an individual decision is involved) and are more easily reached through those more like themselves, a homogenous church would be more effective especially in terms of numerical growth.[2] Many not only question McGavran's emphasis on numerical growth, but also seriously question whether exclusive homogeneity (which readily develops from application of McGavran's theory) as an evangelical strategy is consistent with the ethical teachings of the Christian gospel. Indeed, some wonder if, despite what various strengths it may have, many do or might not use it to veil racism and/or classicism in churches.

Thirdly, the concept of the kingdom of God[3] is open to a wide assortment of interpretations that can be described or differentiated not only as previously discussed (i.e., relative to eschatology), but also in terms of internally- and externally- related concepts. Though the former definition certainly apply to the issue of vision among Evangelical Protestants, these latter definitions have particular application at this point.

The kingdom can be understood as having something to do with matters internal to the life of the believer, though admittedly Evangelical Protestants are virtually universal in assuming that such might have many possible forms of external manifestation. Often this would be characterized as one's citizenship in the kingdom and has to do with one's station and one's attitude and behavior. Evangelical Protestants tend to agree that the individual becomes a citizen of the kingdom at the point of conversion. The questions remains, however, as to whether the kingdom is something one enters or that which one becomes—or both. The latter perspective stresses the role of the individual's commitment and submission to the Lordship of Jesus in the conversion and continuing salvation experience. Simply argued, regardless of geographical location and, in fact, separate from the very issue of geography, wherever a citizen lives in obedience and submission to her/his ruler, there is that ruler's dominion. This idea is similar to that expressed in Rupert Brooke's poem, "The Soldier": "If I should die, think only this of me: That there's some corner of a foreign field that is forever England." More importantly for Evangelical Protestants, it is consistent with 1 John 2:3: "Now by this we may be sure that we know him, if we obey his commandments" and Luke 17:20-21: "Once Jesus was asked by the Pharisees when the kingdom of God was coming, and he answered, 'The kingdom of God is not coming with things that can be observed; nor will they say, 'Look, here it is,' or 'There it is!' For, in fact, the kingdom of God is among you."

On the other hand, the former perspective—that of entering the kingdom—focuses on the corporate aspect or consequence of the individual commitment involved in conversion. It also fits with the numerical focus in church growth. It, too, has its biblical precedents such as the following:

> And the disciples were perplexed at these words. But Jesus said to them again, "Children, how hard it is to enter the kingdom of God! It is easier for a camel to go through the eye of a needle than for someone who is rich to enter the kingdom of God. (Mark 10:24-25)

> And Jesus answered, "Very truly, I tell you, no one can enter the kingdom of God without being born of water and Spirit." (John 3:5)

Externally-related concepts regarding the kingdom also have to do with matters of citizenship for Evangelical Protestants, especially in terms of outwardly manifested obedience in submission to the Lordship of Jesus. Of course, this was somewhat at the root of the attempts of the Reformation progenitors of Evangelical Protestantism in working toward establishing the kingdom in the forms of communities, cities, states, and nations as theocracies. Moreover, there is an element of this in some of the political activism among many contemporary Evangelical Protestants and much of that among others. However, in the minds of most Evangelical Protestants, the immediate, earthly manifestation of the kingdom is found in the corporate experience of the church. Though Evangelical Protestantism generally recognizes that the church exists in the universal sense in the fellowship of all Christians, the focus remains the local church.

These many differing perspectives and their various interactions provide much grist for theological reflection and debate. They and the reflection and debate they engender significantly influence pedagogy and many other faces of religious education.

VISION AND PEDAGOGY

Looking toward what is yet to be realized as integral to pedagogy, most philosophies of education address the issue of vision, at least by some definition of the term. What follows is but a sampling and a brief review or explanation of how they apply or inform vision as an aspect of and as related to various facets of educational methodology.

Seeing that which is beyond the immediately perceived by the senses is at the heart of idealism. However, according to its critics who charge idealism with irrelevancy, this form of vision relates more to that which is past rather than the present and even much less the future. Nonetheless, others recognize that a strength of idealism is to be found in its potential emphasis on self-realization in which "the individual self is subsumed under a larger and more important concern, that is, the universal self or God."[4] This places the teacher in the place of role model, leader, and guide. The idealist curriculum does confront the student with the history and literature related to the content, but it is the teacher who is expected to embody the ideal so that the students can more readily perceive it. Similarly, realism focuses on discerning the "forms" or "essences" that exist separate from or beyond (behind?) that which is materially experienced, but—especially as expressed in modern and contemporary realism—primarily as connected with the experiences of the student. This is attractive particularly to those who, for example, see God as revealed in nature. They would differ with the idealists in that they would stress the role of the teacher as a more experienced fellow pilgrim vested with the responsibility of imparting to their students facts and frameworks by and through which the learners may comprehend (or, within this context, envision) the principles and laws that are ultimately reality.

Pragmatism rejects idealism and realism in their quest for universals, but addresses vision nonetheless, though in its own particular way. Realism shares with realism attention to the experience of the learner. However, pragmatism is concerned with the immediacy of that experience not so much as a study of life, but as a part of it. By this approach the student is encouraged to seek out and examine that which is most purposeful. This experiential methodology is toward the purpose of enabling a student to build a type of data base from everyday life on which to learn and on which to draw when confronted with the need to deal with new problems. This purpose, then, can be said to enable the learner to envision answers to new questions and situations and to learn from the implementation and living out of that vision. Thereby, the vision itself becomes a subsequent learning experience.

INTERNALLY-RELATED CONCEPTS OF THE KINGDOM OF GOD AND PEDAGOGY

The internally-related concepts of the kingdom, particularly as related to individual citizenship of kingdom can significantly influence differing approaches to pedagogy. It may be true that, to some extent, both the concepts of the kingdom and the pedagogical forms are so flexible that compatibility is always possible. However, it seems that—within the context of Evangelical Protestantism—some of each group are more adaptable to and accommodating of certain ones of the other. Before proceeding with some examples, it is vital to remember that, given the continuing Evangelical Protestant emphasis on the authority of Scripture, that their methodology will always—though not at every moment—involve attention to biblical teaching and principles.

The kingdom as something that one subjectively enters has numerous implications regarding curriculum, content, the teacher, and methodology. For most Evangelical Protestants, this decision to enter the kingdom is the most important an individual could possibly make, for it deals with ultimate and eternal issues. Therefore, teaching regarding this decision and the doctrines surrounding it, must subsume the entire curriculum. It often will be the primary focus of the content either as the end itself or the foundation on which attitudinal or behavioral lesson goals are built. When not, at least it will be an auxiliary matter. From this perspective the role of the teacher remains somewhat flexible and very important. In this sense, it is vital that the teacher has made that personal commitment. This would be true not only for the spiritual sake of the teacher as an individual, but also for the teacher's pedagogical role. Evangelical Protestants would see its educational importance first as a "witness." In terms of the educational philosophies described above this would involve the teacher's function as a role model and example. There is also the sense of the teacher being a guide and fellow pilgrim, though, in the sense of "having been there," less for those who have not "entered" the kingdom and more so for those who have. The methodology of this perspective among Evangelical Protestants focuses more on the study of literature and especially the Bible because it almost exclusively drives the vast majority of the truth they hold at this point. What other literature might be studied—other than curricular material—would be historical and contemporary reflections on biblical doctrine on the kingdom and how it might be entered and conversion stories of historical and contemporary personalities. There is less use of classically understood experiential methodology, because of its danger that human experience may be regarded as authoritative. Especially at this crucial point, human experience must be measured in terms of Scripture and not the reverse.

The kingdom as something that individuals become has similar pedagogical implications for Evangelical Protestants. The conversional or salvific issues remain the same, but now with more behavioral connotations. The matter is still personal and subjective, but has more to do with particular attitudes. The curriculum and content are still driven by the common experience of those who are or have or would become the kingdom. Similarly and for like reasons, the teacher functions as role model and example. However, due to this being a behavioral and attitudinal perspective, there is more need for the teacher to function as a guide and fellow pilgrim. The methodology among Evangelical Protestants still requires initial and continuing consideration of the Bible (as core authority), but is more amenable to experiential learning.

EXTERNALLY-RELATED CONCEPTS OF THE KINGDOM OF GOD AND PEDAGOGY

The externally-related concepts of the kingdom also influence pedagogy. Whether understood as something to enter or to become, how broadly or narrowly the church as the universal fellowship of Christians may be defined or emphasized will impact content and curriculum significantly. The most constricted ecumenical perspective would limit the "church universal" to believers of the same denomination and creedal orientation. (The local church as an expression of the kingdom as something one enters may be considered the most closely defined sense of the term, especially when membership in a church is deemed important.) The least constrained perspective delimits the church in much broader and, arguably, more basic terms such as anyone accepting Jesus as Lord. (Of course, Evangelical Protestants can be found at both ends of that spectrum and at all points between, but generally tend to be much more comfortable with other Evangelical Protestants.) The more limiting view requires more narrowly defined, more apologetic, and more catechetical curricula and content, because the issue is consistency not only with the Bible but also with the community. Likewise, the less restrictive perspective would attend to more general and basic doctrinal matters in its curriculum and content. Who may serve as teachers and their respective roles are similarly influenced. Though either view would demand of teachers some level of accountability, a more restrictive ecumenical outlook tends to have more limits on who serve as teachers because they are seen as role models and examples as well as guides and fellow pilgrims, and the goal of education at this point is more closely construed. These limits can include various degrees of required creedal adherence and/or certain levels of spiritual maturity however that may be measured. The less restrictive outlook has fewer creedal limits, but as with curriculum and content, looks to basic issues. However, it may have and, perhaps, because it focuses more on the basics of the faith, a like requirement regarding the spiritual maturity of teachers. Regardless of the ecumenical perspective, among Evangelical Protestants the methodology remains centered on the Bible, because it must be consistent with theology in both substance and source. The more narrow the perspective, the more important that some attention be given to the history and literature of the more closely defined family of faith.

A GIFT TO RELIGIOUS EDUCATION

At the heart of religion and religious experience is coming to grips with the transcendent. This, in and of itself, demands a type of vision in that it challenges one to see that which is beyond immediate perception. Moreover, any type of education, growth, or maturity such as that involved in the spiritual formation that is the main task of religious education also requires that one see not only one's immediate condition and situation, but also what is not already existent—the possible—and work toward that vision. The vision of

Evangelical Protestants has to do with their core experience and their core mission. Perhaps it is partially due to their differences as to the meaning of all those terms that it is a matter that is ever before them. Whatever the case, this gift to religious education is one that seeks to maintain consistency among its doctrine, purpose, and pedagogy as a matter not only of personal vision and possibility, but also as a vision for relationships with others and the transcendent. By this, religious education can be a prophetic voice and engender among adherents a sense of the "big picture" and, more likely, the willingness to learn how to affect the future positively.

NOTES

[1] Ray S. Anderson, *The Soul of Ministry: Forming Leaders for God's People* (Louisville KY: Westminster/John Knox Press, 1997) 198.

[2] Thom S. Rainer, *The Book of Church Growth: History, Theology, and Principles* (Nashville: Broadman Press, 1993) 35.

[3] For the sake of simplicity, from this point on—unless specified otherwise—the term "kingdom" should be understood as referring to the kingdom of God.

[4] Howard Ozman and Samuel Craver, *Philosophical Foundations of Education*, 4th ed. (Columbus OH: Merrill Publishing Co., 1990) 30.

GIFTS OF OPPORTUNITY

[CHAPTER 17]

OPPORTUNITY FOR RESPONSE

William James wrote that the basic nature of religion was that which evoked response: "The divine shall mean for us only such a primal reality as the individual feels impelled to respond to solemnly and gravely, and neither by a curse nor a jest."[1]

The opportunity for response is woven into the fabric of Evangelical Protestantism and, for many outside that fellowship, is one of its most obvious characteristics. The image that most readily comes to mind is that of the climactic moment toward the end of an evangelistic sermon (e.g., one given by Billy Graham in one of his crusades, which are often nationally or internationally televised). At that point the preacher encourages those who are so moved—and all are exhorted to permit God to move them—to come to the front of the congregation. During the playing or singing of a particular hymn to give indication of some form of personal decision in response to the message or sermon. In these settings the "invitations" usually focus on responses and commitments related to conversions, or, as often expressed by Evangelical Protestants, professing faith in Jesus Christ as Lord. Of course, these invitations come in myriad forms other than that just depicted. They are not always so explicit nor do they occur only during such services or settings. Often they are implicit or more subtle and can be found in many differing settings in the lives of Evangelical Protestant congregations. However, so connected in people's minds and thought with the salvific or conversionist aspect of the gospel is the opportunity to or for response—and especially in the form of the invitation—that often overlooked or lost is its value in religious education in general and schooling in particular. After examining the theological and historical roots of the invitation to response and its place and many expressions in Evangelical Protestantism, this chapter will explore its pedagogical value and its place as a gift to all religious education.

ROOTS

The theological and historical roots of opportunities for response among Evangelical Protestants are somewhat intertwined, especially when discussed in connection with the Bible. can be traced to their core authority, the Bible.

For our purposes those bases found in Scripture will be spoken of as theological even though, strictly understood, they would otherwise be referred to as historical. This is because, despite their distinctly historical nature, the fact that they are contained in Scripture renders them theological for most Evangelical Protestants. For this reason as well as limited space, those foundations that are both extrabiblical and realized within the history of the Christian church (especially post-Reformation) will be discussed as the historical roots.

The Old Testament addresses the issue in terms of God's self-disclosure as Redeemer who called the people of Israel to respond to this through or by covenant. In some sense this response was marked by the preexilic Hebrew observation of rituals and other cultic activity, feasts and festivals, lives of devotion, etc. Postexilic Jewish life was marked by attention to writing, studying, interpreting, and observing the Law. For them, this was life lived in response to God in covenant and in history. Significant is what has been referred to as the "golden age of prophecy" that, beginning in the eighth century BCE, spanned the late preexilic and early postexilic periods of biblical and Hebrew history. The general message of the preexilic prophets (e.g., Amos, Hosea, Isaiah, Micah) was that Israel had not lived as God had directed them. They were to have lived as God's special people and the object of God's love. However, rather than living as monotheists, seekers of justice, or champions of the oppressed, they had become infected with the idolatry (esp., that of the fertility cults of Baal and Astarte) and often had been themselves—somewhat as a consequence of that idolatry—the oppressors of the less fortunate and the perpetrators of injustice. This relational and moral failure would incur the judgment and wrath of God. The prophetic oracles of judgment for these failures were linked to varying levels and expressions of hope for the future. However, often what hope there might have been was predicated on a response of repentance. It has been said that the common theme of the four eighth-century prophets of Israel and Judah (Isaiah, Micah, Hosea, and Amos) was "return." Their messages, however, were not simply that God's people would return to their land after a period of judgment and punishment, but that the people should respond by repenting of their errant ways and return to God. The exilic prophets (e.g., Jeremiah, Deutero-Isaiah, Ezekiel, Zechariah) could have looked on the judgment as already having come to pass, but what hope they offered for the future also was couched in terms of appropriate response in the form of godly living on the part of the covenant community.

The New Testament offers Evangelical Protestants further bases for response. The essence of much of the ministry of Jesus as recorded in the Gospels is often couched in terms inviting response. Jesus' call to his disciples was, as recorded in Matt 4:19, "Follow me, and I will make you fish for people." The explicit summons was to follow not only physically, but also spiritually, and mentally by becoming students. The implicit challenge was for the disciples' lives, perspectives, calling, and goals to be changed.

Jesus' many encounters and dialogues with people usually culminated in his offering an opportunity for response. Typical would be Jesus' discussion with a "rich young man" in Matt 19:16-21. Their conversation hinged on the issue of "doing good" and seeking "eternal life." Verse 21 reports that, bringing the conversation to a close, Jesus challenged the man, "If you wish to be perfect, go, sell your possessions, and give the money to the poor, and you will have treasure in heaven; then come, follow me." The further teachings of Jesus—especially those that deal with such issues as relationships and ethics—invariably invited response, and some may be said to have demanded it. Even the stories of the miracles of Jesus frequently have at their core allusions to some form of invitation to respond in faith. Similar patterns emerge in the New Testament historical book of Acts. On the Jewish holiday of Pentecost and in the Temple in Jerusalem, the apostle Simon Peter preached the first recorded Christian sermon. Peter recounted the prophet Joel's oracle that, when God's spirit would be poured out on everyone, everyone would have the opportunity for a faith response (cf. Joel 2:28, 32). According to Acts 2:38, Peter ended his sermon with the call to response: "Repent, and be baptized every one of you in the name of Jesus Christ so that your sins may be forgiven." Additional opportunities for response as recorded in Acts, as with the gospel, had to do with varying appeals including professing faith, living rightly, and committing to mission. The same is true in the various letters of the New Testament with frequent additional calls to right belief and practice. Even the apocalyptic literature of the New Testament, i.e., the book of Revelation, calls Christians to response—with steadfastness and commitment in the face of persecution and other problems they faced. Among the letters from Jesus to the seven churches in Revelation, that to Laodicea (in Rev 3:20) includes the call, "Listen! I am standing at the door, knocking; if you hear my voice and open the door, I will come in to you and eat with you, and you with me." Further, the final chapter of Revelation in verse 17 invites readers to response this way: "The Spirit and the bride say, 'Come.' And let everyone who hears say, 'Come.' And let everyone who is thirsty come. Let anyone who wishes take the water of life as a free gift."

In summary, for Evangelical Protestants, the nature of the relationship to which God, in Scripture, invites all humanity requires some form of answer on the part of humanity. It may come as one enters into that relationship either through the covenant of the Old Testament or the profession of faith as found in the New Testament. However, as demonstrated in the entire Bible, that response both requires and rises from the very personal nature of the relationship that God seeks with humankind. That is, as Martin Buber noted, a relationship of the "I-Thou" demands that neither party objectify the other, but that each recognizes and respects the person of the other. The importance of Buber's approach at this point is that an object can neither respond nor, in and of its own volition, elicit response. This is what lies at the heart of what Evangelical Protestants see as their core and common mission and purpose. Their efforts toward accomplishing that mission are, in fact, their own response to their understanding of it. Further, they cannot comprehend the nature of that mission and purpose separate from calling others to response.

The practice of the "invitation" as the culminating moment of a worship service or a sermon cannot be traced to the early church, but is a much more recently-established practice, finding its roots it the revivalism of the Great Awakenings of the eighteenth and nineteenth centuries.[2] In that earlier time, calls to response through repentance saturated the forceful preaching of Jonathan Edwards and George Whitefield. The prevailing mode of preaching of the day appealed more to the intellect alone. However, these preachers, though somewhat dismayed by the excessive displays of emotionalism that frequented the revival meetings of the time and committed to addressing the intellect, determined to move people to action. Of course, the most immediate call would be that to repentance, faith, and conversion. It has been reported that John Wesley, at Whitefield's death, eulogized, "Have we read or heard of any person since the apostles, who…called so many thousands, so many myriad of sinners to repentance?"[3] Later, during the Second Great Awakening of the early nineteenth century, Charles G. Finney included in his evangelistic services and methods practices that elicited responses in the forms of "…praying for persons by name, allowing women to pray and testify, encouraging people under conviction to come forward…"[4] The last of those was characterized by Finney's "anxious benches" that, patterned after those of an earlier Congregational preacher, Asahael Nettleton, were located at the front of the congregation. At the end of the sermon Finney would invite those concerned with their salvation or in the need of prayer to come to these benches for those needs to be met. For similar purposes, ensuing evangelists and preachers such as A. B. Earle, Dwight L. Moody, Billy Sunday, and Billy Graham initiated their own distinctive types of invitational innovations. Earle had respondents come forward to sign cards that indicated the nature of their individual decisions and commitments in that service. Moody invited those making decisions not only to walk the aisle to the front of the auditorium or sanctuary, but also from there to proceed to an "inquiry room" for further counseling. When his invitations did not elicit what he considered enough response, Billy Sunday had assistants go into the congregation to make specific, personal appeals to individuals. Billy Graham's approach has evolved to include the use of counselors from the area in which his crusade is being held.[5] These counselors, including both laity and clergy, are enlisted and trained months ahead of time and for the explicit purpose of advising, praying with, and otherwise ministering to those who respond to the invitation.

EXPRESSIONS

Regardless of the venue, the most obvious and frequently heard call to and opportunity for response among Evangelical Protestants is that regarding personal salvation. This is also where, ideally and either directly or indirectly, they make the greatest investment of resources. As one Evangelical Protestant put it, "We must prioritize our time, money, and effort to evangelize before time as we know it ends. No task is more urgent than evangelism."[6] For both biblical and psychological purposes, this response is deemed vital for Evangelical Protestants. Many would point to passages such as Rom 10:9-10, which declares, "because if you confess with your lips that Jesus is Lord and believe in your heart that God raised him from the dead, you will be saved. For one believes with the heart and so is justified, and one confesses with the mouth and so is saved." The psychological value of this response was described by William James this way:

> To be converted, to be regenerated, [etc.], are so many phrases which denote the process, gradual or sudden, by which a self hitherto divided, and consciously wring inferior and unhappy, becomes unified and consciously right superior and happy, in consequence of its firmer hold upon religious realities.[7]

Evangelical Protestants, however, frequently offer opportunities for other types of responses: confession, rededication, vocational and other types of commitment, and general or specific acts of ministry. Two of these—confession and rededication—may require a little further explanation. Due to their nature, the others will be dealt with in the next chapter.

The opportunity for confession (i.e., of some type of sin or shortcoming) invites persons to fulfill what is called for in James 5:16—"Therefore confess your sins to one another, and pray for one another, so that you may be healed"—and holds potential for strengthening corporate spiritual ties and engendering mutual understanding and appreciation within the fellowship of believers as well as restoration to it. Similarly, in that it is often predicated on the confession of personal failure or sin, rededication is a type of response that addresses the theological issue of sanctification and the psychological issue of developmental maturity. It offers occasion for those already converted to confess, repent, and share with others a reaffirmation of an earlier profession of faith or the personal life consistent with that profession. It may also consist of a commitment to further spiritual growth without the significance of confession. Both are consistent with spiritual growth and the process of sanctification. Rededication also offers opportunities for the expansion and deepening of one's commitment to the Lordship of Jesus as one advances through the developmental stages as described by any of the major developmental theories. For example, a child who makes a commitment of faith (i.e., is saved) at the age of nine or ten can scarcely commit what he/she cannot conceive (e.g., her/his sexuality) to Jesus' Lordship. For such a person, a rededication at a more mature age would make public that additional promise. This is partially the impact that is to be found in the youth-oriented program/ministry, "True Love Waits" (TLW), which originated with an Evangelical Protestant, Richard Ross, and has spread throughout the Evangelical Protestant fellowship and beyond. TLW is a program of sexual awareness that stresses the importance of premarital sexual abstinence. As designed, the program culminates in an invitation for the young people involved to commit themselves to abstinence and to make that known publicly in response to an invitation in a worship service. Though this obviously is a response in the form of a type of commitment, for many youth it is tantamount to a rededication.

Despite the public and obvious nature of those opportunities characterized by invitations in Evangelical Protestant worship services, it would not be safe to assume that those would be the only occasions for some type of overt and explicit response. Rather, they exist throughout the curricula, ministries, and events of Evangelical Protestant Christian education. Their presence in the curricula is made obvious through attention to specific activities and methodologies suggested in printed curriculum pieces common to Evangelical Protestants—often (as if a reflection of the invitation in a worship service) at the end of the lesson. This is what Maria Harris refers to as the "explicit curriculum," which "refers to what is actually presented, consciously and with intention."[8]

However, opportunities for response are so much a part of Evangelical Protestant life that they are in the implicit curriculum as described by Harris: "the patterns or organizations or procedures that frame the explicit curriculum."[9] Importantly, many Evangelical Protestants would be quite concerned if there were not present within the context of most congregational activities consistent opportunities for response. Their fear at this point would be that by not offering such, their church would be teaching its members that response was either not important or unnecessary. Such concern would resonate with the null curriculum as defined by Harris.[10] Their stress is for the sake of the accountability, the witness, and the example offered by the public nature of commitment and response.

PEDAGOGICAL VALUE

One obvious pedagogical advantage of consistent opportunities for response is that it encourages a type of active or experiential learning related very much to the basic educational philosophy of pragmatism. That is, the content is much less apt to be seen as simply an abstraction or a sterile matter of objective study that isolates the learner from the subject matter. Rather, when a learner is continually exposed to calls to response, she/he becomes sensitized in such a way that, when in any learning setting, the anticipation of such a call will compel him/her to consider how what is being studied should or will apply to her/his life. The pedagogical event, then, is no longer separate from life. It becomes life itself.

Further, by this means, students (both those in or observing of the congregation) benefit from the modeling that occurs. Rather than being restrictive to a static view of a person, it recognizes that, whether youth or adults, they are capable and in need of growth and development. Regardless of age, as one observes the public nature of another's commitment (whatever the context or setting) in response to what has been learned, one learns and is reminded by the example that has been set.

A GIFT TO RELIGIOUS EDUCATION

The religious education of many faiths have, within their contexts, various forms of catechisms in which their doctrines are taught through a verbal dialogue of question/answer. Though with potential for some level of learning, unfortunately, some have found that this method can degenerate into learning by rote, with no real internalization nor application to the life of the learner. What Evangelical Protestants, by their consistent implementation of opportunities for response is offer to religious education what may safely be called a "catechism of life." Whether in their preaching or their teaching they are asking persons "What will you do with this truth?" The learners answer by embodying their responses. By this, they are continuously confronted with the need to adhere not only mentally to a set of beliefs, but also to live them experientially. Whatever the core authority, mission, or purpose of a faith perspective, its religious education must communicate and teach to its adherents that it is a life to be lived—in response to those teachings. A sports event can easily become boring and/or terribly discouraging to an athlete who has practiced and has the ability, but has no opportunity to "get into the game." The same is true with people in relation to religion. When any religious education offers its believers or inquirers opportunities for response, it is encouraging participation and enabling the excitement and learning that involvement engenders.

NOTES

[1] William James, *The Varieties of Religious Experience* (New York: Random House/The Modern Library, 1902) 39.

[2] Delos Miles, *Introduction to Evangelism* (Nashville: Broadman Press, 1983) 302.

[3] "Deep Mourning," *Christian History* 12, no. 2 (1993) 15.

[4] "Charles Grandison Finney and the Second Phase of the Second Great Awakening," Christian History 8, no. 3 (1989) 30.

[5] Miles, 302-303.

[6] Thom S. Rainer, *The Book of Church Growth: History, Theology, and Principles* (Nashville: Broadman Press, 1993) 167.

[7] James, 186.

[8] Maria Harris, *Fashion Me a People: Curriculum in the Church* (Louisville KY: Westminster/John Know Press, 1989) 68.

[9] Harris, 68-69.

[10] Ibid., 69.

[CHAPTER 18]

OPPORTUNITY FOR SERVICE

Opportunities abound for response in the forms of vocational and other types of commitment and general or specific acts of ministry. These relate to the issue of service—whether in the church, community, or world—rather than to spiritual commitments regarding such things as attitudes and ethics. Further, though as with all Evangelical Protestant gifts to religious education, they are grounded in commitment to authority of Scripture, they also rise from another vital Evangelical Protestant doctrine—the priesthood of all believers—along with their concept of their common purpose and mission. Because of this they have a widespread and distinct impact on Evangelical Protestantism and deserve special attention as gifts. Attention will first be given to how Evangelical Protestant theology affects the emphasis on opportunities for service in terms of both quality and quantity as well as at various levels and in differing venues. Specific examples of the many types of service will help one understand how the interplay of theologies influences how Evangelical Protestants discern the types of service and respond to opportunities to be involved in them. Important to note will be the significance these opportunities have not only for fulfillment of Evangelical Protestant theology, but also as expressions of both pedagogical theory and philosophy and as pedagogical tools affecting the respective roles of the teacher and the student and influencing the teacher/student relationship. Crucial will be to note that, with the lack of ecclesiastical hierarchy or, at the least, a "flat" hierarchical structure (as called for by the priesthood of all believers), students involved in religious education are compelled to become active learners with all the rights, responsibilities, and privileges appertaining thereto. Also important will be the accountability demanded by the doctrine of the priesthood of all believers and its specific role in the pedagogical process.

THEOLOGY

Opportunities for service among Evangelical Protestants center directly on the comprehensive understandings of the priesthood of all believers and their common purpose and mission. The priesthood of all believers has numerous connotations and implications, of which "soul competency" is the most often discussed and claimed. The idea of soul competency states that all persons have ultimate freedom of conscience in that they are directly responsible to (and believers have direct access to) God. As a result, every Christian has not only the right, but also the responsibility to study and interpret the Bible for her/himself. (Baptists are among the Evangelical Protestants who give particular emphasis to this dimension of the doctrine.)

Another dimension of this belief, however, addresses the issue of service and, unfortunately, is sometimes lost. Often cited by Evangelical Protestants regarding the hermeneutical aspect of the priesthood of all believers is Paul's statement to his protégé Timothy: "All Scripture is inspired by God and is useful for teaching, for reproof, for correction and for training in righteousness" (2 Tim 3:16) Yet Paul continues by adding that the result of such study is "so that everyone who belongs to God may be proficient, equipped for every good work" (v. 17). Though some see this verse as a vestigial implication or indication of clericalism and has specific reference to one who is a minister, it can refer to any Christian.[1] Of course, this latter interpretation is consistent with the myriad calls to service found throughout the Bible and issued to all of God's people as well as the various references that point to and undergird the priesthood of all believers. One specific example that echoes the language of Paul is the challenge issued by Jesus in Matt 5:16 to those who would be citizens of his kingdom: "In the same way, let your light shine before others, so that they may see your good works and give glory to your Father in heaven." Paul's admonishment in Rom 12:4-8 bespeaks the variety of gifts as tools for service and the need for both the gifted and others to permit and to encourage those gifts to be used in service.

Biblical references to the call of God's people (and, therefore, all believers) to service includes those to ministries that could be categorized as social/physical (e.g., Matt 25:31ff) or evangelistic and didactic (e.g. Matt 28:19-20). The latter of these examples reminds one of the centrality of Evangelical Protestants' understanding of their core mission and purpose to their calls to and opportunities for service. Though their emphases will vary widely, Evangelical Protestants almost universally see any service or ministry in terms of, as an expression of, or in connection with their respective understandings of the gospel and the kingdom of God.

Even if the interaction of these two core beliefs does not do away with ecclesiological hierarchy, it at least either diminishes its importance or underscores the importance of the laity in service. While this can be construed as focusing on individual hermeneutical rights and engendering a type of ecclesiastical and theological anarchy (or opening the door for such), it is better seen as emphasizing responsibility for service on the parts of all members of a congregation. Especially when this aspect is held in tension with that of accountability, it is not independence that is realized, but interdependence. That is, each believer is responsible to serve the others and, alongside and with the others, to serve the congregation, community, and world. Ideally, and as an important part of that cooperative and interdependent relationship, each is accountable to the other regarding all aspects of spiritual life including that of service and its many differing expressions.

EXAMPLES

The most apparent and commonly understood opportunities for service among Evangelical Protestants are those expressed within the fellowship of the local congregation. This is one of the many points at which they stress the diversity and importance of all gifts. Of course, relying on laity is quite common in most congregations regardless of theological orientation. Significant for Evangelical Protestants is that, whether consciously or otherwise, it is basic to their doctrinal perspective as described above. For this reason, the opportunities for service—regardless of the nature of the work involved—are seen not so much as rising from necessity (though that, too, is often the case). Rather, occasions for service are frequently stated, offered, or announced as spiritual responsibilities and privileges.

The variety of opportunities for service will differ from congregation to congregation depending on setting, size, and other factors, all of which are seen as important for both the church and the one serving. A passage often employed to affirm the significance of each gift used in the function of the church is 1 Cor 12:4-6 and 25-26, in which the apostle Paul wrote:

> Now there are varieties of gifts, but the same Spirit; and there are varieties of services, but the same Lord; and there are varieties of activities, but it is the same God who activates all of them in everyone...[so] that there may be no dissension within the body, but the members may have the same care for one another. If one member suffers, all suffer together with it; if one member is honored, all rejoice with it.

Though Evangelical Protestants tend to affirm the importance of each gift and the service through which it is expressed and used, of particular importance for them and for these purposes are those opportunities for service through the curricula, ministries, and programs of religious education. It is not unusual in Evangelical Protestant congregations for laity along with clergy to serve as worship leaders through music performance, voicing corporate prayer, Scripture reading, and even preaching. The area of service that most obviously is affected by and has its own influence on religious education is that in and through which the church is schooling. This area would include the sundry Bible study, missions education, and Christian growth (often referred to as discipleship training) ministries of the church. Examples of these would be Sunday School, Vacation Bible School, weekday studies, and special emphases and events. The vast majority of the teachers in these instances will be laity with greatly differing levels of training and preparation. As a result, the teachers and leaders of the church are more likely to be seen as fellow pilgrims in spiritual formation. This has many pedagogical implications and is of tremendous value for the religious education ministry of each church as will be discussed below.

Other opportunities for service among Evangelical Protestants include those external to congregation but within the denomination with which the local church is affiliated. Of course, the form and structure of each denomination, the relationships that exist between the denomination as an institution and the churches of which it is comprised, and the relationships that exist among those churches will combine to influence what opportunities for service of this type there might be. These can range from membership on committees and boards governing and/or advising programs and/or institutions of the denomination to teaching and counseling at denominational conferences, camps, assemblies, and worker training events. Many Evangelical Protestant denominations develop, recruit, and train cadres of lay and clergy workers for such purposes. Such training typically includes that necessary in the respective areas of expertise and, where appropriate, education and training in pedagogy, leadership roles, and denominational polity.

Most Evangelical Protestant churches will also offer to their respective members opportunities for service through ministries external to the congregation, but within the community in which they live. These, too, come in many forms and require differing types of training and preparation. Some ministries, such as working in a community clothes closet, will require training in awareness and general organization and procedural skills or, at least, those specific to the program in which they serve. Not unusual is it for these to receive some level of training in counseling as might be needed in situations they may encounter. Also, Evangelical Protestant churches teach and train persons so serving in more obviously religious education-related matters such as evangelism or the biblical basis for the particular ministry in which they are involved. Of course, service in special settings such as that characterized by counseling respondents and inquirers in, for example, a Billy Graham evangelistic crusade (as mentioned in the previous chapter) demands equipping in a number of skill and knowledge areas.

Similarly, many Evangelical Protestant congregations and denominations are increasingly offering their people—again, both laity and clergy—opportunities for service that are external to the congregation, but expressed through short-term and volunteer as well as career missions. Some of the growth in this area is due to the increase in the relative ease of domestic and overseas travel and the increase in disposable income. Other factors and to varying degrees among differing Evangelical Protestant individuals and groups are the urgency experienced in anticipation of the end of the century and millennium and/or an expanding appreciation for the potential of lay involvement in missions not only for the immediate lay service itself, but also for the general support for and awareness of missions it engenders. The avenue for training and preparation for any of these avenues of service depends on the nature and structure of the missions agency, denomination, or church in question. Further, the necessary content, curriculum, and orientation for such service—as those described in the preceding paragraph—can vary widely. Short-term, volunteer missionaries are often lay people who may, for example, use vacation or retirement time for from a few days or weeks to several months of missionary service. Another example of short-term missions service is characterized by "mission trips" in which a group of church members travel together to a missions setting (national or international) for the sake of some type of ministry. The missions "team" may be comprised primarily of youth with a number of adult leaders, or, as is often the case, may be deliberately cross-generational. In either case, there is particular opportunity for intergenerational religious education.

Whatever the context, any of the foregoing varieties of missions service may be done through such activities as construction, teaching, distinctly evangelistic efforts, and religious surveys. Some will require use of personal or professional skills already applied in one's current or past vocation. Others will demand that a particular skill or awareness (e.g., those related to cultural context) or a specific body of secular or religious knowledge be taught.

Related to the above, but of a distinct nature, are missions opportunities offered for lay people involved in careers that take them into missions settings, however that might be understood. Characteristic of this are what many denominations and churches, whether or not they be Evangelical Protestant, refer to as "tentmaker" missions. Modeled after the example given by the Apostle Paul (who was simply following the pattern of many rabbis of his day) who, while on his various missionary journeys, supported himself by working as a tentmaker (cf. Acts 18:1-3). The concept is to encourage and equip Christian business people who might be assigned by their corporations to Singapore, for example, to both network with and support missionaries there and to communicate the gospel within the context of that culture. It may be assumed that certain aspects of the cultural orientation would be given by the corporation itself. However, how that compares and contrasts to one's personal faith would be a matter to be addressed by the person as she/he accesses a particular missions resource.

Of course, it should be mentioned that Evangelical Protestants, despite the many avenues of and opportunities for nonprofessional service that they offer, continue to stress and invite adherents to service through professional and/or bivocational (sometimes called "dual-career") ministry. This is what has traditionally been referred to among them in considering the issue of vocation. The training and education they make available to those called to professional ministry has been discussed in a previous chapter.

What all the foregoing demonstrate is the tremendous variety of opportunities for service offered by and to Evangelical Protestants. The diversity rises from the doctrine of priesthood of all believers in at least two ways. First, it affirms that each believer is not only capable of but also responsible for serving in ministry. Second, it allows each believer to discern for him/herself God's vocational claim on her/his life, how that calling is being expressed at any point in life, and the appropriate response to that call. Further, the diversity offers continuous reminders that God's call and their core mission and purpose extend to every area of life. Finally, the variety presents to Evangelical Protestants almost countless types, ways, means, reasons, settings, and goals for religious education.

PEDAGOGY

Pedagogically, opportunities for service go one step (potentially several steps) beyond that of response as described in the preceding chapter. Response alone affords occasion for learning to remain at the affective level with nothing being accomplished beyond that. Service, on the other hand, requires more consistently applied engagement and activity that can lead to further learning in three ways. First, preparation for the service in question more often than not requires some level of education or training as described above in connection with almost every example given. Second, the service itself can be a learning event. Third, as the individual engages in and performs the service in question, the need for additional knowledge or skills often surfaces. This is a natural occasion for praxis as described by Thomas Groome:

> I claim that a praxis way of knowing is most capable of meeting the task [i.e., a 'way of knowing that can hold past, present, and future in fruitful tension']. It is a relational, reflective, and experiential way of knowing in which by critical reflection on lived experience people discover and name their own story and vision...[2]

Moreover, the lack of hierarchy that affords or requires service on the parts of all—and the commiserate responsibility, rights, and accountability—affords the pedagogically liberating force of praxis as described by Paolo Friere. Formed by liberation theology, Friere held that, because education itself was not neutral, it could be used as a means to free people.[3] Within the context of Evangelical Protestant, this freedom means, among other things, that to be what is called for by the priesthood of all believers.

The active learning involved in service reflects Friere's attention to the role of teacher and the teacher/student relationship. Rather than relegating learners to inactive roles, his methodology called for a horizontal (i.e., among equals) relationship that would employ a "problem-posing" dialogue.[4] This empowers the learner involved in service to become more self-directed toward further learning and service.

Additionally, even more so than opportunities for response, service naturally follows the pedagogical precepts of pragmatism. Through service the individual naturally integrates knowledge, faith, and life. That which is realized are the importance and reinforcement nature of teacher/leader training. Championing this perspective as a means to church renewal, Findley B. Edge wrote that the church should function as a "miniature theological seminary," since "in the seminary, students realize that the responsibility for carrying out 'the ministry' is theirs" and "the function of the seminary faculty is to equip (train) the students (ministers) for their ministry."[5] Finally, many if not most of the opportunities for service to be found among Evangelical Protestants offer occasion for intergenerational experiences in religious education. The intergenerational value can be experienced both when laity teach laity (and clergy) and laity work with laity and clergy—all as co-equals, fellow-pilgrims, and co-learners.

A GIFT TO RELIGIOUS EDUCATION

A faith community need not have the same theological orientation as Evangelical Protestants to appreciate the value of offering its adherents opportunities for service. Its value is especially evident in the potential that can be realized through application in and through religious education. Pedagogically, it is a freeing approach that demonstrates for learners how faith can be integrated with life and the continuing motivation to do so. It has a broadening effect on curriculum and content. Moreover, since it calls for dialogue between teacher and student in every aspect of the educational process from curriculum design to content selection and dialogue in instruction, it enhances their relationship as partners in pedagogy and in the faith. Even a faith with a hierarchical ecclesiastical governance can benefit from this—especially in an age and in settings in which persons are seeking a voice toward personal empowerment. For the religious education of faith communities oriented toward more democratic forms of governance or any concerned that adherents learn to integrate faith with life—such as demanded by the priesthood of all believers—it is vital.

NOTES

[1] E. Glenn Hinson, "2 Timothy," in *Broadman Bible Commentary*, vol. 11 (Nashville: Broadman Press, 1971) 354.

[2] Thomas H. Groome, *Christian Religious Education: Sharing Our Story and Vision* (San Francisco: Harper & Row, 1980) 149.

[3] Mary C. Boys, *Educating in Faith: Maps and Visions* (San Francisco: Harper & Row, 1989) 124.

[4] Paulo Freire, *Education for Critical Consciousness* (New York: The Seabury Press, 1973) 126.

[5] Findley B. Edge, *The Greening of the Church* (Waco TX: Word Books, 1971) 178-79.

[CHAPTER 19]

OPPORTUNITY FOR LEADERSHIP

Issues surrounding opportunities for leadership among Evangelical Protestants serve as grist for much dialogue and controversy among those of that fellowship and especially within many Evangelical Protestant denominations and churches. One reason for the divisiveness of the issue is related to hermeneutics. Whatever the context or arena, differing factions among and within Evangelical Protestant bodies refer to specific Bible passages in support of their views. These passages focus especially on issues relating to appropriate leadership roles for women, the pastor, and other ministers. Further complicating the matter are the contrasting means by which conclusions on these and other concerns are held in tension with the doctrine of the priesthood of all believers. The following examination of the theological issues surrounding Evangelical Protestant opportunities for leadership is not for the purpose of proving one side or the other. Rather, it demonstrates how those theological and hermeneutical approaches influence what opportunities for leadership are open to whom, how that leadership is allowed to function, and, subsequently, what role that leadership can play in religious education and in the application of gifts discovered, developed, and empowered through religious education.

LEADERSHIP DEFINED

Whatever the particular view of the issues enumerated above, leadership—as related to religious education—affects curriculum, programs, and schooling. It is more a macrosystemic pedagogical matter (as opposed—or in addition—to certain aspects of opportunities for service as discussed in the previous chapter).

The study of leadership theories and styles has been the focus and subject of myriad books aimed at readerships from corporate and institutional executives to both laity and clergy as leaders. Leadership is often confused with administration or management. The terms are certainly related. Management can be described as the work of one person achieving goals through other people.[1] Leadership, often an element of management or administration, is a more strategic matter. One definition of leadership is "the ability to influence a group toward the achievement of goals."[2] Other general definitions of leadership are similar but also include various allusions to or emphases on relationships, interaction, context, and empowerment.

The responsibilities of leaders of faith communities, according to one writer, are "the operations and health of the institution as well as the personal safety of members, guests, and property [of the local congregation]."[3] Toward this end, Walter C. Jackson has observed that, though leaders in congregations should incorporate what may be learned and what may be learned from "secular" leadership theories, they should still be faithful to the core of the gospel and employ "Christian wisdom for the strategies to design, equip, empower, and accomplish Christ's desires for his disciples."[4]

THEOLOGICAL ISSUES

Evangelical Protestants may agree on the above description or definition of leadership, or what may be called the "why" of leadership in the Christian community. However, there is much more diversity on the issues that deal with the who, where, when, and how of opportunities for leadership to be exercised. These address matters of leadership roles, and Evangelical Protestants again look to the Bible as their authority for the basis of their belief and practice. As is true in many areas of life in their faith communities, even this does not affect uniformity among them. Rather, their respective hermeneutical perspectives—especially those that incorporate cultural influences on the context in which the Bible was written and the subsequent interpretations within contemporary culture—are held in tension with the priesthood of all believers. These combine to produce not only differing interpretations of any particular passage that might address the issue, but also what passages they will refer in defense of whatever their respective practices might be as related to leadership and opportunities for it. This is one significant example of the development of a "canon within the canon." The results are diverse understandings of ecclesiology. That is, though Evangelical Protestants generally are of the "free church" tradition, how they employ various biblical models of church governance on the local and denominational level (whether explicitly or implicitly) will influence what opportunities for leadership are available to whom and in which situations.

Nevertheless, the theological issues surrounding opportunities for leadership that focus on appropriate leadership roles for women tend to be the most divisive. However, also important are the differing views on how divorce influences to whom leadership opportunities are made available and how the role of the pastoral ministry fits with the priesthood of all believers.

Of initial concern regarding biblically acceptable leadership roles for women is how women are perceived and portrayed, generally, by the biblical witness. Those who are more restrictive considering leadership roles for women tend to note that the Bible is likewise limiting and connect such with an interpretation of the account of "the Fall" in Gen 3. They sometimes understand it as women, through Eve, having brought sin into the world and, so, are limited by God: "[Paul] excludes women from pastoral leadership (1 Tim. 2:12) to preserve a submission to God because the man was the first in creation and the woman was first in the Edenic fall (v. 13ff)..."[5] They especially refer to as normative Gen 3:17 in which God tells Eve that her husband would rule over her. Those who differ and, so, are more open to women in leadership answer that such passages, though inspired, are to be interpreted within the context in which they were written: the ancient Middle East in which women were seen as inferior to men (at best) or as somewhat subhuman (at worst) and, so, treated as property. The more restrictive interpreters also note that the vast numbers of leaders of God's people, as recorded in the Old Testament, were men. Others once again note the cultural bias and remind us that, despite that bent, the Old Testament does contain instances of women as leaders (Deborah the judge and Huldah the prophet are two examples). They also may refer to such passages as Joel 2:28-29 in which God says through the prophet that when His day comes, "I will pour out my Spirit on all flesh; your sons and your daughters shall prophesy, your old men shall dream dreams and your young men shall see visions. Even on the male and female slaves, in those days, I will pour out my Spirit."

Within the context of the New Testament there are arguments made from both sides of the issue that make general reference to the Gospels and specific reference to various passages and most of those within the Pauline corpus. The more restrictive view points out that Jesus included only men in his inner circle of twelve disciples. Yet others note that, though not of "the twelve," there were women (e.g., Mary and Martha) who were close to Jesus and whose work Jesus affirmed.

A few of the specific passages used as references in debate on women as leaders—all written by Paul—are 1 Cor 14:34-35, Gal 3:28 , and 1 Tim 2:11-15 and 3:2, 12. 1 Cor 14:34-35 states,

> Women should be silent in the churches. For they are not permitted to speak, but must be in subordinate, as the law also says. If there is anything they desire to know, let them ask their husbands at home. For it is shameful for a woman to speak in church.

Moreover, 1 Tim 3: 2, 12 limits the roles of "bishops" (from the Greek *episkopos*, sometimes translated or interpreted as "pastor") and deacons to "men with one wife" [the NRSV translates it "married only once"]. A restrictive perspective of the issue sees this passage as fairly clear-cut and, as noted in the Southern Baptist Convention statement cited above, view 1 Tim 2: 11-15 as not only an obvious restraint on women as leaders, but also an explanation of appropriate gender and marital roles and an explanation of at least part of the reason for such. However, other groups point to the cultural context and interpret Paul's strictures in 1 Corinthians as situational and not normative.[6] Many also cite Gal 3:28 as offering an organizing principle: "There is no longer Jew or Greek, there is no longer slave or free, there is no longer male and female; for all of you are one in Christ Jesus." As one writer with such a perspective put it, "We deal with these passages [those from 1 Corinthians and 1 Timothy as cited above] by affirming the biblical ideal of equality of all persons. We see it in the Old Testament; we see it in the life of Jesus; we see it in Paul. This ideal is our guide."[7]

Though often resulting from individual preferred managerial style, particular personality traits, or local church tradition/preference/style, the issue of pastoral authority influences what opportunities for leadership are offered among Evangelical Protestants and shapes how that leadership is exercised. Where the matter becomes one of theological reflection and dialogue is in the context of ministerial education and when it is brought into tension with the priesthood of all believers. It is this latter situation that is of concern at this point. For example, in 1988, the Southern Baptist Convention, an Evangelical Protestant denomination, passed a resolution (albeit nonbinding) that stated a concern that "the doctrine of the priesthood of the believer can be used to justify the undermining of pastoral authority in the local church" and resolved that, in light of Heb 13:17, pastoral authority supersedes the priesthood of all believers.[8]

The diversity of perspectives on the biblical and theological issues related to leadership in the church is more multifarious than described above. Moreover, the variety is reflected not only in differing tendencies among Evangelical Protestant fellowships and denominations, but also within them.

OPPORTUNITIES FOR EVANGELICAL PROTESTANTS

The most obvious opportunities for leadership among Evangelical Protestants are those afforded their ordained ministers. Further, the one most often considered is that of pastor. However, there is an increasing diversity of what is considered pastoral leadership. Not until late in the twentieth century were the Christian educators among Evangelical Protestants considered "clergy" by many and, often, vested with such titles as "minister of education." Among some this has shifted even further so that these same leaders might be known as "associate pastor for Christian education." Of course, this can be no more than a titular issue, but can reflect a shift in how those other than the "senior pastor" are perceived and received as leaders. Also, many Evangelical Protestant pastors, through the study of the Bible and secular and religious books on leadership, are concluding as Paul Chaffee has observed that "most effective leadership is shared leadership."[9] Their study of biblical models demonstrates that, though there are diverse gifts and roles, "wherever the faith went [as recorded in Acts], partnerships in ministry developed."[10] The result is that both formally and informally there are more and differing leadership roles and opportunities being exercised among Evangelical Protestant clergy.

Within congregational and denominational contexts, leadership vested in clergy is a matter of position, status, or expertise. Chaffee has noted that "the greatest difference between clergy and laity comes from the personal trust and authority vested in the clergy by the laity."[11] That is, though the priesthood of all believers is among the most significant tenets held by Evangelical Protestants, their laity still vest the majority of the privileges of and responsibilities for leadership in their clergy (mostly the pastor) due to the office, the theological status it is afforded, and/or the expertise expected of the minister whether it be obtained through experience, education, or training. One leadership scholar, Sally Helgesen, has written regarding the importance of status—and especially that which derives from expertise,

> Position is a crude way of measuring power.... An organization that permits people to manifest and develop these kinds of power [power from expertise, relationships, knowledge, skills, etc.] without regard to their official status will have a head start in nurturing leadership within the ranks.[12]

Arguably the most important leadership opportunities afforded among Evangelical Protestants are those afforded the laity, because it is most consistent with the entire meaning and priesthood of all believers. Depending on the theological and biblical perspective and the individual and corporate styles and preferences noted above, these can span virtually the entire spectrum on congregational life. It can include both formal and informal leadership through service on congregational or denominational boards and committees. Leadership also can be exercised through particular church and denominational offices and worship services. Congregational offices through which laity often exert leadership are those of deacons, elders, and trustees. Further, many pastors—again, depending on their respective styles of and approaches to their own leadership—will informally use specific laypersons who are *de facto* congregational leaders in administration and strategizing although those persons may not hold a particular leadership office.

PEDAGOGY AND OPPORTUNITIES FOR LEADERSHIP

As is the case with opportunities for service, opportunities for leadership require attention by the curriculum and the content of religious education. Findley Edge described the leadership role of the clergy in this regard—relying on the metaphor of the church as a "miniature seminary"—as one of equipping the laity to do their work as leaders/ministers.[13] Unfortunately, according to Chaffee, "most religious communities make too little provision for training lay leaders."[14]

Though some may suggest that leaders are "born and not made" and, within Christian circles, observe that the matter is one of giftedness, leadership and management guru Peter F. Drucker wrote that "leadership must be learned and can be learned."[15] The issue is not denying the importance of spiritual giftedness. Rather, one might say that though a person may be gifted for leadership, training and equipping are necessary for that gift to be "unwrapped" and put into action.

Once the myriad opportunities for leadership are exercised, there is further influence as that leadership affects programs and strategies. Robert Dale, a writer widely read by Evangelical Protestant ministers, wrote that lay leaders can "help the church evaluate its ministry opportunities and resources and then capitalize on its possibilities."[16] The effect of wide-ranging leadership on the pedagogical process is both strategic and a matter of investment and ownership. It offers learners a reason to learn and, through the application of leadership gifts and the learned skills by which the potential of those gifts can be realized, opportunities to put them into practice. Indeed, this is encouraged and, in many cases, expected. In this sense it is a matter of immediate effect in the classroom (such as found with opportunities for service and many of the other gifts). However, it is also more macro-systemic and can be seen as a means for corporate self-directed learning. This is integral to keeping programs, curricula, and content of religious education applicable to the learners. Not only are they more likely to be specifically equipped to function as leaders in the faith community, but also they are empowered to influence religious education to speak to their life needs. Moreover, this addresses James Michael Lee's concern that religious education (more specifically religious instruction) nurture the creative, rational, and conceptual potential of learners.[17]

A GIFT TO RELIGIOUS EDUCATION

Regardless of how they may be interpreted by adherents, each faith community must be faithful to and consistent with its theological foundations in determining its own ecclesiology. Obviously, these interpretations, whatever they may be and however they may differ, will affect the who, what, where, when, and how of leadership within the faith community. This is demonstrated by the consequences of their wide diversity at this point and the many differing ways in which opportunities for leadership are made available among Evangelical Protestants.

The gift of Evangelical Protestants to religious education is one that demonstrates that, beyond immediate issues of ecclesiology, that leadership and opportunities for it have important implications for the religious education of any faith. First, religious education serves as an agent by which a faith community conveys not only its affective and cognitive traditions, but also its practices and—of especial importance at this juncture—how its adherents may participate in its corporate life. This is done both by precept and by example. The former, of course, has particular effect on the content and curriculum of religious education as appropriate skills and knowledge necessary to leadership within a specific faith community. It all has particular impact on how religious education addresses the issue of vocation. Further, a learner's sense of investment and involvement as encouraged by opportunities for leadership serves to enhance learning.

Opportunities for leadership, however, may have a singular benefit for religious education in a contemporary culture that has been described as "post-denominational." The theory is that, for any number of reasons, people today are much less concerned with identifying with any one religious tradition or faith community. As a result, some congregations or broader faith communities—as a matter of either survival or simply seeking to address the needs/requirements of contemporary culture—address the issue by deemphasizing the traditions of their faith by attempting to be "all things to all people" in order to attract or retain membership. However, if a faith community and its religious education, regardless of the particularities of its theological foundations, can devise more ways to involve more of its people through more opportunities for leadership—and equipping, empowering, and encouraging them through its religious education—the resulting sense of investment can serve as force for retention, growth, and strategizing and planning for the future while maintaining faithfulness to it foundations.

NOTES

[1] Stephen P. Robbins, *Organizational Behavior: Concepts, Controversies, Applications*, 7th ed. (Englewood Cliffs NJ: Prentice Hall, 1996) 5.

[2] Ibid., 413.

[3] Paul Chaffee, *Accountable Leadership: A Resource Guide for Sustaining Legal, Financial, and Ethical Integrity in Today's Congregations* (San Francisco: Jossey-Bass, 1997) xi.

[4] Walter C. Jackson, "Church Ministry Leadership," *Preparing for Christian Ministry: An Evangelical Approach (Formation for Ministry in the 21st Century)*, ed. David P. Gushee and Walter C. Jackson (Wheaton IL: BridgePoint/Victor Books, 1996) 170.

[5] Resolution No. 3, 1984 *Southern Baptist Convention Annual* (Nashville: Southern Baptist Convention, 1984) 65.

[6] Raymond Bryan Brown, "1 Corinthians," in *Broadman Bible Commentary*, vol. 10 (Nashville: Broadman Press, 1971) 352.

[7] Sheri Adams, *What the Bible Really Says about Women* (Macon GA: Smyth & Helwys, 1994) 87.

[8] Resolution No. 5, 1988 *Southern Baptist Convention Annual* (Nashville: Southern Baptist Convention, 1988) 68-69.

[9] Chaffee, 9.

[10] William J. Carter, *Team Spirituality: A Guide for Staff and Church* (Nashville: Abingdon Press, 1997) 13.

[11] Chaffee, 9.

[12] Sally Helgesen, "Leading from the Grass Roots," *The Leader of the Future*, ed. Frances Hesselbein, Marshall Goldsmith, and Richard Beckhard (San Francisco: Jossey-Bass, 1996) 23.

[13] Findley B. Edge, *The Greening of the Church* (Waco TX, Word Books, 1971) 179.

[14] Chaffee, xv.

[15] Peter F. Drucker, "Foreword," *The Leader of the Future*, ed. Frances Hesselbein, Marshall Goldsmith, and Richard Beckhard (San Francisco: Jossey-Bass, 1996) xi.

[16] Robert Dale, Leading Edge: *Leadership Strategies from the New Testament* (Nashville: Abingdon Press, 1996) 12.

[17] James Michael Lee, *The Content of Religious Education* (Birmingham AL: Religious Education Press, 1973) 129-34.

[CHAPTER 20]

OPPORTUNITY FOR CULTURAL SENSITIVITY

Culture is a matter that encompasses the cognitive, affective, and behavioral aspects of life. As Craig Sorti put it, culture is "a system of beliefs and values shared by a particular group of people, [that] is an abstraction which can be appreciated intellectually, but it is behavior, the principal manifestation and most significant consequence of culture, that we actually experience."[1]

The confluence of the common purpose and mission of Evangelical Protestants with their core authority offers to them opportunity for cultural sensitivity—albeit (and unfortunately) an opportunity that is not universally embraced among them. This gift offers freedom from bondage to tradition and one culture and, arguably, demands of them contextualization. This has become even more significant over the past fifty years in which "no trend is more apparent, more unequivocal, and more predictive of the future than the trend toward cultural change."[2]

Whether understood in terms of making "disciples of all nations" (cf. Matt 28:18) or being "witness in Jerusalem, and in all Judea and Samaria, and to the ends of the earth" (cf. Acts 1:8), the essence of what Evangelical Protestants often refer to as "the Great Commission" summarizes their purpose in terms of cultural encounter. This has obvious missiological implications and is based in hermeneutical issues that influence not only apologetic, ecclesiological, and evangelistic theory and practice, but also the didactic and pedagogical work of the faith community through religious education. Moreover, and more specifically, cultural sensitivity will impact the shape of the content, curriculum, and methodology of religious education.

An important caveat is warranted at this point. When considering issues of cultural sensitivity, one is tempted to think exclusively in terms of major cultural differences and shifts experienced, for example, between WASPs (White-Anglo-Saxon-Protestants) of North America and the indigenous people groups of any Asian country. Certainly, the encounter of such diverse cultures offers its own distinct challenges and opportunities for sensitivity. However, to relegate cultural sensitivity solely to such instances is to lose touch with the basic and broader-ranging implications of cultural sensitivity that deserve attention much more often—almost daily—in religious education. That is, opportunities for cultural sensitivity also abound in intergenerational religious education when a given culture shifts, when the rural meets the urban.

This broader view puts beyond doubt the immediacy of the issue for not only Evangelical Protestants, but also to any faith community and its religious education. Whether within the context of the "foreign missions field" or when a local, rural congregation uses printed curriculum written by a suburban writer and produced in an urban publishing house—or any of the other countless possibilities—cultural sensitivity is an opportunity that religious education can ill-afford to ignore.

THEOLOGICAL FOUNDATIONS AND IMPLICATIONS

As has been evident at several points in the preceding chapters, almost paradoxically holding to the authority of Scripture often serves to divide rather than unite Evangelical Protestants on certain issues. The reason relates to hermeneutics and to issues of cultural sensitivity. Often couched in terms of interpreting the Bible literally and normative as such, on the other hand, the matter could be expressed as understanding the Bible through the lens of the culture in which it was written, discovering whatever universal principle might exist behind that cultural lens, and applying that principle within the context of a contemporary culture. Regardless of the hermeneutical approach, the immediacy of the authority of Scripture mandates that it be applied and its truths lived out within cultures very different than and chronologically separated from that in which it originated.

Interesting to note is that the breadth of the cultural variety that exists is part of the creative work of God: "It was God who authored human diversity. This fact calls us to deal with cultural diversity, see it as he sees it—as good—and honor it as the handiwork of the wise and sovereign Creator."[3] Further, despite the covenant relationship between God and Israel which set that nation/people apart, God called them to be sensitive to "the nations" or noncovenant peoples. Certainly Israel was commanded to be holy and "apart," but there were also many laws concerning the right treatment of the "sojourner," "stranger," "foreigner," or "alien." The biblical term connoted the status of a person different than those of the covenant community and was not the casual "passer-through," but a resident alien.[4] The sojourners resided within boundaries of Israel, but remained distinct. Exod 22:21 commanded Israel not to mistreat the sojourner and reminded them that they had once been sojourners themselves, and Lev 19:34 required Israel to love sojourners just as they love themselves.[5] "The Israelites are urged to drop their prejudices and selfish notions."⁶ Prophets such as Jeremiah, who lists proper treatment of the sojourner as a prerequisite to Judah's being allowed to remain in God's land (Jer 7:5-7), shared a similar concern.

In Matt 25, Jesus uses the term "the Son of Man " (Jesus' favorite self-designation) to identify himself with the "stranger" or those who were different. "The point of Matt 25 is clear: not only does Jesus identify with the strangers among us, but he also expects his followers to treat strangers as they would treat him."⁷ This is basic to an understanding of Jesus' ethical teaching.

Cultural sensitivity is at the heart of missiological concerns related to strategy and methodology. One of the most significant related missiological issues is that of communication. Consideration of the three basic elements of communicating a message—its source or sender, the means or medium by which it is sent, and the one who receives it—and the cultural differences that can and often do exist among all three reveals the complexity of communicating crossculturally and highlights the importance of cultural sensitivity. (Indeed, historically it was cultural confusion that led to misunderstanding the message of the early Christian church and required response by the apologists who were some of the earliest Christian writers.) Since all three are inevitably culturally weighted or formed, it is vital that the process take this into account.

Among those three elements of communication, Evangelical Protestants would identify the message (i.e., the gospel) as having singular importance. What this requires, then, is that soteriology be distilled to its essence to be as devoid of cultural baggage as is possible. The theological task for communicating the gospel is the discernment of the absolute core of the gospel and the discovery of what norms, values, and symbols of the receiving culture are consistent with that core so that it might be shared in that context. Of course, this theological undertaking has particular significance for Evangelical Protestant religious education and is more difficult and complex than is already apparent from even a cursory consideration.

Beyond soteriology, cultural sensitivity affects how a faith community understands such doctrines as authority of Scripture and the priesthood of all believers and how it sees their implementation in individual and corporate lives. As an extreme example, how and at what point does one explain authority of Scripture to those who have no written language? Another: how can a tribal people given to what one might call "blind obedience" to a local chief in all civil and spiritual matters grasp the concept of the priesthood of all believers or accept the responsibility for which it calls? This latter example has more frequent expression in ecclesiology and its many surrounding issues such as leadership and church governance. Diane Elmer observed, "In the Two-Thirds World where collectivism (acting as a group in solidarity) is preferred to individualism, the majority-rule procedure is seen as schismatic and disruptive of harmony."[8]

OPPORTUNITIES AMONG EVANGELICAL PROTESTANTS

One response to the theological questions surfaced by the interface of differing cultures is offered by Evangelical Protestant scholarship. There exists within Evangelical Protestant academia a growing appreciation for the significance of both the advances in communication technology and transportation and the increasing heterogeneity of the particular societies in which Evangelical Protestants reside. What these factors have produced is what might be called a "global village," a term often bandied about—for obvious reasons—in discussions on international missions. However, the concept also redefines traditionally-understood, geographically-related terms such as "the Bible Belt." Bob Lupton, a minister in Atlanta, Georgia, in his search "for a theology that causes Christian churches to be agents of transformation of the neighborhoods in which they are located," noted the challenge for doing so posed by a Jewish synagogue in suburban Atlanta and a Muslim mosque in Atlanta's innercity.[9] This kind of quest—and that of discerning how to rid the theological core of the gospel of cultural baggage and to communicate it within a particular cultural context—requires that theology be increasingly informed by anthropology and sociology.

This need is being addressed among Evangelical Protestants by their sponsorship and/or participation in networks and consultations such as The Gospel and Our Culture Network (GOCN). Just one example, GOCN is headquartered and sponsored by Western Theological Seminary in Holland, Michigan. It sponsors national and regional consultations and publishes a newsletter toward its purpose of encouraging "the encounter of the gospel with North American culture."[10] Another example of an interdenominational network in which Evangelical Protestants participate for the sake of cultural study and sensitivity is the Rural Church Network. Similar concerns are also the focus of denominational and inter- and nondenominational missions agencies as well as graduate and undergraduate emphases, courses, curricula, and programs in theological higher education. Wartburg Theological Seminary's Center for Theology and the Land is one instance. One would expect this to be a part of those educational institutions and contexts in which missiology has been consistently emphasized or has been the primary subject of study. What is significant, however, is the increasing integration of cultural sensitivity into a broader range of courses and the growth of crosscultural study and/or experiences being required in the general curriculum. Moreover, Evangelical Protestant scholars, ministers, and leaders also frequently interact with and participate in anthropologically- and sociologically-based programs of study at state universities. For instance, Texas A & M University sponsors a rural studies institute that often includes the culture of rural churches in the programs, papers, and theses that fall under its aegis.

Such emphases among Evangelical Protestant scholars and educators either filter down to the churches (i.e., through either the graduates who go on to minister in the churches, or denominational emphases and programs, or publishing houses that produce a variety of literature accessed by the churches) or surface on their own. The latter may occur as a response to a given circumstance in which a church is confronted with an immediate situation that demands attention to cultural issues such as a family of immigrants—from a culture vastly different from that of the church in question—moving into the community. Opportunities for cultural sensitivity also arise within a local church when the culture of a church changes or when a differing culture arises to compete with the one already established. This is the basic issue when a rural church is transformed into a suburban one or when the makeup of a church "ages" and the generational cultures (at best) enter into dialogue or (at worst) vie for dominance.

A major movement among Evangelical Protestant churches that illustrates cultural sensitivity across virtually the entire spectrum of congregational life is that which incorporates the "seeker-sensitive" approach. Borne in and exemplified by rapidly-growing suburban churches such as Saddleback Valley Community Church in Orange County, California, and Willow Creek Community church near Chicago, this approach eschews "traditional" forms of worship, Bible teaching, and ministry. Rather, they utilize forms of music, worship, and communication that are more understandable and attractive to a contemporary, suburban, secular culture. Few established churches are totally abandoning traditional congregational practices in such a drastic way. Some are experimenting with the seeker-sensitive approach in new churches or additional services and ministries they are starting. A few have begun alternative worship services and ministries centered around "themes" such as "contemporary" and "country-western."

Most Evangelical Protestant congregations, however, have been more selective in their application of cultural sensitivity to existing corporate functions, forms, and ministries. These churches blend traditional with contemporary and/or ethnic forms, thereby producing eclectic programs and services of worship and evangelism. Because the tension between the traditional and contemporary culture sometimes rises to an unhealthy level, the blended approach is seen by some as a matter of negotiation or compromise. However, it could be said to avoid being sensitive to one culture at the expense of the other.

Cultural sensitivity finds many other expressions among Evangelical Protestant congregations, however. With cultures increasingly coming into interface and more of their laity and clergy serving in short-term missions, it is not surprising that those so serving will bring to their "home" congregations the cultural sensitivity they learned in missions service and that was necessary to at least some measure of success. This can influence what music they sing, how their Bible study lessons are taught, the content of those lessons, and the new ministries in which they engage. For example, having ministered in a particular country on a mission trip or in short-term missions sensitizes individuals in a number of ways. Persons are more inclined to recognize those in their community from that culture—that they may not have otherwise noticed—and, as a result, be both more inclined to involve them in the local church. Also, they are more apt to understand what it is like to be "a stranger in a strange land" and how it feels to be unable to read traffic signs and food labels. Such awareness has compelled some Evangelical Protestant churches to establish literacy schools to teach adults literacy skills and (in North America) English as a second language to immigrants, international university students and their families and others.

Though sensitivity to cultural issues may once have affected the content of only those educational ministries and programs in support of missions, burgeoning heterogeneity in almost every context requires the same awareness in the content, curricula, and methodology of all religious education and schooling within Evangelical Protestantism. Some of this has been addressed through support for the translation of the Bible and religious education literature and media in an increasing number of vernaculars. (Among Evangelical Protestants there is widespread support for societies and organizations whose primary purposes are translation and distribution of Scripture. These include Wycliffe Bible Translators, United Bible Societies, American Bible Society, and Slavic Gospel.) Moreover, many of those who publish curricular literature in varying languages do contextualize the pedagogy of their material, adjusting methodology to reflect learning styles more prevalent in the cultures in which the language in question is the vernacular. Unfortunately, sometimes translation is done directly from English with little modification for a culturally sensitive pedagogy. Where this is done, however, materials often include teacher and leader training material designed for that same cultural context.

PEDAGOGICAL IMPLICATIONS

Communication as part of the essence of pedagogy. Further, it could be said (perhaps in slight overstatement) that, since no two individuals or their experiences or values are exactly alike, every teaching situation is crosscultural in some measure. Even if seen as hyperbole, this at least demonstrates the common concerns and parallel issues inherent in all teaching. This being the case, the model provided by cultural sensitivity serves any pedagogical situation.

Cultural sensitivity demands that pedagogy be more attentive to contextualization of the content, curriculum, participants, and media of instruction. This calls for all pedagogy to be better informed by anthropology and sociology. Concurrently, it requires that one reflect on one's own culture to discern the difference from that of the other. When this reflection is brought to bear on the content and the curriculum, what *needs* to be taught is clarified. When brought to bear on methodology and the respective roles of the teacher and the learner, it reveals that one's personal experiences and inclinations are not normative or universal. Luis Bush put it this way to Evangelical Protestants: "In my view, one of the greatest hopes for the church in the West is transformation through exposure to what the Spirit of God is doing in the non-Western world."[11] The result can be that the learning situation is personalized and the participants humanized. An inherent feature of such pedagogy is that it moves toward the goals praxis and conscientization as proposed by Friere, Groome, and others.

A GIFT TO RELIGIOUS EDUCATION

Opportunities for cultural sensitivity exist among Evangelical Protestants for a variety of reasons—though the primary one is their sense of mission and purpose as related to spreading the gospel. Whatever the reason may be, the significance is that those opportunities exist. The importance of this gift to religious education—regardless of the underlying theology—is threefold. First, it is pragmatic and preparation for life in that it reflects the current reality—especially given the postdenominationalism of today that is characterized by, among other descriptors, decreasing implicit loyalty to the faith traditions of one's birth or rearing. No longer can any religious education be satisfied with remaining and conducting itself within the context of an isolated culture or religiocultural enclave. This is a disservice to adherents, for their lives will involve interacting with people of increasingly diverse cultures (though even the nuances of differences among subcultures can be significant and can divide people). Second, it is a pedagogical model that serves well in any educational or communication situation, because it compels one to learn more about oneself and the person with whom one is in dialogue. Third, as a result of this second factor, it frees both subjects in dialogue and learning from the constraints of cultural ignorance and stereotypes and, thus, empowers their humanity.

NOTES

[1] Craig Storti, *The Art of Crossing Cultures* (Yarmouth ME: Intercultural Press, Inc., 1990) 14.

[2] Barbara Wilkerson, "Introduction," *Multicultural Religious Education*, Barbara Wilkerson, ed. (Birmingham AL: Religious Education Press, 1997) 1.

[3] Duane Elmer, *Cross-Cultural Conflict: Building Relationships for Effective Ministry* (Downers Grove IL: InterVarsity Press, 1993) 23.

[4] Frank E. Eakin, Jr., "Stranger," *Mercer Dictionary of the Bible*, Watson E. Mills, ed. (Macon GA: Mercer University Press, 1990) 858.

[5] A. O. Collins, "Sojourner/Resident Alien," *Mercer Dictionary*, 840.

[6] John D. W. Watts, "Deuteronomy," in *The Broadman Bible Commentary*, vol. 2, ed. Clifton J. Allen (Nashville: Broadman Press, 1970) 233.

[7] Ronnie Prevost and Kevin Dellaria, "The Bible and the 'Other': Foundation for Theologizing in a Global Context," *Review & Expositor* 94, no. 3 (Summer 1997) 449-50.

[8] Elmer, 56-57.

[9] Bob Lupton, "Community-Friendly Theology," *The Gospel and Our Culture*, 11:1 (March, 1999) 1-2.

[10] *The Gospel and Our Culture* is published quarterly by GOCN and contains this statement in its masthead and in an informational box usually found on page 2 of an issue.

[11] Luis Bush, "Greater Glory Yet to Come: Trends Regarding Indigenous Ministries," *Supporting Indigenous Ministries*, Daniel Rickett and Dotsey Welliver, eds. (Wheaton IL: The Billy Graham Center, 1997) 13.

[CHAPTER 21]

SEPARATION OF CHURCH AND STATE

Separation of church and state is not an ethical or doctrinal perspective that is universally held or recognized among Evangelical Protestants. However, it is a distinctive mark of those loyal to their Baptist and Anabaptist roots. Further, the separation of church and state as delineated by the framers of the United States Constitution owes much to the support, requests, and encouragement of Baptists of the early U.S. and, so, is one of their unique contributions to U.S. history. Significant is that, though not common to all Evangelical Protestants, separation of church and state directly derives from at least two of their core beliefs: authority of Scripture and the priesthood of all believers. This is particularly evident from Baptist and Anabaptist heritage and thought and will be the first matter examined in this chapter.

The second matter will be how separation of church and state affects contemporary public discourse—especially as it applies to public and religious education in the U.S., for few public concerns evoke more emotional, religious, and political rhetoric than this subject in its many expressions and manifestations. The overview will refer mostly to U.S. Supreme Court cases that reflect issues directly related to the concerns of religious education. The aim is not polemic, but descriptive. This will provide the backdrop by which one can see that, rather than being a limiting force, separation of church and state offers an opportunity for freedom that has significant pedagogical value especially for religious education. This pedagogical benefit is seldom mentioned in dialogue regarding either religious education or the theology and ethics of the issue. That is why it is important to highlight it here regardless of how one may view the issue of separation of church and state or whether one's perspective be for theological, legal, political, ethical, or cultural reasons. Therefore, the pedagogical benefit that emanates from separation of church and state will be the final matter examined before summarizing the gift in terms of the opportunities it holds for all religious education.

THEOLOGICAL AND HISTORICAL FOUNDATIONS

Often credited as one of the first English Baptists, John Smyth wrote in *Propositions and Conclusions concerning True Christian Religion, containing a Confession of Faith of certain English people, living in Amsterdam* (1612):

> That the magistrate is not by virtue of his office to meddle with religion, or matters of conscience, to force or compel men to this or that form of religion, or doctrine: but to leave Christian religion free, to every man's conscience, and to handle only civil transgressions (Rom. xiii), injuries and wrongs of man against man, in murder adultery, theft, etc., for Christ only is the king, and law giver of the church and conscience.[1]

Edgar Young Mullins, one of the most important Baptist apologists of the nineteenth and twentieth centuries, in *Axioms of Religion* noted six general truths basic to faith. His "Religious Axiom" was based on the priesthood of all believers, and his "Moral Axiom" was that "To be responsible man must be free." His "Religio-civic Axiom" called for "a free Church in a free State" and, for that, Mullins seemed to draw on Smyth when he explained:

> The Church is a voluntary organization, the State compels obedience.... The direct allegiance in the Church is to God, in the State it is to law and government. One is for the protection of life and property, the other for the promotion of spiritual life. An established religion, moreover, subverts the principle of equal rights and equal privileges to all which is part of our organic law. Both on its political and on its religious side the doctrine of separation of Church and State holds good. Civil liberty and religious liberty alike forbid their union.[2]

George W. Truett, long-time pastor of First Baptist Church, Dallas, Texas, noted that the doctrine of biblical authority was foundational to the priesthood of all believers and the separation of church and state.[3] Truett felt that, if one is to be able to look to the Bible as one's core authority, one must be free from externally-imposed beliefs, traditions, practices, confessions, and ecclesiastical formulations. Only if this freedom is realized can one be governed "simply and solely [by] the will of Christ as they find it revealed in the New Testament."[4] Truett once summarized the matter this way: "God wants free worshippers and no other kind."[5] The Southern Baptist *Faith and Message*, adopted by the Southern Baptist Convention in 1963, was a revision of the statement adopted in 1925 that had been influenced by Mullins and based on the New Hampshire Confession of Faith of 1833. The ninth article stated that "the Kingdom of God includes both His general sovereignty over the universe and His particular kingship over men who willfully acknowledge Him as King."[6] The seventeenth article on "Religious Liberty" stated:

> God alone is Lord of the conscience, and He has left it free from the doctrines and commandments of men which are contrary to His Word or not contained in it. Church and state should be separate.... The church should not resort to the civil power to carry on its work.... A free church in a free state is the Christian ideal, and this implies the right of free and unhindered access to God on the part of all men, and the right to form and propagate opinions in the sphere of religion without interference by the civil power.[7]

Herschel H. Hobbs, chair of the committee that developed the 1963 revised *Faith and Message*, explained an important, broad-ranging, and practical dimension of the issue:

> Baptists insist upon religious freedom, not for themselves alone, but for all people. They witness to the lost. But they insist that a person has the right to be a Jew, Catholic, Protestant, Muslim, Hindu, or atheist as he [sic] so chooses.[8]

Over issues such as pedobaptism and separation of church and state, Baptists and Anabaptists in Reformation and Post-Reformation Europe endured varying kinds of persecution and martyrdom at the hands of Catholic, Lutheran, Calvinist, and Zwinglian state-established churches. Some of this continued in the American colonies, of which the strictures imposed on Roger Williams, Obadiah Holmes, Henry Dunster, and others in Massachusetts are some of the better known examples. Baptist leadership regarding the specific issue of separation of church and state and their influence on the U.S. Constitution resided in Virginia and the other southern colonies. They spoke against taxation in support of the Anglican Church. And John Leland, an important leader of Baptists, is known to have influenced Thomas Jefferson and James Madison. Jefferson's Bill for Religious Freedom of 1785 and Madison's authorship of the First Amendment to the Constitution can be attributed partly to Leland's persuasion. In 1802 Thomas Jefferson wrote a letter responding to concerns raised by the Danbury (Connecticut) Baptist Association. In it he said,

I contemplate with sovereign reverence that act of the whole American people which declared that their legislature should "make no law respecting an establishment of religion, or prohibiting the free exercise thereof," thus building a wall of separation between Church and State.[9]

CONTEMPORARY UNITED STATES EDUCATION

Though it dealt with issues related to schools, but not pedagogy, the landmark Supreme Court decision *Everson v. Board of Education* is often cited, even by opposing sides in support of their respective positions.[10] The significance of *Everson v. Board of Education* is to be found in the decision's use of the Jefferson's "wall of separation" concept regarding the Establishment Clause, i.e., that part of the first Amendment that reads, "Congress shall make no law respecting an establishment of religion,…" (The "Free Exercise Clause" of the First Amendment continues, "…or prohibiting the free exercise thereof;….")[11]

Everson v. Board of Education dealt with the practice of the Board of Education of Ewing Township in New Jersey to reimburse parents for bus fares incurred transporting their children to and from public schools and to students attending specific Roman Catholic schools. It was claimed that the new practice violated the Establishment Clause of the First Amendment. Decided on February 10, 1947, the Court found that the practice was constitutionally valid. The opinion of the Court, delivered by Justice Black, was based on "public safety" or "public interest."[12] However, Black invoked Jefferson in writing that "the clause against establishment of religion by law was intended to erect "a wall of separation between Church and State."[13]

Justice Jackson wrote a dissenting opinion, calling the Court's advocacy of separation of church from state, "utterly discordant with its conclusion yielding support to their commingling in educational matters" and rejected the public safety argument.[14] Justice Rutledge also dissented and noted that "New Jersey's action therefore exactly fits the type of exaction and the kind of evil at which Madison and Jefferson struck"[15] and compared the provisions of the New Jersey law to "an appropriation from the public treasury to pay the cost of transportation to Sunday School, to weekday special classes at the church or parish house…"[16]

In 1947 the Court considered the case of *McCollum v. Board of Education of School District*, 333 U.S. 203 (1948). The issue was "released time" by which the school board of Champaign, Illinois, had been allowing the Champaign Council of Religious Education to offer classes in religion at the public elementary schools taught by religion teachers not already serving in the public school (but approved by the district superintendent). The case was decided (by the same justices that ruled in *Everson*) on March 8, 1948. Justice Black wrote the opinion of the Court that "released time" was "beyond all question a utilization of the tax-established and tax-supported public school system to aid religious groups to spread their faith. And its falls squarely under the ban of the First Amendment."[17] A separate majority opinion stated, "We renew our conviction that we have staked the very existence of our country on the faith that complete separation between the state and religion is best for the state and best for religion.... If nowhere else, in the relation between Church and state, 'good fences make good neighbors.' "[18] In dissenting, Justice Reed saw released time more as an "opportunity to present religion as an optional, extracurricular subject during released school time in public school buildings, was equivalent to an establishment of religion."[19]

Zorach v. Clauson 343 U.S. 306 (1952) came to the Court and related to "dismissed time" (as opposed to "released time"). The program at issue was one in New York City in which the voluntary religious instruction was given during school hours, but at religious centers. Handed down on April 8, 1952, the decision upheld dismissed time as constitutional. Justice Douglas, writing the opinion of the Court, noted that *Zorach* differed from *McCollum* in two significant ways: the classes in question were not held in the public school buildings, and there was less involvement of public school administration and personnel. Justice Black wrote a dissent, viewing the Court's decision as an "abandonment" of neutrality in religious matters that "...is all the more dangerous to liberty because of the Court's legal exaltation of the orthodox and its derogation of unbelievers."[20]

Among the most significant, most controversial, and least understood, decisions of the Court is that of *Engel v. Vitale* 370 U.S. 421 (1962). *Engel* concerned a prayer the New York Board of Regents had composed (assisted by several from among Jewish and Christian clergy). This "Regents' Prayer" was to be recited aloud by students and led by a teacher at the start of each school day.[21] This practice was challenged and eventually came before the Court, which ruled the practice in violation of the Establishment Clause. Justice Black wrote the opinion of the Court in which, he observed: "an establishment of religion must at least mean that in this country it is no part of the business of government to compose official prayers for any group of the American people to recite as a part of a religious program carried on by government."[22] Justice Stewart dissented: "I cannot see how an 'official religion' is established by letting those who want to say a prayer say it. On the contrary, I think that to deny the wish of these school children to join in reciting this prayer is to deny them the opportunity of sharing in the spiritual heritage of our nation."[23]

The Court later combined two cases—*Abington School District v. Schempp*, 374 U.S. 203 (1963) and *Murray v. Curlett* 374 U.S. 203 (1963)—and voted, with only Justice Stewart dissenting, that both school-sponsored prayer (the prayer in question was the Lord's Prayer) and Bible reading were unconstitutional, based on the Establishment Clause. (Interesting to note at this point is that many years before E. Y. Mullins had written:

> As to the Bible in public schools there has been much difference of opinion among Americans. Baptists very generally and consistently oppose the reading of the Bible in the schools, because they respect the consciences of all others.[24]

A more recent but related court case, *Wallace v. Jaffree* 472 U.S. 38 (1985), dealt with an Alabama law passed in 1981, Alabama Statute (16-1-20.1), that allowed public schools to have one minute of silence "for meditation or voluntary prayer." It followed two laws, enacted in 1978 and 1982, that had similar purposes. *Wallace v. Jaffree*, handed down on June 4, 1985, declared unconstitutional all three of the laws in question. While Alabama governor George Wallace (who was named in the complaint) contended that the laws should be understood as accommodation so as to allow for "free exercise," Justice O'Connor's opinion was that ". . . neither history nor the Free Exercise Clause of the First Amendment validates the law struck down by the Court today."[25]

PEDAGOGY AND SEPARATION OF CHURCH AND STATE

Though there are many people who view as harmless school-sponsored prayer and Bible reading or other religious practices and observances in public schools, the separation of church and state offers pedagogical opportunities that are often lost or overlooked in the rhetoric over the specific issues. Whether articulated within the context of a court decision (as in the above examples) or of some other discourse on the issue, much of the concern for separation of church and state is rooted in what could simply be stated in terms of control versus freedom. Questions of control have significant implications for the institutions, curricula, and content of religious education. Freedom from incursions from government or other religions frees any religious education to reflect its own particularity, thereby implying agreement with this concept.

However, the more narrow concern here is the effect on pedagogy. Opportunities deriving from separation of church and state are based in freedom plays in pedagogy particularly that of the affective domain whether in the secular or the religious arena. Plato's allegory of the cave implies that at the root of education and learning is freeing one from the constraints that may be limiting their vision to the "shadows" rather than the ideal. Subsequent philosophers and philosophers such as John Locke and Baruch Spinoza likewise addressed human freedom, but saw it as limited either in terms of experience or social interaction. John Dewey differed from Locke in that he did not limit freedom to the ability to act on one's choices. He also rejected the limiting of the individual to servility within external structures as found in Spinoza. Rather, response to a continually changing environment and improving it demanded extensive freedom for the individual to choose in any number of dimensions of life and learning. Immanuel Kant related freedom more directly to values as "a necessary condition of morality."[26] Of course, for Freire, freedom was both the means and the end of pedagogy. Even developmentalists such as Piaget and Kohlberg have related morality or moral reasoning to one's freedom, either in terms of the cognitive ability, upon understanding "the rules" and the consequences of the alternatives (as with Piaget) or that freedom found in differentiation (as with Kohlberg).

Carl R. Rogers defined values as preferences for certain actions or objects. Rogers expressed the two types of preferences with which he was most concerned as "operative values" (those behaviorally expressed) and "conceived values" (principles affirmed in principle separate from an event).[27] The work of Louis E. Raths, Merrill Harmin, and Sidney B. Simon on values education was influenced by both Dewey and Rogers. They described the process of valuing as a sequence of steps:

- choosing freely
- choosing from among alternatives
- choosing after thoughtful consideration of each alternative
- prizing and cherishing
- affirming
- acting upon choices
- repeating[28]

Though some Evangelical Protestants have denounced this approach as "liberal" or "secular humanism," whether intentional or not, it closely follows the model of Jesus in dialogue with persons. This is most explicitly reflected in Jesus' conversation with a wealthy man (in Matt 19:16ff) and the Samaritan woman at the well of Sychar (in John 4:5ff). In neither instance did Jesus command. Rather, he made the inquirers aware of their alternatives and freed them to choose. For Rogers, the effect of this pedagogical approach is that "curiosity is unleashed" and the learners "become explorers"[29] This terminology, in turn, seems to reflect much of the intent of Jesus by calling individuals to discipleship. The end for his disciples, then, is to reclaim the image of God and to explore how that may be manifested in each of them individually. Of course, freedom and the benefit and potential it offers for learning is not always wanted by individuals. Teachers attempting, through their methodology, to implement it should remember what Rogers noted: "It does not seem reasonable to impose freedom on anyone who does not desire it...there should also be provision for those who do not wish or desire this freedom and prefer to be instructed and guided."[30]

A GIFT TO RELIGIOUS EDUCATION

Religious education must be free to function within the theological, ecclesiological, and pedagogical constraints consistent with and originating in the faith community in and for which it exists. The separation of church and state protects that freedom and offers religious education the opportunity to do its work free from external impositions. The result is that the content and character of religious education will be unique to each faith community as its theology is brought to bear on the context in which it lives.

The strictures that rise from the same separation offer similar opportunities for the curriculum, content, and pedagogy of any religious education. For example, that government-mandated prayers are not allowed in U.S. public schools does not disallow prayer (nor any religious practice that does not impose on others, pose a danger to them, or otherwise violate legitimate regulations consistently applied). Rather, it frees religious educators to teach their adherents about prayer as consistent with their faith. It makes those things learned about prayer (whether they be about style, circumstance, form, formula, etc.) something to be valued by being freely chosen. On the other hand, it further frees adherents to pray (even at school[31]) without the impositions of government, another individual, or another faith.

Finally, the freedom allowed by the separation of church and state is both a model and a reminder for religious education. Religious education is affectively- and values-laden. Therefore, particularly if one accepts how freedom benefits learning in general and is required in the valuing process, the pedagogy of religious education must take this into account and provide at least a measure of freedom to the learner. Only by this freedom will the results of religious education be adherents that not only enunciate a faith, but also live it daily and, so, influence their respective worlds.

NOTES

[1] Excerpt from William L. Lumpkin, *Baptist Confessions of Faith* (Philadelphia: Judson Press, 1959) 140.

[2] Edgar Young Mullins, *The Axioms of Religion* (Philadelphia: American Baptist Publication Society, 1908) 196.

[3] George W. Truett, *God's Call to America*, ed. J. B. Cranfill (Nashville: The Sunday School Board of the Southern Baptist Convention, 1923) 38-39.

[4] Ibid., 35.

[5] Ibid., 33.

[6] *The Baptist Faith and Message* (Nashville: The Sunday School Board of the Southern Baptist Convention, 1963) 14.

[7] Ibid., 19.

[8] Herschel H. Hobbs, "The People Called Baptists: Whence, Who, What, Whither," in *The Fibers of Our Faith*, vol. I, ed. Dick Allen Rader (Franklin TN: Providence House Publishers, 1995) 20.

[9] Thomas Jefferson, *Writings of Thomas Jefferson*, vol. 16, ed. Albert Ellery Bergh (Washington DC: The Thomas Jefferson Memorial Association, 1905) 281-82.

[10] Harry W. Jones, "The Constitutional Status of Public Funds for Church-Related Schools," *Journal of Church and State* 6, no. 1 (Winter 1964): 63.

[11] Leo Pfeffer, "Everson v. Board of Education of Ewing Township," in *The Oxford Companion to the Supreme Court of the United States*, ed. Kermit L. Hall (New York: Oxford University Press, 1992) 263.

[12] Ibid., 9.

[13] Everson v. Board of Education.330 U.S. 1, 15-16 (1947).

[14] Ibid., 20.

[15] Ibid., 43.

[16] Ibid., 44.

[17] McCollum v. Board of Education, 333 U.S. 203, 210 (1948).

[18] Ibid., 232.

[19] Ibid., 244.

[20] Ibid., 320.

[21] The prayer read: "Almighty God, we acknowledge our dependence on Thee, and we beg Thy blessings upon us, our parents, our teachers, and our country."

[22] *Engel v. Vitale* 370 U.S. 421, 425 (1962).

[23] Ibid., 445.

[24] Mullins, 197.
[25] Ibid., 67.
[26] Thomas Groome, *Sharing Faith: A Comprehensive Approach to Religious Education and Pastoral Ministry: The Way of Shared Praxis* (San Francisco: HarperSanFrancisco, 1991) 70.
[27] Carl R. Rogers, *Freedom to Learn* (Columbus OH: Charles E. Merrill Publishing Co., 1969) 241-42.
[28] Louis E. Raths, Merrill Harmin, and Sidney B. Simon, *Values and Teaching: Working with Values in the Classroom* (Columbus OH: Charles E. Merrill Publishing Co., 1966) 28-29.
[29] Rogers, 232.
[30] Ibid., 134.
[31] As has often been noted and reflects the reality of the situation, "as long as there are exams there will be prayer in schools, whether public or private."

Printed in the United States
18934LVS00003B/73-117